The Heart of the
Buddha's Teaching

Other Books by Thich Nhat Hanh

Be Still and Know

Being Peace

The Blooming of a Lotus

Breathe! You Are Alive

Call Me by My True Names

Cultivating the Mind of Love

The Diamond That Cuts through Illusion

For a Future To Be Possible

Fragrant Palm Leaves

The Heart of Understanding

Hermitage among the Clouds

Interbeing

Living Buddha, Living Christ

The Long Road Turns to Joy

Love in Action

The Miracle of Mindfulness

Old Path White Clouds

Our Appointment with Life

Peace Is Every Step

Plum Village Chanting and Recitation Book

Present Moment Wonderful Moment

Stepping into Freedom

The Stone Boy

The Sun My Heart

Sutra on the Eight Realizations of the Great Beings

A Taste of Earth

Teachings on Love

Thundering Silence

Touching Peace

Transformation and Healing

Zen Keys

The Heart of the Buddha's Teaching

TRANSFORMING SUFFERING INTO
PEACE, JOY, & LIBERATION:
THE FOUR NOBLE TRUTHS,
THE NOBLE EIGHTFOLD PATH, AND
OTHER BASIC BUDDHIST TEACHINGS

Thich Nhat Hanh

BROADWAY BOOKS

New York

BROADWAY

A hardcover edition of this book was originally published in 1998 by Parallax Press. It is here reprinted by arrangement with Parallax Press.

Broadway Books titles may be purchased for business or promotional use or for special sales. For information, please write to: Special Markets Department, Random House, Inc., 1540 Broadway, New York, NY 10036.

BROADWAY BOOKS and its logo, a letter B bisected on the diagonal, are trademarks of Broadway Books, a division of Random House, Inc.

First Broadway Books trade paperback edition published 1999.

Significant portions of this text were translated by Sister Annabel Laity from the Vietnamese book, *Trai tim cua But.*
Edited by Arnold Kotler.

Figures by Gay Reineck.
Book design by Legacy Media.
Index by Brackney Indexing Service.
Chinese characters courtesy of Rev. Heng Sure.
Wheel of Life on p. 228 from *Cutting Through Spiritual Materialism,* by Chögyam Trungpa, © 1973. Published by arrangement with Shambhala Publications, Inc., Boston.

Library of Congress Cataloging-in-Publication Data

Nhat Hanh, Thich
    The heart of the Buddha's teaching: transforming suffering into peace, joy, and liberation: the four noble truths, the noble eightfold path, and other basic Buddhist teachings/by Thich Nhat Hanh.
        p. cm.
    Originally published: Berkeley, Calif.: Parallax Press, 1998.
    Includes index.
    ISBN 0-7679-0369-2 (pbk.)
    1. Four Noble Truths.   2. Buddhism—Doctrines.
BQ4230.N53   1999
294.'34—dc21   98-10883
                                                           CIP

06 20 19 18 17 16 15 14 13

To the reader:
Unless otherwise noted, the terms that appear in parentheses throughout the text are in Sanskrit. Sanskrit has been transliterated informally, without the diacritical marks. The s and ś have been written as sh. Sanskrit and other foreign terms are italicized the first time they appear, and definitions are provided at that time. Textual sources are provided in full the first time they are cited; after that, only author and title are noted.

Contents

PART ONE   *The Four Noble Truths*

1. Entering the Heart of the Buddha   3
2. The First Dharma Talk   6
3. The Four Noble Truths   9
4. Understanding the Buddha's Teachings   12
5. Is Everything Suffering?   19
6. Stopping, Calming, Resting, Healing   24
7. Touching Our Suffering   28
8. Realizing Well-Being   41

PART TWO   *The Noble Eightfold Path*

9. Right View   51
10. Right Thinking   59
11. Right Mindfulness   64
12. Right Speech   84
13. Right Action   94
14. Right Diligence   99
15. Right Concentration   105
16. Right Livelihood   113

PART THREE   *Other Basic Buddhist Teachings*

17. The Two Truths   121
18. The Three Dharma Seals   131
19. The Three Doors of Liberation   146

20.	The Three Bodies of Buddha	156
21.	The Three Jewels	161
22.	The Four Immeasurable Minds	169
23.	The Five Aggregates	176
24.	The Five Powers	184
25.	The Six Paramitas	192
26.	The Seven Factors of Awakening	214
27.	The Twelve Links of Interdependent Co-Arising	221
28.	Touching the Buddha Within	250

PART FOUR *Discourses*

1.	Turning the Wheel of the Dharma (*Dhamma Cakka Pavattana Sutta*)	257
2.	The Great Forty (*Mahacattarisaka Sutta*)	263
3.	Right View (*Sammaditthi Sutta*)	271

Index 277

Figures

1.	The Four Noble Truths	10
2.	The Twelve Turnings of the Wheel	30
3.	The Interbeing of the Eight Elements of the Path	57
4.	The Six Paramitas	193
5.	Seeds of Mindfulness	208
6.	The Wheel of Life	228
7.	The Three Times and Two Levels of Cause and Effect	233
8.	The Interbeing of the Twelve Links	235
9.	Twelve Links: The Two Aspects of Interdependent Co-Arising	246
10.	Twelve Links: The Two Aspects of Interdependent Co-Arising	247

The Heart of the
Buddha's Teaching

ॐ

PART ONE

The Four Noble Truths

CHAPTER ONE

Entering the Heart of the Buddha

Buddha was not a god. He was a human being like you and me, and he suffered just as we do. If we go to the Buddha with our hearts open, he will look at us, his eyes filled with compassion, and say, "Because there is suffering in your heart, it is possible for you to enter my heart."

The layman Vimalakirti said, "Because the world is sick, I am sick. Because people suffer, I have to suffer." This statement was also made by the Buddha. Please don't think that because you are unhappy, because there is pain in your heart, that you cannot go to the Buddha. It is exactly because there is pain in your heart that communication is possible. Your suffering and my suffering are the basic condition for us to enter the Buddha's heart, and for the Buddha to enter our hearts.

For forty-five years, the Buddha said, over and over again, "I teach only suffering and the transformation of suffering." When we recognize and acknowledge our own suffering, the Buddha — which means the Buddha in us — will look at it, discover what has brought it about, and prescribe a course of action that can transform it into peace, joy, and liberation. Suffering is the means the Buddha used to liberate himself, and it is also the means by which we can become free.

The ocean of suffering is immense, but if you turn around, you can see the land. The seed of suffering in you may be strong, but don't wait until you have no more suffering before allowing yourself to be happy. When one tree in the garden is sick, you have to care for it. But don't overlook all the healthy trees. Even while you have pain in your heart, you can enjoy the many wonders of life — the beautiful sunset, the smile of a child, the many flowers and trees. To suffer is not enough. Please don't be imprisoned by your suffering.

If you have experienced hunger, you know that having food is a miracle. If you have suffered from the cold, you know the preciousness of warmth. When you have suffered, you know how to appreciate the elements of paradise that are present. If you dwell only in your suffering, you will miss paradise. Don't ignore your suffering, but don't forget to enjoy the wonders of life, for your sake and for the benefit of many beings.

When I was young, I wrote this poem. I penetrated the heart of the Buddha with a heart that was deeply wounded.

My youth
an unripe plum.
Your teeth have left their marks on it.
The tooth marks still vibrate.
I remember always,
remember always.

Since I learned how to love you,
the door of my soul has been left wide open
to the winds of the four directions.
Reality calls for change.
The fruit of awareness is already ripe,
and the door can never be closed again.

Fire consumes this century,
and mountains and forests bear its mark.
The wind howls across my ears,
while the whole sky shakes violently in the snowstorm.

Winter's wounds lie still,
Missing the frozen blade,
Restless, tossing and turning
in agony all night.[1]

I grew up in a time of war. There was destruction all around — children, adults, values, a whole country. As a young person, I suffered a lot. Once the door of awareness has been opened, you cannot close it. The wounds of war in me are still not all healed. There are nights I lie awake and embrace my people, my country, and the whole planet with my mindful breathing.

Without suffering, you cannot grow. Without suffering, you cannot get the peace and joy you deserve. Please don't run away from your suffering. Embrace it and cherish it. Go to the Buddha, sit with him, and show him your pain. He will look at you with loving kindness, compassion, and mindfulness, and show you ways to embrace your suffering and look deeply into it. With understanding and compassion, you will be able to heal the wounds in your heart, and the wounds in the world. The Buddha called suffering a Holy Truth, because our suffering has the capacity of showing us the path to liberation. Embrace your suffering, and let it reveal to you the way to peace.

---

[1] "The Fruit of Awareness Is Ripe," in *Call Me By My True Names: The Collected Poems of Thich Nhat Hanh* (Berkeley: Parallax Press, 1993), p. 59.

CHAPTER TWO

The First Dharma Talk

Siddhartha Gautama was twenty-nine years old when he left his family to search for a way to end his and others' suffering. He studied meditation with many teachers, and after six years of practice, he sat under the bodhi tree and vowed not to stand up until he was enlightened. He sat all night, and as the morning star arose, he had a profound breakthrough and became a Buddha, filled with understanding and love. The Buddha spent the next forty-nine days enjoying the peace of his realization. After that he walked slowly to the Deer Park in Sarnath to share his understanding with the five ascetics with whom he had practiced earlier.

When the five men saw him coming, they felt uneasy. Siddhartha had abandoned them, they thought. But he looked so radiant that they could not resist welcoming him. They washed his feet and offered him water to drink. The Buddha said, "Dear friends, I have seen deeply that nothing can be by itself alone, that everything has to inter-be with everything else. I have seen that all beings are endowed with the nature of awakening." He offered to say more, but the monks didn't know whether to believe him or not. So the Buddha asked, "Have I ever lied to you?" They knew that he hadn't, and they agreed to receive his teachings.

The Buddha then taught the Four Noble Truths of the existence of suffering, the making of suffering, the possibility of restoring well-being, and the Noble Eightfold Path that leads to well-being. Hearing this, an immaculate vision of the Four

Noble Truths arose in Kondañña, one of the five ascetics. The Buddha observed this and exclaimed, "Kondañña understands! Kondañña understands!" and from that day on, Kondañña was called "The One Who Understands."

The Buddha then declared, "Dear friends, with humans, gods, brahmans, monastics, and maras[1] as witnesses, I tell you that if I have not experienced directly all that I have told you, I would not proclaim that I am an enlightened person, free from suffering. Because I myself have identified suffering, understood suffering, identified the causes of suffering, removed the causes of suffering, confirmed the existence of well-being, obtained well-being, identified the path to well-being, gone to the end of the path, and realized total liberation, I now proclaim to you that I am a free person." At that moment the Earth shook, and the voices of the gods, humans, and other living beings throughout the cosmos said that on the planet Earth, an enlightened person had been born and had put into motion the wheel of the *Dharma*, the Way of Understanding and Love. This teaching is recorded in the *Discourse on Turning the Wheel of the Dharma (Dhamma Cakka Pavattana Sutta)*.[2] Since then, two thousand, six hundred years have passed, and the wheel of the Dharma continues to turn. It is up to us, the present generation, to keep the wheel turning for the happiness of the many.

Three points characterize this sutra. The first is the teaching of the Middle Way. The Buddha wanted his five friends to be free from the idea that austerity is the only correct practice. He had learned firsthand that if you destroy your health, you have no energy left to realize the path. The other ex-

---

[1] See footnote number 7 on p. 17.

[2] *Samyutta Nikaya* V, 420. See p. 257 for the full text of this discourse. See also the *Great Turning of the Dharma Wheel* (*Taisho Revised Tripitaka* 109) and the *Three Turnings of the Dharma Wheel* (*Taisho* 110). The term "discourse" (*sutra* in Sanskrit, *sutta* in Pali) means a teaching given by the Buddha or one of his enlightened disciples.

treme to be avoided, he said, is indulgence in sense pleasures — being possessed by sexual desire, running after fame, eating immoderately, sleeping too much, or chasing after possessions.

The second point is the teaching of the Four Noble Truths. This teaching was of great value during the lifetime of the Buddha, is of great value in our own time, and will be of great value for millennia to come. The third point is engagement in the world. The teachings of the Buddha were not to escape from life, but to help us relate to ourselves and the world as thoroughly as possible. The Noble Eightfold Path includes Right Speech and Right Livelihood. These teachings are for people in the world who have to communicate with each other and earn a living.

The *Discourse on Turning the Wheel of the Dharma* is filled with joy and hope. It teaches us to recognize suffering as suffering and to transform our suffering into mindfulness, compassion, peace, and liberation.

CHAPTER THREE

The Four Noble Truths

After realizing complete, perfect awakening *(samyak sambodhi)*, the Buddha had to find words to share his insight. He already had the water, but he had to discover jars like the Four Noble Truths and the Noble Eightfold Path to hold it. The Four Noble Truths are the cream of the Buddha's teaching. The Buddha continued to proclaim these truths right up until his Great Passing Away *(mahaparinirvana)*.

The Chinese translate Four Noble Truths as "Four Wonderful Truths" or "Four Holy Truths." Our suffering is holy if we embrace it and look deeply into it. If we don't, it isn't holy at all. We just drown in the ocean of our suffering. For "truth," the Chinese use the characters for "word" and "king." No one can argue with the words of a king. These Four Truths are not something to argue about. They are something to practice and realize.

The First Noble Truth is suffering *(dukkha)*. The root meaning of the Chinese character for suffering is "bitter." Happiness is sweet; suffering is bitter. We all suffer to some extent. We have some malaise in our body and our mind. We have to recognize and acknowledge the presence of this suffering and touch it. To do so, we may need the help of a teacher and a *Sangha,* friends in the practice.

The Second Noble Truth is the origin, roots, nature, creation, or arising *(samudaya)* of suffering. After we touch our suffering, we need to look deeply into it to see how it came to

9

The Four Noble Truths & the Noble Eightfold Path

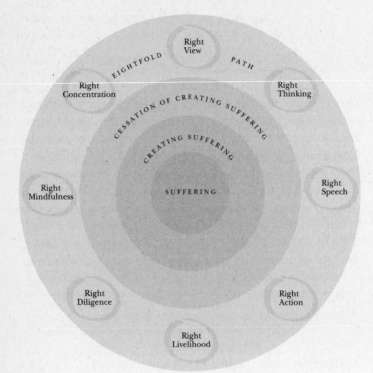

Figure One

be. We need to recognize and identify the spiritual and material foods we have ingested that are causing us to suffer.

The Third Noble Truth is the cessation *(nirodha)* of creating suffering by refraining from doing the things that make us suffer. This is good news! The Buddha did not deny the existence of suffering, but he also did not deny the existence of joy and happiness. If you think that Buddhism says, "Everything is suffering and we cannot do anything about it," that is the opposite of the Buddha's message. The Buddha taught us how to recognize and acknowledge the presence of suffering, but he also taught the cessation of suffering. If there were no possibility of cessation, what is the use of practicing? The Third Truth is that healing is possible.

The Fourth Noble Truth is the path *(marga)* that leads to refraining from doing the things that cause us to suffer. This is the path we need the most. The Buddha called it the Noble Eightfold Path. The Chinese translate it as the "Path of Eight Right Practices": Right View, Right Thinking, Right Speech, Right Action, Right Livelihood, Right Diligence, Right Mindfulness, and Right Concentration.[1]

---

[1] The Pali word for "Right" is *samma* and the Sanskrit word is *samyak*. It is an adverb meaning "in the right way," "straight," or "upright," not bent or crooked. Right Mindfulness, for example, means that there are ways of being mindful that are right, straight, and beneficial. Wrong mindfulness means that there are ways to practice that are wrong, crooked, and unbeneficial. Entering the Eightfold Path, we learn ways to practice that are of benefit, the "Right" way to practice. Right and wrong are neither moral judgments nor arbitrary standards imposed from outside. Through our own awareness, we discover what is beneficial ("right") and what is unbeneficial ("wrong").

CHAPTER FOUR

Understanding the Buddha's Teachings

When we hear a Dharma talk or study a sutra, our only job is to remain open. Usually when we hear or read something new, we just compare it to our own ideas. If it is the same, we accept it and say that it is correct. If it is not, we say it is incorrect. In either case, we learn nothing. If we read or listen with an open mind and an open heart, the rain of the Dharma will penetrate the soil of our consciousness.[1]

> *The gentle spring rain permeates the soil of my soul.*
> *A seed that has lain deeply in the earth for many years just smiles.*[2]

While reading or listening, don't work too hard. Be like the earth. When the rain comes, the earth only has to open herself up to the rain. Allow the rain of the Dharma to come in and penetrate the seeds that are buried deep in your consciousness. A teacher cannot give you the truth. The truth is

---

[1] According to Buddhist psychology, our consciousness is divided into eight parts, including mind consciousness *(manovijñana)* and store consciousness *(alayavijñana)*. Store consciousness is described as a field in which every kind of seed can be planted — seeds of suffering, sorrow, fear, and anger, and seeds of happiness and hope. When these seeds sprout, they manifest in our mind consciousness, and when they do, they become stronger. See fig. 5 on p. 208.

[2] From Thich Nhat Hanh, "Cuckoo Telephone," in *Call Me By My True Names*, p. 176.

already in you. You only need to open yourself — body, mind, and heart — so that his or her teachings will penetrate your own seeds of understanding and enlightenment. If you let the words enter you, the soil and the seeds will do the rest of the work.

⌁

The transmission of the teachings of the Buddha can be divided into three streams: Source Buddhism, Many-Schools Buddhism, and Mahayana Buddhism. Source Buddhism includes all the teachings the Buddha gave during his lifetime. One hundred forty years after the Buddha's Great Passing Away, the Sangha divided into two schools: *Mahasanghika* (literally "majority," referring to those who wanted changes) and *Sthaviravada* (literally, "School of Elders," referring to those who opposed the changes advocated by the Mahasanghikas). A hundred years after that, the Sthaviravada divided into two branches — *Sarvastivada* ("the School that Proclaims Everything Is") and *Vibhajyavada* ("the School that Discriminates"). The Vibhajyavadins, supported by King Ashoka, flourished in the Ganges valley, while the Sarvastivadins went north to Kashmir.

For four hundred years during and after the Buddha's lifetime, his teachings were transmitted only orally. After that, monks in the *Tamrashatiya* School ("those who wear copper-colored robes") in Sri Lanka, a derivative of the Vibhajyavada School, began to think about writing the Buddha's discourses on palm leaves, and it took another hundred years to begin. By that time, it is said that there was only one monk who had memorized the whole canon and that he was somewhat arrogant. The other monks had to persuade him to recite the discourses so they could write them down. When we hear this, we feel a little uneasy knowing that an arrogant monk may not have been the best vehicle to transmit the teachings of the Buddha.

13

Even during the Buddha's lifetime, there were people such as the monk Arittha, who misunderstood the Buddha's teachings and conveyed them incorrectly.[3] It is also apparent that some of the monks who memorized the sutras over the centuries did not understand their deepest meaning, or at the very least, they forgot or changed some words. As a result, some of the Buddha's teachings were distorted even before they were written down. Before the Buddha attained full realization of the path, for example, he had tried various methods to suppress his mind, and they did not work. In one discourse, he recounted:

> I thought, Why don't I grit my teeth, press my tongue against my palate, and use my mind to repress my mind? Then, as a wrestler might take hold of the head or the shoulders of someone weaker than he, and, in order to restrain and coerce that person, he has to hold him down constantly without letting go for a moment, so I gritted my teeth, pressed my tongue against my palate, and used my mind to suppress my mind. As I did this, I was bathed in sweat. Although I was not lacking in strength, although I maintained mindfulness and did not fall from mindfulness, my body and my mind were not at peace, and I was exhausted by these efforts. This practice caused other feelings of pain to arise in me besides the pain associated with the austerities, and I was not able to tame my mind.[4]

---

[3] *Arittha Sutta (Discourse on Knowing the Better Way to Catch a Snake), Majjhima Nikaya* 22. See Thich Nhat Hanh, *Thundering Silence: Sutra on Knowing the Better Way to Catch a Snake* (Berkeley: Parallax Press, 1993), pp. 47–49.

[4] *Mahasaccaka Sutta, Majjhima Nikaya* 36.

Obviously, the Buddha was telling us not to practice in this way. Yet this passage was later inserted into other discourses to convey exactly the opposite meaning:

> Just as a wrestler takes hold of the head or the shoulders of someone weaker than himself, restrains and coerces that person, and holds him down constantly, not letting go for one moment, so a monk who meditates in order to stop all unwholesome thoughts of desire and aversion, when these thoughts continue to arise, should grit his teeth, press his tongue against his palate, and do his best to use his mind to beat down and defeat his mind.[5]

Often, we need to study several discourses and compare them in order to understand which is the true teaching of the Buddha. It is like stringing precious jewels together to make a necklace. If we see each sutra in light of the overall body of teachings, we will not be attached to any one teaching. With comparative study and looking deeply into the meaning of the texts, we can surmise what is a solid teaching that will help our practice and what is probably an incorrect transmission.

By the time the Buddha's discourses were written down in Pali in Sri Lanka, there were eighteen or twenty schools, and each had its own recension of the Buddha's teachings. These schools did not tear the teachings of the Buddha apart but were threads of a single garment. Two of these recensions exist today: the Tamrashatiya and Sarvastivada canons. Recorded at about the same time, the former was written down

---

[5] *Vitakka Santhana Sutta, Majjhima Nikaya* 20. This same passage was inserted into a Sarvastivada version of the Buddha's discourse on mindfulness, *Nian Chu Jing, Madhyama Agama* 26, *Taisho Revised Tripitaka.*

in Pali and the latter in Sanskrit and Prakrit. The sutras that were written down in Pali in Sri Lanka are known as the Southern transmission, or "Teachings of the Elders" *(Theravada)*. The Sarvastivada texts, known as the Northern transmission, exist only in fragmented form. Fortunately, they were translated into Chinese and Tibetan, and many of these translations are still available. We have to remember that the Buddha did not speak Pali, Sanskrit, or Prakrit. He spoke a local dialect called Magadhi or Ardhamagadhi, and there is no record of the Buddha's words in his own language.

By comparing the two extant sutra recensions, we can see which teachings must have preceded Buddhism's dividing into schools. When the sutras of both transmissions are the same, we can conclude that what they say must have been there before the division. When the recensions are different, we can surmise that one or both might be incorrect. The Northern transmission preserved some discourses better, and the Southern transmission preserved others better. That is the advantage of having two transmissions to compare.

The third stream of the Buddha's teaching, Mahayana Buddhism, arose in the first or second century B.C.E.[6] In the centuries following the Buddha's life, the practice of the Dharma had become the exclusive domain of monks and nuns, and laypeople were limited to supporting the ordained Sangha with food, shelter, clothing, and medicine. By the first century B.C.E., many monks and nuns seemed to be practicing only for themselves, and reaction was inevitable. The ideal put forth by the Mahayanists was that of the bodhisattva, who practiced and taught for the benefit of everyone.

These three streams complement one another. It was impossible for Source Buddhism to remember everything the

---

[6] See Thich Nhat Hanh, *Cultivating the Mind of Love: The Practice of Looking Deeply in the Mahayana Buddhist Tradition* (Berkeley: Parallax Press, 1996).

Buddha had taught, so it was necessary for Many-Schools Buddhism and Mahayana Buddhism to renew teachings that had been forgotten or overlooked. Like all traditions, Buddhism needs to renew itself regularly in order to stay alive and grow. The Buddha always found new ways to express his awakening. Since the Buddha's lifetime, Buddhists have continued to open new Dharma doors to express and share the teachings begun in the Deer Park in Sarnath.

Please remember that a sutra or a Dharma talk is not insight in and of itself. It is a means of presenting insight, using words and concepts. When you use a map to get to Paris, once you have arrived, you can put the map away and enjoy being in Paris. If you spend all your time with your map, if you get caught by the words and notions presented by the Buddha, you'll miss the reality. The Buddha said many times, "My teaching is like a finger pointing to the moon. Do not mistake the finger for the moon."

In the Mahayana Buddhist tradition, it is said, "If you explain the meaning of every word and phrase in the sutras, you slander the Buddhas of the three times — past, present, and future. But if you disregard even one word of the sutras, you risk speaking the words of Mara."[7] Sutras are essential guides for our practice, but we must read them carefully and use our own intelligence and the help of a teacher and a Sangha to understand the true meaning and put it into practice. After reading a sutra or any spiritual text, we should feel lighter, not heavier. Buddhist teachings are meant to awaken our true self, not merely to add to our storehouse of knowledge.

From time to time the Buddha refused to answer a question posed to him. The philosopher Vatsigotra asked, "Is there a self?" and the Buddha did not say anything.

---

[7] Mara: the Tempter, the Evil One, the Killer, the opposite of the Buddha nature in each person. Sometimes personalized as a deity.

Vatsigotra persisted, "Do you mean there is no self?" but the Buddha still did not reply. Finally, Vatsigotra left. Ananda, the Buddha's attendant, was puzzled. "Lord, you always teach that there is no self. Why did you not say so to Vatsigotra?" The Buddha told Ananda that he did not reply because Vatsigotra was looking for a theory, not a way to remove obstacles.[8] On another occasion, the Buddha heard a group of disciples discussing whether or not he had said such and such, and he told them, "For forty-five years, I have not uttered a single word." He did not want his disciples to be caught by words or notions, even his own.

When an archaeologist finds a statue that has been broken, he invites sculptors who specialize in restoration to study the art of that period and repair the statue. We must do the same. If we have an overall view of the teachings of the Buddha, when a piece is missing or has been added, we have to recognize it and repair the damage.

---

[8] *Samyutta Nikaya* XIV, 10.

CHAPTER FIVE

Is Everything Suffering?

If we are not careful in the way we practice, we may have the tendency to make the words of our teacher into a doctrine or an ideology. Since the Buddha said that the First Noble Truth is suffering, many good students of the Buddha have used their skills to prove that everything on Earth is suffering. The theory of the Three Kinds of Suffering was such an attempt. It is not a teaching of the Buddha.

The first kind of suffering is "the suffering of suffering" *(dukkha dukkhata),* the suffering associated with unpleasant feelings, like the pain of a toothache, losing your temper, or feeling too cold on a winter's day. The second is "the suffering of composite things" *(samskara dukkhata).* Whatever comes together eventually has to come apart; therefore, all composite things are described as suffering. Even things that have not yet decayed, such as mountains, rivers, and the sun, are seen to be suffering, because they will decay and cause suffering eventually. When you believe that everything composed is suffering, how can you find joy? The third is "the suffering associated with change" *(viparinama dukkhata).* Our liver may be in good health today, but when we grow old, it will cause us to suffer. There is no point in celebrating joy, because sooner or later it will turn into suffering. Suffering is a black cloud that envelops everything. Joy is an illusion. Only suffering is real.

For more than two thousand years, students of Buddhism have been declaring that the Buddha taught that all objects of perception — all physical (table, sun, moon) and physi-ological phenomena and all wholesome, unwholesome, and neutral states of mind — are suffering. One hundred years after the Buddha passed away, practitioners were already re-peating the formula, "This is suffering. Life is suffering. *Everything* is suffering." They thought that to obtain insight into the First Noble Truth, they had to repeat this formula. Some commentators said that without this constant repetition, the Four Noble Truths could not be realized.[1]

Today, many people invoke the names of the Buddha or do similar practices mechanically, believing that this will bring them insight and emancipation. They are caught in forms, words, and notions, and are not using their intelli-gence to receive and practice the Dharma. It can be danger-ous to practice without using your own intelligence, without a teacher and friends who can show you ways to practice cor-rectly. Repeating a phrase like "Life is suffering" might help you notice when you are about to become attached to some-thing, but it cannot help you understand the true nature of suffering or reveal the path shown to us by the Buddha.

This dialogue is repeated in many sutras:

> "Monks, are conditioned things permanent or im-permanent?"
> "They are impermanent, World-Honored One."

---

[1] *Points of Controversy (Kathavatthu)*, a work belonging to the Southern Transmission that enumerates points on which the various schools of Bud-dhism differed, says that the question, "Does the realization of the truth of suffering depend on the repetition of the words, *'Idam dukkham ti.'* (This is suffering.)?" was answered affirmatively by many schools, including the Purvashaila, Aparashaila, Rajagirika, and Siddharthika. Also, when Mahadeva of the Mahasanghika School listed five reasons that an arhat is not fully awakened, one of the reasons he gave was that an arhat needs to repeat something constantly in order to be able to realize it.

"If things are impermanent, are they suffering or well-being?"

"They are suffering, World-Honored One."

"If things are suffering, can we say that they are self or belong to self?"

"No, World-Honored One."

When we read this, we may think that the Buddha is offering a theory — "All things are suffering" — that we have to prove in our daily life. But in other parts of the same sutras, the Buddha says that he only wants us to recognize suffering when it is present and to recognize joy when suffering is absent. By the time the Buddha's discourses were written down, seeing all things as suffering must have been widely practiced, as the above quotation occurs more frequently than the teaching to identify suffering and the path to end suffering.

The argument, "Impermanent, therefore suffering, therefore nonself" is illogical. Of course, if we believe that something is permanent or has a self, we may suffer when we discover that it is impermanent and without a separate self. But, in many texts, suffering is regarded as one of the Three Dharma Seals, along with impermanence and nonself. It is said that all teachings of the Buddha bear the Three Dharma Seals.[2] To put suffering on the same level as impermanence and nonself is an error. Impermanence and nonself are "universal." They are a "mark" of all things. Suffering is not. It is not difficult to see that a table is impermanent and does not have a self separate of all non-table elements, like wood, rain, sun, furniture maker, and so on. But is it suffering? A table will only make us suffer if we attribute permanence or separateness to it. When we are attached to a certain table, it is not the table that causes us to suffer. It is our attachment. We

---

[2] For an explication of the Three Dharma Seals, see chap. 18.

can agree that anger is impermanent, without a separate self, and filled with suffering, but it is strange to talk about a table or a flower as being filled with suffering. The Buddha taught impermanence and nonself to help us not be caught in signs.

The theory of the Three Kinds of Suffering is an attempt to justify the universalization of suffering. What joy is left in life? We find it in nirvana. In several sutras the Buddha taught that nirvana, the joy of completely extinguishing our ideas and concepts, rather than suffering, is one of the Three Dharma Seals. This is stated four times in the *Samyukta Agama* of the Northern transmission.[3] Quoting from yet another sutra, Nagarjuna listed nirvana as one of the Three Dharma Seals.[4] To me, it is much easier to envision a state where there are no obstacles created by concepts than to see all things as suffering. I hope scholars and practitioners will begin to accept the teaching that all things are marked by impermanence, nonself, and nirvana, and not make too great an effort to prove that everything is suffering.

Another common misunderstanding of the Buddha's teaching is that all of our suffering is caused by craving. In the *Discourse on Turning the Wheel of the Dharma*, the Buddha did say that craving is the cause of suffering, but he said this because craving is the first on the list of afflictions *(kleshas)*. If we use our intelligence, we can see that craving can be a cause of pain, but other afflictions such as anger, ignorance, suspicion, arrogance, and wrong views can also cause pain and suffering. Ignorance, which gives rise to wrong perceptions, is responsible for much of our pain. To make the sutras shorter and therefore easier to memorize, the first item on a list was often used to represent the whole list. The word "eyes," for example, is used in many sutras to represent all six

---

[3] *Tsa A Han* 262 *(Taisho 99).*

[4] *Mahaprajñaparamita Shastra.* See Étienne Lamotte, *Le Traité de La Grande Vertu de Sagesse* (Louvain, Belgium: Institut Orientaliste, 1949).

sense organs[5] and "form" is often used to represent all Five Aggregates *(skandhas)*.[6] If we practice identifying the causes of our suffering, we will see that sometimes it is due to craving and sometimes it is due to other factors. To say, "Life is suffering," is too general. To say that craving is the cause of all our suffering is too simplistic. We need to say, "The basis for this suffering is such and such an affliction," and then call it by its true name. If we have a stomachache, we need to call it a stomachache. If it is a headache, we need to call it a headache. How else will we find the cause of our suffering and the way to heal ourselves?

It is true that the Buddha taught the truth of suffering, but he also taught the truth of "dwelling happily in things as they are"*(drishta dharma sukha viharin)*.[7] To succeed in the practice, we must stop trying to prove that everything is suffering. In fact, we must stop trying to prove anything. If we touch the truth of suffering with our mindfulness, we will be able to recognize and identify our specific suffering, its specific causes, and the way to remove those causes and end our suffering.

---

[5] Six sense organs: eyes, ears, nose, tongue, body, and mind.

[6] The Five Aggregates are the elements that constitute a person, namely form, feelings, perceptions, mental formations, and consciousness. See chap. 23.

[7] *Samyutta Nikaya* V, 326, and many other places.

CHAPTER SIX

Stopping, Calming, Resting, Healing

Buddhist meditation has two aspects — *shamatha* and *vipashyana*. We tend to stress the importance of vipashyana ("looking deeply") because it can bring us insight and liberate us from suffering and afflictions. But the practice of shamatha ("stopping") is fundamental. If we cannot stop, we cannot have insight.

There is a story in Zen circles about a man and a horse. The horse is galloping quickly, and it appears that the man on the horse is going somewhere important. Another man, standing alongside the road, shouts, "Where are you going?" and the first man replies, "I don't know! Ask the horse!" This is also our story. We are riding a horse, we don't know where we are going, and we can't stop. The horse is our habit energy pulling us along, and we are powerless. We are always running, and it has become a habit. We struggle all the time, even during our sleep. We are at war within ourselves, and we can easily start a war with others.

We have to learn the art of stopping — stopping our thinking, our habit energies, our forgetfulness, the strong emotions that rule us. When an emotion rushes through us like a storm, we have no peace. We turn on the TV and then we turn it off. We pick up a book and then we put it down. How can we stop this state of agitation? How can we stop our fear, despair, anger, and craving? We can stop by practicing mindful breathing, mindful walking, mindful smiling, and deep looking in order to understand. When we are mindful, touching deeply the present moment, the fruits are always understanding, acceptance, love, and the desire to relieve suffering and bring joy.

But our habit energies are often stronger than our volition. We say and do things we don't want to and afterwards we regret it. We make ourselves and others suffer, and we bring about a lot of damage. We may vow not to do it again, but we do it again. Why? Because our habit energies *(vashana)* push us.

We need the energy of mindfulness to recognize and be present with our habit energy in order to stop this course of destruction. With mindfulness, we have the capacity to recognize the habit energy every time it manifests. "Hello, my habit energy, I know you are there!" If we just smile to it, it will lose much of its strength. Mindfulness is the energy that allows us to recognize our habit energy and prevent it from dominating us.

Forgetfulness is the opposite. We drink a cup of tea, but we do not know we are drinking a cup of tea. We sit with the person we love, but we don't know that she is there. We walk, but we are not really walking. We are someplace else, thinking about the past or the future. The horse of our habit energy is carrying us along, and we are its captive. We need to stop our horse and reclaim our liberty. We need to shine the light of mindfulness on everything we do, so the darkness of forgetfulness will disappear. The first function of meditation — shamatha — is to stop.

The second function of shamatha is calming. When we have a strong emotion, we know it can be dangerous to act, but we don't have the strength or clarity to refrain. We have to learn the art of breathing in and out, stopping our activities, and calming our emotions. We have to learn to become solid and stable like an oak tree, and not be blown from side to side by the storm. The Buddha taught many techniques to help us calm our body and mind and look deeply at them. They can be summarized in five stages:

(1) Recognition — If we are angry, we say, "I know that anger is in me."

(2) Acceptance — When we are angry, we do not deny it. We accept what is present.

(3) Embracing — We hold our anger in our two arms like a mother holding her crying baby. Our mindfulness embraces our emotion, and this alone can calm our anger and ourselves.

(4) Looking deeply — When we are calm enough, we can look deeply to understand what has brought this anger to be, what is causing our baby's discomfort.

(5) Insight — The fruit of looking deeply is understanding the many causes and conditions, primary and secondary, that have brought about our anger, that are causing our baby to cry. Perhaps our baby is hungry. Perhaps his diaper pin is piercing his skin. Our anger was triggered when our friend spoke to us meanly, and suddenly we remember that he was not at his best today because his father is dying. We reflect like this until we have some insights into what has caused our suffering. With insight, we know what to do and what not to do to change the situation.

After calming, the third function of shamatha is resting. Suppose someone standing alongside a river throws a pebble in the air and it falls down into the river. The pebble allows itself to sink slowly and reach the riverbed without any effort. Once the pebble is at the bottom, it continues to rest, allowing the water to pass by. When we practice sitting meditation, we can allow ourselves to rest just like that pebble. We can allow ourselves to sink naturally into the position of sitting — resting, without effort. We have to learn the art of resting, allowing our body and mind to rest. If we have wounds in our body or our mind, we have to rest so they can heal themselves.

Calming allows us to rest, and resting is a precondition for healing. When animals in the forest get wounded, they find a place to lie down, and they rest completely for many days. They don't think about food or anything else. They just rest, and they get the healing they need. When we humans get sick, we just worry! We look for doctors and medicine, but we don't stop. Even when we go to the beach or the mountains for a vacation, we don't rest, and we come back more tired than before. We have to learn to rest. Lying down is not the only position for resting. During sitting or walking meditation, we can rest very well. Meditation does not have to be hard labor. Just allow your body and mind to rest like an animal in the forest. Don't struggle. There is no need to attain anything. I am writing a book, but I am not struggling. I am resting also. Please read in a joyful, yet restful way. The Buddha said, "My Dharma is the practice of non-practice."[1] Practice in a way that does not tire you out, but gives your body, emotions, and consciousness a chance to rest. Our body and mind have the capacity to heal themselves if we allow them to rest.

Stopping, calming, and resting are preconditions for healing. If we cannot stop, the course of our destruction will just continue. The world needs healing. Individuals, communities, and nations need healing.

---

[1] *Dvachatvarimshat Khanda Sutra (Sutra of Forty-Two Chapters). Taisho* 789.

CHAPTER SEVEN

Touching Our Suffering

In the Pali version of the *Discourse on Turning the Wheel of the Dharma,* the Buddha told the five monks,

> As long as the insight and the understanding of these Four Noble Truths in their three stages and twelve aspects, just as they are, had not been fully realized, I could not say that in this world with its gods, maras, brahmas, recluses, brahmans, and men, someone had realized the highest awakening. Monks, as soon as the insight and understanding of the Four Noble Truths in their three stages and twelve aspects, just as they are, had been realized, I could say that in this world with its gods, maras, brahmas, recluses, brahmans, and men, someone had realized the highest awakening.

In the Chinese version of the sutra, the Buddha said,

> Monks, the experience of the three turnings of the wheel with regard to each of the Four Truths gives rise to eyes of awakened understanding, and therefore I declare before gods, spirits, shramanas, and brahmans of all times that I have destroyed all afflictions and reached full awakening.

The wheel of the Dharma was put in motion twelve times

— three for each of the Four Noble Truths. To understand the Four Noble Truths, not just intellectually but experientially, we have to practice the twelve turnings of the wheel.

The first turning is called "Recognition." We sense that something is wrong, but we are not able to say exactly what it is. We make some effort to escape, but we cannot. We try to deny our suffering, but it persists. The Buddha said that to suffer and not know that we are suffering is more painful than the burden endured by a mule carrying an unimaginably heavy load. We must, first of all, recognize that we are suffering and then determine whether its basis is physical, physiological, or psychological. Our suffering needs to be identified.

Recognizing and identifying our suffering is like the work of a doctor diagnosing an illness. He or she says, "If I press here, does it hurt?" and we say, "Yes, this is my suffering. This has come to be." The wounds in our heart become the object of our meditation. We show them to our doctor, and we show them to the Buddha, which means we show them to ourselves. Our suffering is us, and we need to treat it with kindness and nonviolence. We need to embrace our fear, hatred, anguish, and anger. "My dear suffering, I know you are there. I am here for you, and I will take care of you." We stop running from our pain. With all our courage and tenderness, we recognize, acknowledge, and identify it.

The second turning of the wheel is called "Encouragement." After recognizing and identifying our pain, we take the time to look deeply into it in order to understand its true nature, which means its causes. After observing our symptoms, the doctor says, "I will look deeply into it. This illness can be understood." It may take him a week to conduct tests and inquire about what we have been eating, our attitudes, how we spend our time, and so on. But he is determined to understand our illness.

Our suffering — depression, illness, a difficult relation-

The Twelve Turnings of the Wheel

FOUR NOBLE TRUTHS	TWELVE TURNINGS
Suffering	Recognition: This is suffering.
	Encouragement: Suffering should be understood.
	Realization: Suffering is understood.
Arising of suffering	Recognition: There is an ignoble way that has led to suffering.
	Encouragement: That ignoble way should be understood.
	Realization: That ignoble way is understood.
Cessation of suffering (well-being)	Recognition: Well-being is possible.
	Encouragement: Well-being should be obtained.
	Realization: Well-being is obtained.
How well-being arises	Recognition: There is a noble path that leads to well-being.
	Encouragement: This noble path has to be lived.
	Realization: This noble path is being lived.

Figure Two

ship, or fear — needs to be understood and, like a doctor, we are determined to understand it. We practice sitting and walking meditation, and we ask for guidance and support from our friends and, if we have one, our teacher. As we do this, we see that the causes of our suffering are knowable, and we make every effort to get to the bottom of it. At this stage, our practice can still be "set back" *(ashrava).*

The third turning of the wheel is called "Realization" and can be expressed as, "This suffering has been understood." We realize the efforts begun during the second turning. The doctor tells us the name and all the characteristics of our illness. After studying, reflecting upon, and practicing the First Noble Truth, we realize that we have stopped running away from our pain. We can now call our suffering by its specific name and identify all of its characteristics. This alone brings us happiness, joy "without setbacks" *(anashrava).*

Still, after we have successfully diagnosed our ailment, for a time we continue to create suffering for ourselves. We pour gasoline on the fire through our words, thoughts, and deeds and often don't even realize it. The first turning of the wheel of the Second Noble Truth is the "Recognition": I am continuing to create suffering. The Buddha said, "When something has come to be, we have to acknowledge its presence and look deeply into its nature. When we look deeply, we will discover the kinds of nutriments that have helped it come to be and that continue to feed it."[1] He then elaborated four kinds of nutriments that can lead to our happiness or our suffering — edible food, sense impressions, intention, and consciousness.

The first nutriment is edible food. What we eat or drink can bring about mental or physical suffering. We must be able to distinguish between what is healthful and what is harmful. We need to practice Right View when we shop, cook, and eat. The Buddha offered this example. A young couple and their two-year-old child were trying to cross the desert, and they ran out of food. After deep reflection, the parents realized that in order to survive they had to kill their son and eat his flesh. They calculated that if they ate such

---

[1] *Samyutta Nikaya* II, 47. See also p. 269, *Discourse on Right View.*

and such a proportion of their baby's flesh each day and carried the rest on their shoulders to dry, it would last the rest of the journey. But with every morsel of their baby's flesh they ate, the young couple cried and cried. After he told this story, the Buddha asked, "Dear friends, do you think the young man and woman enjoyed eating their son's flesh?" "No, Lord, it would not be possible for them to enjoy eating their son's flesh." The Buddha said, "Yet many people eat the flesh of their parents, their children, and their grandchildren and do not know it."[2]

Much of our suffering comes from not eating mindfully. We have to learn ways to eat that preserve the health and well-being of our body and our spirit. When we smoke, drink, or consume toxins, we are eating our own lungs, liver, and heart. If we have children and do these things, we are eating our children's flesh. Our children need us to be healthy and strong.

We have to look deeply to see how we grow our food, so we can eat in ways that preserve our collective well-being, minimize our suffering and the suffering of other species, and allow the earth to continue to be a source of life for all of us. If, while we eat, we destroy living beings or the environment, we are eating the flesh of our own sons and daughters. We need to look deeply together and discuss how to eat, what to eat, and what to resist. This will be a real Dharma discussion.

The second kind of nutriment is sense impressions. Our six sense organs — eyes, ears, nose, tongue, body, and mind — are in constant contact *(sparsha)* with sense objects, and these contacts become food for our consciousness. When we drive through a city, our eyes see so many billboards, and these images enter our consciousness. When we pick up a magazine, the articles and advertisements are food for our

---

[2] *Discourse on the Son's Flesh, Samyukta Agama* 373 (*Taisho* 99). Also *Samyutta Nikaya* II, 97.

consciousness. Advertisements that stimulate our craving for possessions, sex, and food can be toxic. If after reading the newspaper, hearing the news, or being in a conversation, we feel anxious or worn out, we know we have been in contact with toxins.

Movies are food for our eyes, ears, and minds. When we watch TV, the program is our food. Children who spend five hours a day watching television are ingesting images that water the negative seeds of craving, fear, anger, and violence in them. We are exposed to so many forms, colors, sounds, smells, tastes, objects of touch, and ideas that are toxic and rob our body and consciousness of their well-being. When you feel despair, fear, or depression, it may be because you have ingested too many toxins through your sense impressions. Not only children need to be protected from violent and unwholesome films, TV programs, books, magazines, and games. We, too, can be destroyed by these media.

If we are mindful, we will know whether we are "ingesting" the toxins of fear, hatred, and violence, or eating foods that encourage understanding, compassion, and the determination to help others. With the practice of mindfulness, we will know that hearing this, looking at that, or touching this, we feel light and peaceful, while hearing that, looking at this, or touching that, we feel anxious, sad, or depressed. As a result, we will know what to be in contact with and what to avoid. Our skin protects us from bacteria. Antibodies protect us from internal invaders. We have to use the equivalent aspects of our consciousness to protect us from unwholesome sense objects that can poison us.

The Buddha offered this drastic image: "There is a cow with such a terrible skin disease that her skin is almost no longer there. When you bring her close to an ancient wall or old tree, all the living creatures in the bark of the tree come out, cling to the cow's body, and suck. When we bring her into the water, the same thing happens. Even when she is just exposed to the air, tiny insects come and suck." Then the Buddha said, "This is our situation, also."

We are exposed to invasions of all kinds — images, sounds, smells, touch, ideas — and many of these feed the craving, violence, fear, and despair in us. The Buddha advised us to post a sentinel, namely mindfulness, at each of our sense doors to protect ourselves. Use your Buddha eyes to look at each nutriment you are about to ingest. If you see that it is toxic, refuse to look at it, listen to it, taste it, or touch it. Ingest only what you are certain is safe. The Five Mindfulness Trainings[3] can help very much. We must come together as individuals, families, cities, and a nation to discuss strategies of self-protection and survival. To get out of the dangerous situation we are in, the practice of mindfulness has to be collective.

The third kind of nutriment is volition, intention, or will — the desire in us to obtain whatever it is that we want. Volition is the ground of all our actions. If we think that the way for us to be happy is to become president of a large corporation, everything we do or say will be directed toward realizing that goal. Even when we sleep, our consciousness will continue to work on it. Or suppose we believe that all our suffering and the suffering of our family has been brought about by someone who wronged us in the past. We believe we will only be happy if we inflict harm on that person. Our life is motivated solely by the desire for revenge, and everything we say, everything we plan, is to punish that person. At night, we dream of revenge, and we think this will liberate us from our anger and hatred.

Everyone wants to be happy, and there is a strong energy in us pushing us toward what we think will make us happy.

---

[3] See Thich Nhat Hanh, *For a Future To Be Possible: Commentaries on the Five Mindfulness Trainings,* Revised Edition (Berkeley: Parallax Press, 1998). See also chaps. 12 and 13 of this book.

But we may suffer a lot because of this. We need the insight that position, revenge, wealth, fame, or possessions are, more often than not, obstacles to our happiness. We need to cultivate the wish to be free of these things so we can enjoy the wonders of life that are always available — the blue sky, the trees, our beautiful children. After three months or six months of mindful sitting, mindful walking, and mindful looking, a deep vision of reality arises in us, and the capacity of being there, enjoying life in the present moment, liberates us from all impulses and brings us real happiness.

One day, after the Buddha and a group of monks finished eating lunch mindfully together, a farmer, very agitated, came by and asked, "Monks, have you seen my cows? I don't think I can survive so much misfortune." The Buddha asked him, "What happened?" and the man said, "Monks, this morning all twelve of my cows ran away. And this year my whole crop of sesame plants was eaten by insects!" The Buddha said, "Sir, we have not seen your cows. Perhaps they have gone in the other direction." After the farmer went off in that direction, the Buddha turned to his Sangha and said, "Dear friends, do you know you are the happiest people on Earth? You have no cows or sesame plants to lose." We always try to accumulate more and more, and we think these "cows" are essential for our existence. In fact, they may be the obstacles that prevent us from being happy. Release your cows and become a free person. Release your cows so you can be truly happy.

The Buddha presented another drastic image: "Two strong men are dragging a third man along in order to throw him into a fire pit. He cannot resist, and finally they throw him into the glowing embers." These strong men, the Buddha said, are our own volition. We don't want to suffer, but our deep-seated habit energies drag us into the fire of suffering. The Buddha advised us to look deeply into the nature of our volition to see whether it is pushing us in the direction of liberation, peace, and compassion or in the direction of suffering and unhappiness. We need to be able to see the kinds of intention-food that we are consuming.

The fourth kind of nutriment is consciousness.[4] Our consciousness is composed of all the seeds sown by our past actions and the past actions of our family and society. Every day our thoughts, words, and actions flow into the sea of our consciousness and create our body, mind, and world. We can nourish our consciousness by practicing the Four Immeasurable Minds of love, compassion, joy, and equanimity,[5] or we can feed our consciousness with greed, hatred, ignorance, suspicion, and pride. Our consciousness is eating all the time, day and night, and what it consumes becomes the substance of our life. We have to be very careful which nutriments we ingest.[6]

The Buddha offered another dramatic image to illustrate this: "A dangerous murderer was captured and brought before the king, and the king sentenced him to death by stab-

---

[4] See chap. 4, n. 1, on p. 12.

[5] See chap. 22.

[6] In the year 255, Vietnamese Meditation Master Tang Hôi taught that our consciousness is like the ocean with the six rivers of our senses flowing into it. Our mind and our body come from consciousness. They are formed by ourselves and our environment. Our life can be said to be a manifestation of our consciousness. Because of the food that our consciousness consumes, we are the person we are and our environment is what it is. In fact, the edible foods we take into our body and the foods of sense-impression and intention all end up in our consciousness. Our ignorance, hatred, and sadness all flow back to the sea of consciousness. We should know the kinds of food we feed our consciousness every day. When *vijñana* (consciousness) ripens, it brings forth a new form of life, *nama rupa* (mind/body). Rupa is our body or physical aspect, and nama is our mind or mental aspect. Body and mind are manifestations of our consciousness, and our consciousness is made of these kinds of food. We have to look at the Five Aggregates (skandhas) in us — form, feelings, perceptions, mental formations, and consciousness. They are *nama rupa*. The first of the Five Aggregates is rupa, and the other four are nama. They are all products of our alayavijñana, our store consciousness.

bing. 'Take him to the courtyard and plunge three hundred sharp knives through him.' At noon a guard reported, 'Majesty, he is still alive,' and the king declared, 'Stab him three hundred more times!' In the evening, the guard again told the king, 'Majesty, he is not yet dead.' So the king gave the third order: 'Plunge the three hundred sharpest knives in the kingdom through him.'" Then the Buddha said, "This is how we usually deal with our consciousness." Every time we ingest toxins into our consciousness, it is like stabbing ourselves with three hundred sharp knives. We suffer, and our suffering spills out to those around us.

When we practice the first turning of the First Noble Truth, we recognize suffering as suffering. If we are in a difficult relationship, we recognize, "This is a difficult relationship." Our practice is to be with our suffering and take good care of it. When we practice the first turning of the Second Noble Truth, we look deeply into the nature of our suffering to see what kinds of nutriments we have been feeding it. How have we lived in the last few years, in the last few months, that has contributed to our suffering? We need to recognize and identify the nutriments we ingest and observe, "When I think like this, speak like that, listen like this, or act like that, my suffering increases." Until we begin to practice the Second Noble Truth, we tend to blame others for our unhappiness.

Looking deeply requires courage. You can use a pencil and paper if you like. During sitting meditation, if you see clearly a symptom of your suffering, write it down. Then ask yourself, "What kinds of nutriments have I been ingesting that have fed and sustained this suffering?" When you begin to realize the kinds of nutriments you have been ingesting, you may cry. Use the energy of mindfulness all day long to be truly present, to embrace your suffering like a mother holding her baby. As long as mindfulness is there, you can stay with the difficulty. Practice does not mean using only your own mindfulness, concentration, and wisdom. You also have to benefit from the mindfulness, concentration, and wisdom of friends on the path and your teacher. There are things that even a child can see but we ourselves cannot see because we are imprisoned by our notions. Bring what you have written to a friend and ask for his or her observations and insights.

If you sit with a friend and speak openly, determined to discover the roots of your suffering, eventually you will see them clearly. But if you keep your suffering to yourself, it might grow bigger every day. Just seeing the causes of your suffering lessens your burden. Shariputra, one of the Buddha's great disciples, said, "When something takes place, if we look at it deeply in the heart of reality, seeing its source and the food that nourishes it, we are already on the path of liberation." When we are able to identify our suffering and see its causes, we will have more peace and joy, and we are already on the path to liberation.

In the second stage of the Second Noble Truth, "Encouragement," we see clearly that real happiness is possible if we can stop ingesting the nutriments that cause us to suffer. If we know that our body is suffering because of the way we eat, sleep, or work, we vow to eat, sleep, or work in ways that are healthier. We encourage ourselves to put an end to the causes of our suffering. Only by a strong intention not to do things in the same way can we keep the wheel in motion.

Mindfulness is the energy that can help us stop. We investigate the kinds of nutriments we now ingest and decide which ones to continue to eat and which to resist. We sit and look together with our friends, with our family, and as a community. Mindfulness of ingestion, protecting our body and mind, protecting our families, society, and the environment are important topics for us to discuss. When we direct our attention toward our suffering, we see our potential for happiness. We see the nature of suffering *and* the way out. That is why the Buddha called suffering a holy truth. When we use the word "suffering" in Buddhism, we mean the kind of suffering that can show us the way out.

There are many practices that can help us face our suffering, including mindful walking, mindful breathing, mindful sitting, mindful eating, mindful looking, and mindful listening. One mindful step can take us deep into the realization of beauty and joy in us and around us. Tran Thai Tong, a great meditation master of thirteenth-century Vietnam, said, "With every step, you touch the ground of reality." If you practice mindful walking and deep listening all day long, that is the Four Noble Truths in action. When the cause of suffering has been seen, healing is possible. We vow to refrain from ingesting foods that make us suffer, and we also vow to ingest foods that are healthy and wholesome.

In the third turning of the wheel of the Second Noble Truth, "Realization," we not only vow but we actually stop ingesting the nutriments that create our suffering. Some people think that to end suffering, you have to *stop* everything — body, feelings, perceptions, mental formations and consciousness — but that is not correct. The third stage of the Second Noble Truth can be described as, "When hungry, I eat. When tired, I sleep." When someone has realized this stage, she has a certain lightness and freedom. What she wants to do is fully in accord with the mindfulness trainings, and she does nothing to cause herself or others harm.

Confucius said, "At thirty, I was able to stand on my own feet. At forty, I had no more doubts. At fifty, I knew the mandate of Earth and Sky. At sixty, I could do what I wanted without going against the path." The last of the ten ox herding pictures in the Zen tradition is called "Entering the Marketplace with Open Hands." You are free to come and go as you please. This is the action of non-action. Suffering no longer arises. This stage is not something you can imitate. You have to reach this stage of realization within yourself.

At the end of the nineteenth century in Vietnam, Master

Nhat Dinh asked the king for permission to retire from being abbot of a national temple so he could live in a mountain hut and take care of his aging mother. Many officials made offerings to the master and begged him to found another temple, but he preferred to live simply, in great peace and joy. One day his mother fell ill and needed fish to eat. He went down to the marketplace, asked some vendors for a fish, and carried it back up the mountain. Onlookers asked, "What is a Buddhist monk doing with a fish?" But someone of Master Nhat Dinh's realization could do as he pleased without going against the precepts. At the third stage of the Second Noble Truth, you only have to be yourself. The form is not important. But be careful! First there has to be genuine insight, genuine freedom.

CHAPTER EIGHT

Realizing Well-Being

When we have a toothache, we know that not having a toothache is happiness. But later, when we don't have a toothache, we don't treasure our non-toothache. Practicing mindfulness helps us learn to appreciate the well-being that is already there. With mindfulness, we treasure our happiness and can make it last longer. I always ask psychotherapists, "Why do you only talk to your clients about suffering? Why not help them touch the seeds of happiness that are also there?" Psychotherapists need to help their patients be in touch with the Third Noble Truth, the cessation of suffering. I encourage them to practice walking meditation and tea meditation with their patients in order to water the seeds of joy in them.

Please ask yourself, "What nourishes joy in me? What nourishes joy in others? Do I nourish joy in myself and others enough?" These are questions about the Third Noble Truth. The cessation of suffering — well-being — is available if you know how to enjoy the precious jewels you already have. You have eyes that can see, lungs that can breathe, legs that can walk, and lips that can smile. When you are suffering, look deeply at your situation and find the conditions for happiness that are already there, already available.

When we begin the first stage of the Third Noble Truth, we already have some happiness, but we are not exactly aware of it. We are free, but we don't know that we are free. When we are young, we are strong and healthy, but we don't appreciate it. Even if someone tries to tell us, we cannot realize what we have. Only when we have difficulty walking do we realize how wonderful it was to have two healthy legs. The first turning of the Third Noble Truth is the "Recognition" of the possibility of the absence of suffering and the presence of peace. If we do not have peace and joy at this moment, we can at least remember some peace and joy we experienced in the past or observe the peace and joy of others. We see that *well-being is possible.*

The second turning is to "Encourage" ourselves to find peace and joy. If you want to garden, you have to bend down and touch the soil. Gardening is a practice, not an idea. To practice the Four Noble Truths, you yourself have to touch deeply the things that bring you peace and joy. When you do, you realize that walking on the Earth is a miracle, washing the dishes is a miracle, and practicing with a community of friends is a miracle. The greatest miracle is to be alive. We can put an end to our suffering just by realizing that our suffering is not worth suffering for! How many people kill themselves because of rage or despair? In that moment, they do not see the vast happiness that is available. Mindfulness puts an end to such a limited perspective. The Buddha faced his own suffering directly and discovered the path of liberation. Don't run away from things that are unpleasant in order to embrace things that are pleasant. Put your hands in the earth. Face the difficulties and grow new happiness.

One student told me, "When I go to parties, people seem to be enjoying themselves. But when I look beneath the surface, I see so much anxiety and suffering there." At first, your joy is limited, especially the kind of joy that is just covering up suffering. Embrace your suffering, smile to it, and discover the source of happiness that is right there within it. Buddhas and bodhisattvas suffer, too. The difference between them and us is that they know how to transform their suffering into joy and compassion. Like good organic gardeners, they do not discriminate in favor of the flowers or against the garbage. They know how to transform garbage into flowers. Don't throw away your suffering. Touch your suffering. Face it directly, and your joy will become deeper. You know that suffering and joy are both impermanent. Learn the art of cultivating joy.

Practice like this, and you come to the third turning of the Third Noble Truth, the "Realization" that suffering and happiness are not two. When you reach this stage, your joy is no longer fragile. It is true joy.

The Fourth Noble Truth is the way out of suffering. First the doctor looks deeply into the nature of our suffering. Then she confirms that the removal of our pain is possible, and she prescribes a way out. Practicing the first turning of the wheel of the Fourth Noble Truth, we "Recognize" that the Eightfold Path — Right View, Right Thinking, Right Speech, Right Action, Right Livelihood, Right Diligence, Right Mindfulness, and Right Concentration — can lead us out of suffering, but we do not yet know how to practice it.

In the second turning, we "Encourage" ourselves to *practice* this path. This is realized by learning, reflecting, and practicing. As we learn, whether by reading, listening, or discussing, we need to be open so we can see ways to put what we learn into practice. If learning is not followed by reflecting and practicing, it is not true learning.

In this stage, we see that the path has everything to do with our real difficulties in life. A practice that does not concern our real suffering is not a path we need. Many people are awakened during a difficult period in their lives, when they see that living irresponsibly has been the cause of their suffering, and that by transforming their lifestyle they can bring an end to their suffering. Transformation is gradual, but once we see clearly the causes of our suffering, we can make the effort to change our behavior and bring our suffering to an end. If we are aware that our heart is not working well and that alcohol, cigarettes, and cholesterol are causes of this, we try to stop ingesting these things. In the second stage of the path, there is an increase in freedom every day. The path becomes real as we put into practice what we have learned.

The Buddha advised us to identify the kinds of nutriments that have been feeding our pain and then simply to stop ingesting them. We do our best, and we ask our brothers and sisters to help us. We can't expect our difficulties to go away by themselves. We have to do certain things and not do other things. The moment we resolve to stop feeding our suffering, a path appears in front of us, which is the Noble Eightfold Path to well-being. The Buddha is a physician. That is why he invited us to bring our suffering to him. We are also physicians. We must be determined to transform our difficulties, to confirm that well-being is possible. The Buddha identified the Noble Eightfold Path to well-being and urged us to follow it. The third turning of the wheel of the Fourth Noble Truth is the "Realization" that we are practicing this path.

When you are assigned a *kung-an* (koan) by your meditation instructor, such as, "What is the sound of one hand clapping?" or "Why did Bodhidharma come from the West?" you have to ask yourself, What does this have to do with my real suffering — my depression, my fear, or my anger? If it doesn't have anything to do with these real problems, it may not be a path you need. It may be just an escape. Practice your kung-an in a way that your suffering is transformed.

"This is suffering. This suffering needs to be seen clearly. The roots of this suffering need to be clearly understood. I have seen this suffering. I have seen how it manifests. I have seen its content and its roots." These are practices, not mere proclamations. "Understanding things as they are" *(yatha bhuta jñana)* emerges from our life and our practice.

When the monk Gavampati heard his fellow monks say, "Whoever sees suffering sees the making of suffering, the ending of suffering, and the path," he added, "With my own ears I have heard the Buddha say, 'Bhikkhus, whoever sees suffering sees the making of suffering, the ending of suffering, and the path that leads to the end of suffering. Whoever sees the making of suffering sees suffering, the end of suffering, and the path. Whoever sees the ending of suffering sees suffering, the making of suffering, and the path. Whoever sees the path that leads to the end of suffering sees suffering, the making of suffering, and the ending of suffering.'"[1] Interbeing is an important characteristic of all the Buddha's teachings. When you touch one, you touch all.

It is important to understand the interbeing nature of the Four Noble Truths. When we look deeply into any one of the Four Truths, we see the other three. When we look deeply into the truth of suffering, we see how that suffering came to be. When we look deeply into the truth of suffering, we see how to end that suffering and touch well-being. When we look deeply into the truth of suffering, we see the efficacy of the path. Looking into the First Holy Truth, we see in it the Second, Third, and Fourth Truths. The Four Noble Truths are one.

We need suffering in order to see the path. The origin of suffering, the cessation of suffering, and the path leading to the cessation of suffering are all found in the heart of suffering. If we are afraid to touch our suffering, we will not be able to realize the path of peace, joy, and liberation. Don't run away. Touch your suffering and embrace it. Make peace with it. The Buddha said, "The moment you know how your suffering came to be, you are already on the path of release from it."[2] If you know what has come to be and how it has come to be, you are already on the way to emancipation.

Let us reframe the Four Noble Truths. "Cessation," the Third Noble Truth, means the absence of suffering, which is

---

[1] *Gavampati Sutta, Samyutta Nikaya* V, 436.

[2] *Samyutta Nikaya* II, 47.

the presence of well-being. Instead of saying "cessation," we can simply say "well-being." If we do that, we can call the Fourth Noble Truth "the Noble Eightfold Path That Leads to Well-Being." Then, instead of just calling the Second Noble Truth "the origin of suffering," we can say that there is an ignoble eightfold path that leads to suffering, a "path of eight wrong practices" — wrong view, wrong thinking, wrong speech, wrong action, wrong livelihood, wrong diligence, wrong mindfulness, and wrong concentration. We might like to renumber the Four Noble Truths, as follows, for the benefit of the people of our time:

(1) Well-Being (traditionally number three, "cessation of suffering");

(2) Noble Eightfold Path That Leads to Well-Being (traditionally number four);

(3) Suffering (traditionally number one); and

(4) Ignoble Eightfold Path That Leads to Suffering (traditionally number two, "arising of suffering").

If we live according to the Noble Eightfold Path, we cultivate well-being and our life will be filled with joy, ease, and wonder. But if our path is not noble, if there is craving, hatred, ignorance, and fear in the way we live our daily life, if we practice the ignoble eightfold path, suffering will naturally be the outcome. The practice is to face our suffering and transform it in order to bring about well-being. We need to study the Noble Eightfold Path and learn ways to put it into practice in our daily lives.

PART TWO

The Noble Eightfold Path

The Noble Eightfold Path

When the Buddha was eighty years old and about to pass away, a young man named Subhadda came to see him. Ananda, the Buddha's attendant, thought it would be too exhausting for his master to see anyone, but the Buddha overheard Subhadda's request and said, "Ananda, please invite him in." Even as he was dying, the Buddha was willing to give an interview.

Subhadda asked, "World-Honored One, are the other religious teachers in Magadha and Koshala fully enlightened?" The Buddha knew he had only a short time to live and that answering such a question would be a waste of precious moments. When you have the opportunity to ask a teacher about the Dharma, ask a question that can change your life. The Buddha replied, "Subhadda, it is not important whether they are fully enlightened. The question is whether you want to liberate yourself. If you do, practice the Noble Eightfold Path. Wherever the Noble Eightfold Path is practiced, joy, peace, and insight are there."[1] The Buddha offered the Eightfold Path in his first Dharma talk, he continued to teach the Eightfold Path for forty-five years, and in his last Dharma talk, spoken to Subhadda, he offered the Noble Eightfold Path — Right View, Right Thinking, Right Speech, Right Action, Right Livelihood, Right Diligence, Right Mindfulness, and Right Concentration.[2]

---

[1] *Mahaparinibbana Sutta, Digha Nikaya* 16.

[2] See chap. 3, n. 1, on p. 11, regarding the use of the word "Right."

Arya ashtangika marga ("a noble path of eight limbs") suggests the interbeing nature of these eight elements of the path. Each limb contains all the other seven. Please use your intelligence to apply the elements of the Noble Eightfold Path in your daily life.

CHAPTER NINE

Right View

The first practice of the Noble Eightfold Path is Right View *(samyag drishti)*. Right View is, first of all, a deep understanding of the Four Noble Truths — our suffering, the making of our suffering, the fact that our suffering can be transformed, and the path of transformation. The Buddha said that Right View is to have faith and confidence that there are people who have been able to transform their suffering. Venerable Shariputra added that Right View is knowing which of the four kinds of nutriments that we have ingested have brought about what has come to be.[1]

Shariputra described Right View as the ability to distinguish wholesome roots *(kushala mula)* from unwholesome roots *(akushala mula)*. In each of us, there are wholesome and unwholesome roots — or seeds — in the depths of our consciousness. If you are a loyal person, it is because the seed of loyalty is in you. But don't think that the seed of betrayal isn't also in you. If you live in an environment where your seed of loyalty is watered, you will be a loyal person. But if your seed of betrayal is watered, you may betray even those you love. You'll feel guilty about it, but if the seed of betrayal in you becomes strong, you may do it.

The practice of mindfulness helps us identify all the seeds in our store consciousness[2] and water the ones that are the

---

[1] See chap. 7, pp. 31-37. See also *Discourse on Right View*, p. 269.

[2] See chap. 4, n. 1, on p. 12, for an explanation of store consciousness.

most wholesome. When one person comes up to us, the very sight of him makes us uncomfortable. But when someone else walks by, we like her right away. Something in each of them touches a seed in us. If we love our mother deeply, but feel tense every time we think of our father, it is natural that when we see a young lady who looks like our mother, we will appreciate her, and when we see a man who evokes the memory of our father, we will feel uncomfortable. In this way, we can "see" the seeds that are in us — seeds of love for our mother and seeds of hurt vis-à-vis our father. When we become aware of the seeds in our storehouse, we will not be surprised by our own behavior or the behavior of others.

The seed of Buddhahood, the capacity to wake up and understand things as they are, is also present in each of us. When we join our palms and bow to another person, we acknowledge the seed of Buddhahood in him or her. When we bow to a child this way, we help him or her grow up beautifully and with self-confidence. If you plant corn, corn will grow. If you plant wheat, wheat will grow. If you act in a wholesome way, you will be happy. If you act in an unwholesome way, you water the seeds of craving, anger, and violence in yourself. Right View is to recognize which seeds are wholesome and to encourage those seeds to be watered. This is called "selective touching." We need to discuss and share with each other to deepen our understanding of this practice and the practice of the Five Mindfulness Trainings, especially the fifth, about the "foods" we ingest.[3]

At the base of our views are our perceptions *(samjña)*. In Chinese, the upper part of the character for perception 想 is "mark," "sign," or "appearance," and the lower part is "mind" or "spirit." Perceptions always have a "mark," and in many cases that mark is illusory. The Buddha advised us not to be fooled by what we perceive. He told Subhuti, "Where there is

---

[3] See Thich Nhat Hanh, *For a Future To Be Possible.*

perception, there is deception."[4] The Buddha also taught on many occasions that most of our perceptions are erroneous, and that most of our suffering comes from wrong perceptions.[5] We have to ask ourselves again and again, "Am I sure?" Until we see clearly, our wrong perceptions will prevent us from having Right View.

To perceive always means to perceive *something.* We believe that the object of our perception is outside of the subject, but that is not correct. When we perceive the moon, the moon is us. When we smile to our friend, our friend is also us, because she is the object of our perception.

When we perceive a mountain, the mountain is the object of our perception. When we perceive the moon, the moon is the object of our perception. When we say, "I can see my consciousness in the flower," it means we can see the cloud, the sunshine, the earth, and the minerals in it. But how can we see our consciousness in a flower? The flower *is* our consciousness. It is the object of our perception. It is our perception. To perceive means to perceive something. Perception means the coming into existence of the perceiver and the perceived. The flower that we are looking at is part of our consciousness. The idea that our consciousness is outside of the flower has to be removed. It is impossible to have a subject without an object. It is impossible to remove one and retain the other.

The source of our perception, our way of seeing, lies in our store consciousness. If ten people look at a cloud, there will be ten different perceptions of it. Whether it is perceived as a dog, a hammer, or a coat depends on our mind — our sadness, our memories, our anger. Our perceptions carry with them all the errors of subjectivity. Then we praise,

---

[4] See Thich Nhat Hanh, *The Diamond That Cuts through Illusion: Commentaries on the Prajñaparamita Diamond Sutra* (Berkeley: Parallax Press, 1992).

[5] See, e.g., *The Honeyball Sutra, Majjhima Nikaya* 18.

blame, condemn, or complain depending on our perceptions. But our perceptions are made of our afflictions — craving, anger, ignorance, wrong views, and prejudice. Whether
we are happy or we suffer depends largely on our perceptions. It is important to look deeply at our perceptions and
know their source.

We have an idea of happiness. We believe that only certain
conditions will make us happy. But it is often our very idea of
happiness that prevents us from being happy. We have to
look deeply into our perceptions in order to become free of
them. Then, what has been a perception becomes an insight,
a realization of the path. This is neither perception nor non-
perception. It is a clear vision, seeing things as they are.

Our happiness and the happiness of those around us depend on our degree of Right View. Touching reality deeply
— knowing what is going on inside and outside of ourselves
— is the way to liberate ourselves from the suffering that is
caused by wrong perceptions. Right View is not an ideology,
a system, or even a path. It is the insight we have into the reality of life, a living insight that fills us with understanding,
peace, and love.

Sometimes we see our children doing things that we know
will cause them to suffer in the future, but when we try to tell
them, they won't listen. All we can do is to stimulate the seeds
of Right View in them, and then later, in a difficult moment,
they may benefit from our guidance. We cannot explain an
orange to someone who has never tasted one. No matter how
well we describe it, we cannot give someone else the direct
experience. He has to taste it for himself. As soon as we say a
single word, he is already caught. Right View cannot be described. We can only point in the correct direction. Right
View cannot even be transmitted by a teacher. A teacher can
help us identify the seed of Right View that is already in our
garden, and help us have the confidence to practice, to entrust that seed to the soil of our daily life. But we are the gar-

dener. We have to learn how to water the wholesome seeds that are in us so they will bloom into the flowers of Right View. The instrument for watering wholesome seeds is mindful living — mindful breathing, mindful walking, living each moment of our day in mindfulness.

At a peace rally in Philadelphia in 1966, a reporter asked me, "Are you from North or South Vietnam?" If I had said I was from the north, he would have thought I was pro-communist, and if I had said I was from the south, he would have thought I was pro-American. So I told him, "I am from the Center." I wanted to help him let go of his notions and encounter the reality that was right in front of him. This is the language of Zen. A Zen monk saw a beautiful goose fly by and he wanted to share this joy with his elder brother who was walking beside him. But at that moment, the other monk had bent down to remove a pebble from his sandal. By the time he looked up, the goose had already flown by. He asked, "What did you want me to see?" but the younger monk could only remain silent. Master Tai Xu said, "As long as the tree is behind you, you can see only its shadow. If you want to touch the reality, you have to turn around." "Image teaching" uses words and ideas. "Substance teaching" communicates by the way you live.

If you come to Plum Village for one day, you have an idea about Plum Village, but that idea isn't really Plum Village. You might say, "I've been to Plum Village," but in fact you've really only been to your idea of Plum Village. Your idea might be slightly better than that of someone who has never been there, but it's still only an idea. It is not the true Plum Village. Your concept or perception of reality is not reality. When you are caught in your perceptions and ideas, you lose reality.

To practice is to go beyond ideas, so you can arrive at the suchness of things. "No idea" 無念 is the path of non-conception. As long as there is an idea, there is no reality, no truth. "No idea" means no wrong idea, no wrong conception. It does not mean no mindfulness. Because of mindfulness, when something is right, we know it's right, and when something is wrong, we know it's wrong.

We are practicing sitting meditation, and we see a bowl of tomato soup in our mind's eye, so we think that is wrong practice, because we are supposed to be mindful of our breathing. But if we practice mindfulness, we will say, "I am breathing in and I am thinking about tomato soup." That is Right Mindfulness already. Rightness or wrongness is not objective. It is subjective.

Relatively speaking, there are right views and there are wrong views. But if we look more deeply, we see that *all views are wrong views*. No view can ever be the truth. It is just from one point; that is why it is called a "point of view." If we go to another point, we will see things differently and realize that our first view was not entirely right. Buddhism is not a collection of views. It is a practice to help us eliminate wrong views. The quality of our views can always be improved. From the viewpoint of ultimate reality, Right View is the absence of all views.

When we begin the practice, our view is a vague idea about the teachings. But conceptual knowledge is never enough. The seeds of Right View, the seed of Buddhahood, are in us, but they are obscured by so many layers of ignorance, sorrow, and disappointment. We have to put our views into practice. In the process of learning, reflecting, and practicing, our view becomes increasingly wise, based on our real experience. When we practice Right Mindfulness, we see the seed of Buddhahood in everyone, including ourselves. This is Right View. Sometimes it is described as the Mother of All Buddhas *(prajña paramita)*, the energy of love and understanding that has the power to free us. When we practice mindful living, our Right View will blossom, and all the other elements of the path in us will flower, also.

The Interbeing of the Eight Elements of the Path

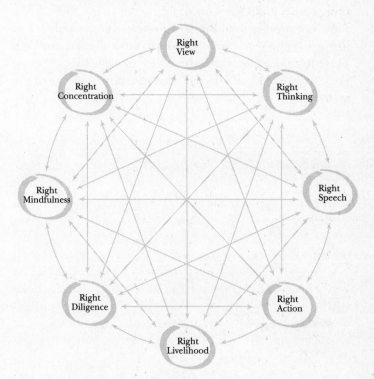

Figure Three

The eight practices of the Noble Eightfold Path nourish each other. As our view becomes more "right," the other elements of the Eightfold Path in us also deepen. Right Speech is based on Right View, and it also nourishes Right View. Right Mindfulness and Right Concentration strengthen and deepen Right View. Right Action has to be based on Right View. Right Livelihood clarifies Right View. Right View is both a cause and an effect of all the other elements of the path.

CHAPTER TEN

Right Thinking

When Right View is solid in us, we have Right Thinking *(samyak samkalpa)*. We need Right View at the foundation of our thinking. And if we train ourselves in Right Thinking, our Right View will improve. Thinking is the speech of our mind. Right Thinking makes our speech clear and beneficial. Because thinking often leads to action, Right Thinking is needed to take us down the path of Right Action.

Right Thinking reflects the way things are. Wrong thinking causes us to see in an "upside-down way" *(viparyasa)*. But to practice Right Thinking is not easy. Our mind is often thinking about one thing while our body is doing another. Mind and body are not unified. Conscious breathing is an important link. When we concentrate on our breathing, we bring body and mind back together and become whole again.

When Descartes said, "I think, therefore I am," he meant that we can prove our existence by the fact that our thinking exists. He concluded that because we are thinking, we are really there, existing. I would conclude the opposite: "I think, therefore I am not." As long as mind and body are not together, we get lost and we cannot really say that we are here. If we practice breathing mindfully and touching the healing and refreshing elements that are already within and around us, we will find peace and solidity. Mindful breathing helps us stop being preoccupied by sorrows of the past and anxieties about the future. It helps us be in touch with life in the present moment. Much of our thinking is unnecessary. Those thoughts are limited and do not carry much understanding in them. Sometimes we feel as though we have a cassette player in our head — always running, day and night — and we cannot turn it off. We worry and become tense and have nightmares. When we practice mindfulness, we begin to hear the cassette tape in our mind, and we can notice whether our thinking is useful or not.

Thinking has two parts — initial thought *(vitarka)* and developing thought *(vichara)*. An initial thought is something like, "This afternoon I have to turn in an essay for literature class." The development of this thought might be to wonder whether we are doing the assignment correctly, whether we should read it one more time before turning it in, whether our teacher will notice if we hand it in late, and so on. Vitarka is the original thought. Vichara is the development of the original thought.

In the first stage of meditative concentration *(dhyana)*, both kinds of thinking are present. In the second stage, neither is there. We are in deeper contact with reality, free of words and concepts. While walking in the woods with a group of children last year, I noticed one of the little girls thinking for a long time. Finally, she asked me, "Grandfather monk, what color is that tree's bark?" "It is the color that you see," I told her. I wanted her to enter the wonderful world that was right in front of her. I did not want to add another concept.

There are four practices related to Right Thinking:

(1) *"Are You Sure?"* — If there is a rope in your path and you perceive it as a snake, fear-based thinking will follow. The more erroneous your perception, the more incorrect your thinking will be. Please write the words "Are you sure?" on a large piece of paper and hang it where you will see it often.

Ask yourself this question again and again. Wrong perceptions cause incorrect thinking and unnecessary suffering.

(2) *"What Am I Doing?"* — Sometimes I ask one of my students, "What are you doing?" to help him release his thinking about the past or the future and return to the present moment. I ask the question to help him *be* — right here, right now. To respond, he only needs to smile. That alone would demonstrate his true presence.

Asking yourself, What am I doing? will help you overcome the habit of wanting to complete things quickly. Smile to yourself and say, Washing this dish is the most important job in my life. When you ask, What am I doing?, reflect deeply on the question. If your thoughts are carrying you away, you need mindfulness to intervene. When you are really there, washing the dishes can be a deep and enjoyable experience. But if you wash them while thinking about other things, you are wasting your time, and probably not washing the dishes well either. If you are not there, even if you wash 84,000 dishes, your work will be without merit.

Emperor Wu asked Bodhidharma, the founder of Zen Buddhism in China, how much merit he had earned by building temples all over the country. Bodhidharma said, "None whatsoever." But if you wash one dish in mindfulness, if you build one small temple while dwelling deeply in the present moment — not wanting to be anywhere else, not caring about fame or recognition — the merit from that act will be boundless, and you will feel very happy. Ask yourself, What am I doing? often. When your thinking is not carrying you away and you do things in mindfulness, you will be happy and a resource for many others.

(3) *"Hello, Habit Energy."* — We tend to stick to our habits, even the ones that cause us to suffer. Workaholism is one example. In the past, our ancestors may have had to work nearly all the time to put food on the table. But today, our

way of working is rather compulsive and prevents us from having real contact with life. We think about our work all the time and don't even have time to breathe. We need to find moments to contemplate the cherry blossoms and drink our tea in mindfulness. Our way of acting depends on our way of thinking, and our way of thinking depends on our habit energies. When we recognize this, we only need to say, "Hello, habit energy," and make good friends with our habitual patterns of thinking and acting. When we can accept these ingrained thoughts and not feel guilty about them, they will lose much of their power over us. Right Thinking leads to Right Action.

(4) *Bodhichitta.* — Our "mind of love" is the deep wish to cultivate understanding in ourselves in order to bring happiness to many beings. It is the motivating force for the practice of mindful living. With bodhichitta at the foundation of our thinking, everything we do or say will help others be liberated. Right Thinking also gives rise to Right Diligence.

The Buddha offered many ways to help us to transform troublesome thoughts. One way, he said, is to replace an unwholesome thought with a wholesome one by "changing the peg," just as a carpenter replaces a rotten peg by hammering in a new one.[1] If we are constantly assailed by unwholesome patterns of thought, we need to learn how to change the peg and replace those patterns with wholesome thoughts. The Buddha also likened unwholesome thinking to wearing a dead snake around your neck. The easiest way, he said, to keep unwholesome thoughts from arising is to live in a wholesome environment, a community that practices mindful living. With the help and presence of Dharma sisters and

---

[1] *Discourse on Removing Distracting Thoughts (Vitakkasanthana Sutta), Majjhima Nikaya* 20.

brothers, it is easy to sustain Right Thinking. Dwelling in a good environment is preventive medicine.

Right Thinking is thinking that is in accord with Right View. It is a map that can help us find our way. But when we arrive at our destination, we need to put down the map and enter the reality fully. "Think non-thinking" is a well-known statement in Zen. When you practice Right View and Right Thinking, you dwell deeply in the present moment, where you can touch seeds of joy, peace, and liberation, heal and transform your suffering, and be truly present for many others.

CHAPTER ELEVEN

Right Mindfulness

Right Mindfulness *(samyak smriti)* is at the heart of the Buddha's teachings. Traditionally, Right Mindfulness is the seventh on the path of eight right practices, but it is presented here third to emphasize its great importance. When Right Mindfulness is present, the Four Noble Truths and the seven other elements of the Eightfold Path are also present. When we are mindful, our thinking is Right Thinking, our speech is Right Speech, and so on. Right Mindfulness is the energy that brings us back to the present moment. To cultivate mindfulness in ourselves is to cultivate the Buddha within, to cultivate the Holy Spirit.

According to Buddhist psychology *(abhidharma,* "super Dharma"), the trait "attention" *(manaskara)* is "universal," which means we are always giving our attention to something. Our attention may be "appropriate" *(yoniso manaskara),* as when we dwell fully in the present moment, or inappropriate *(ayoniso manaskara),* as when we are attentive to something that takes us away from being here and now. A good gardener knows the way to grow flowers from compost. Right Mindfulness accepts everything without judging or reacting. It is inclusive and loving. The practice is to find ways to sustain appropriate attention throughout the day.

The Sanskrit word for mindfulness, *smriti,* means "remember." Mindfulness is remembering to come back to the present moment. The character the Chinese use for "mindfulness" 念 has two parts: the upper part means "now," and the lower part means "mind" or "heart." The First Miracle of Mindfulness is to be present and able to touch deeply the blue sky, the flower, and the smile of our child.

The Second Miracle of Mindfulness is to make the other — the sky, the flower, our child — present, also. In the Vietnamese epic poem *Tale of Kieu,* Kieu returns to the apartment of her beloved, Kim Trong, and finds him fast asleep at his desk, his head resting on a pile of books. Kim Trong hears Kieu's footsteps, but, not quite awake, he asks, "Are you really there, or am I dreaming?" Kieu replies, "Now we have the opportunity to see each other clearly. But if we do not live deeply this moment, it will be only a dream." You and your loved one are here together. You have the chance to see each other deeply. But if you are not fully present, everything will be like a dream.

The Third Miracle of Mindfulness is to nourish the object of your attention. When was the last time you looked into the eyes of your beloved and asked, "Who are you, my darling?" Don't be satisfied by a superficial answer. Ask again: "Who are you who has taken my suffering as your suffering, my happiness as your happiness, my life and death as your life and death? My love, why aren't you a dewdrop, a butterfly, a bird?" Ask with your whole being. If you do not give right attention to the one you love, it is a kind of killing. When you are in the car together, if you are lost in your thoughts, assuming you already know everything about her, she will slowly die. But with mindfulness, your attention will water the wilting flower. "I know you are here, beside me, and it makes me very happy." With attention, you will be able to discover many new and wonderful things — her joys, her hidden talents, her deepest aspirations. If you do not practice appropriate attention, how can you say you love her?

The Fourth Miracle of Mindfulness is to relieve the other's suffering. "I know you are suffering. That is why I am here for you." You can say this with words or just by the way you look at her. If you are not truly present, if you are thinking about other things, the miracle of relieving suffering cannot be realized. In difficult moments, if you have a friend who can be truly present with you, you know you are blessed. To love means to nourish the other with appropriate attention. When you practice Right Mindfulness, you make yourself and the other person present at the same time. "Darling, I know you are there. Your presence is precious to me." If you do not express this while you are together, when she passes away or has an accident, you will only cry, because before the accident happened, you did not know how to be truly happy together.

When someone is about to die, if you sit with him stably and solidly, that alone may be enough to help him leave this life with ease. Your presence is like a mantra, sacred speech that has a transforming effect. When your body, speech, and mind are in perfect oneness, that mantra will have an effect even before you utter a word. The first four miracles of mind-fulness belong to the first aspect of meditation, shamatha — stopping, calming, resting, and healing. Once you have calmed yourself and stopped being dispersed, your mind will be one-pointed and you will be ready to begin looking deeply.

The Fifth Miracle of Mindfulness is looking deeply (vipashyana), which is also the second aspect of meditation. Because you are calm and concentrated, you are really there for deep looking. You shine the light of mindfulness on the object of your attention, and at the same time you shine the light of mindfulness on yourself. You observe the object of your attention and you also see your own storehouse full of precious gems.

The Sixth Miracle of Mindfulness is understanding. When we understand something, often we say, "I see." We see some-thing we hadn't seen before. Seeing and understanding come from within us. When we are mindful, touching deeply the present moment, we can see and listen deeply, and the fruits are always understanding, acceptance, love, and the desire to relieve suffering and bring joy. Understanding is the very foundation of love. When you understand someone, you cannot help but love him or her.

The Seventh Miracle of Mindfulness is transformation. When we practice Right Mindfulness, we touch the healing and refreshing elements of life and begin to transform our own suffering and the suffering of the world. We want to overcome a habit, such as smoking, for the health of our body and mind. When we begin the practice, our habit energy is still stronger than our mindfulness, so we don't expect to stop smoking overnight. We only have to know that we are smoking when we are smoking. As we continue to practice, looking deeply and seeing the effects that smoking has on our body, mind, family, and community, we become determined to stop. It is not easy, but the practice of mindfulness helps us see the desire and the effects clearly, and eventually we will find a way to stop. Sangha is important. One man who came to Plum Village had been trying to stop smoking for years, but he couldn't. At Plum Village, he stopped his first day, because the group energy was so strong. "No one is smoking here. Why should I?" It can take years to transform a habit energy, but when we do, we stop the wheel of *samsara*, the vicious cycle of suffering and confusion that has gone on for so many lifetimes.

Practicing the Seven Miracles of Mindfulness helps us lead a happy and healthy life, transforming suffering and bringing forth peace, joy, and freedom.

৵

In the *Discourse on the Four Establishments of Mindfulness (Satipatthana Sutta)*,[1] the Buddha offers four objects for our

---

[1] *Majjhima Nikaya* 10. In Chinese, *Madhyama Agama* 98. See Thich Nhat Hanh, *Transformation and Healing: Sutra on the Four Establishments of Mindfulness* (Berkeley: Parallax Press, 1990).

mindfulness practice: our body, our feelings, our mind, and the objects of our mind. Monks and nuns in many Buddhist countries memorize this discourse, and it is the text that is read to them as they leave this life. It is helpful to read the *Discourse on the Four Establishments of Mindfulness* at least once a week, along with the *Discourse on the Full Awareness of Breathing*[2] and the *Discourse on Knowing the Better Way to Live Alone*.[3] You might like to keep these three books by your bedside and take them with you when you travel.

The Four Establishments of Mindfulness are the foundation of our dwelling place. Without them, our house is abandoned; no one is sweeping, dusting, or tidying up. Our body becomes unkempt, our feelings full of suffering, and our mind a heap of afflictions. When we are truly home, our body, mind, and feelings will be a place of refuge for ourselves and others.

The first establishment is "mindfulness of the body *in the body*." Many people hate their bodies. They feel their body is an obstacle, and they want to mistreat it. When Sister Jina, a nun at Plum Village, teaches yoga, she always begins by saying, "Let us be aware of our bodies. Breathing in, I know I am standing here in my body. Breathing out, I smile to my body." Practicing this way, we renew our acquaintance with our body and make peace with it. In the *Kayagatasati Sutta*, the Buddha offers methods to help us know what is happening in our body.[4] We observe nondualistically, fully in our

---

[2] *Anapanasati Sutta, Majjhima Nikaya* 118. See Thich Nhat Hanh, *Breathe! You Are Alive: Sutra on the Full Awareness of Breathing* (Berkeley: Parallax Press, 1996). The *Anapanasati Sutta* was available in Vietnam as early as the third century. Dhyana master Tang Hôi, the first Dhyana patriarch of Vietnam, wrote a preface to this sutra that is still available in the Chinese Canon.

[3] *Bhaddekaratta Sutta, Majjhima Nikaya* 131. See Thich Nhat Hanh, *Our Appointment with Life: The Buddha's Teaching on Living in the Present* (Berkeley: Parallax Press, 1990).

[4] *Majjhima Nikaya* 119.

body even as we observe it. We begin by noting all of our body's positions and movements. When we sit, we know we are sitting. When we stand, walk, or lie down we know we are standing, walking, or lying down. When we practice this way, mindfulness is there. This practice is called "mere recognition."

The second way the Buddha taught us to practice mindfulness of the body in the body is to recognize all of our body's parts, from the top of our head to the soles of our feet. If we have blonde hair, we recognize and smile to that. If we have gray hair, we recognize and smile to that. We observe whether our forehead is relaxed and whether it has wrinkles. With our mindfulness, we touch our nose, mouth, arms, heart, lungs, blood, and so on. The Buddha described the practice of recognizing thirty-two parts of our body as being like a farmer who goes up to his loft; brings down a large bag of beans, grains, and seeds; puts the bag on the ground; opens it; and, as the contents fall onto the floor, recognizes rice as rice, beans as beans, sesame as sesame, and so on. In this way, we recognize our eyes as our eyes and our lungs as our lungs. We can practice this during sitting meditation or while lying down. Scanning our body with our mindfulness in this way might take half an hour. As we observe each part of our body, we smile to it. The love and care of this meditation can do the work of healing.

The third method the Buddha offered for practicing mindfulness of the body in the body is to see the elements that it is made of: earth, water, fire, and air. "Breathing in, I see the earth element in me. Breathing out, I smile to the earth element in me." "Earth element" refers to things that are solid. When we see the earth element inside and outside of us, we realize that there is really no boundary between us and the rest of the universe. Next, we recognize the water element inside and outside of us. "Breathing in, I am aware of the element of water in my body." We meditate on the fact that our body is more than seventy percent water. After that, we recognize the fire element, which means heat, inside and outside of us. For life to be possible, there must be heat. Practicing this, we see over and over that the elements inside and outside our body belong to the same reality, and we are no longer confined by our body. We are everywhere.

The fourth element of our body is air. The best way to experience the air element is the practice of mindful breathing. "Breathing in, I know I am breathing in. Breathing out, I know I am breathing out." After saying these sentences, we can abbreviate them by saying "In" as we breath in, and "Out" as we breath out. We don't try to control our breathing. Whether our in-breath is long or short, deep or shallow, we just breathe naturally and shine the light of mindfulness on it. When we do this, we notice that, in fact, our breathing does become slower and deeper naturally. "Breathing in, my in-breath has become deep. Breathing out, my out-breath has become slow." Now we can practice, "Deep/slow." We don't have to make an effort. It just becomes deeper and slower by itself, and we recognize that.

Later on, you will notice that you have become calmer and more at ease. "Breathing in, I feel calm. Breathing out, I feel at ease. I am not struggling anymore. Calm/ease." And then, "Breathing in, I smile. Breathing out, I release all my worries and anxieties. Smile/release." We are able to smile to ourselves and release all our worries. There are more than three hundred muscles in our face, and when we know how to breath in and smile, these muscles can relax. This is "mouth yoga." We smile and we are able to release all of our feelings and emotions. The last practice is, "Breathing in, I dwell deeply in the present moment. Breathing out, I know this is a wonderful moment. Present moment/wonderful moment." Nothing is more precious than being in the present moment, fully alive and fully aware.

In, out
Deep, slow
Calm, ease
Smile, release
Present moment, wonderful moment

If you use this poem during sitting or walking meditation, it can be very nourishing and healing. Practice each line for as long as you wish.

Another practice to help us be aware of our breathing is counting. As you breathe in, count "one," and as you breathe out, count "one" again. Then "Two/two," "Three/three," until you arrive at ten. After that, go back in the other direction: "Ten/ten," "Nine/nine," and so on, until you arrive back at one. If you don't get lost, you know that you have good concentration. If you do get lost, go back to "one," and begin again. Relax. It's only a game. When you succeed in counting, you can drop the numbers if you like and just say "in" and "out." Conscious breathing is a joy. When I discovered the *Discourse on the Full Awareness of Breathing*, I felt I was the happiest person on Earth. These exercises have been transmitted to us by a community that has been practicing them for 2,600 years.[5]

The second establishment is mindfulness of the feelings *in the feelings*. The Abhidharma authors listed fifty-one kinds of mental formations. Feelings *(vedana)* is one of them. In us, there is a river of feelings in which every drop of water is a different feeling. To observe our feelings, we just sit on the riverbank and identify each feeling as it flows by and disappears. Feelings are either pleasant, unpleasant, or neutral.

When we have a pleasant feeling, we may have a tendency to cling to it, and when we have an unpleasant feeling, we may be inclined to chase it away. But it is more effective in

---

[5] See Thich Nhat Hanh, *Breathe! You Are Alive.*

both cases to return to our breathing and simply observe the feeling, identifying it silently: "Breathing in, I know a pleasant (or unpleasant) feeling is in me. Breathing out, I know there is a pleasant (or unpleasant) feeling in me." Calling a feeling by its name, such as "joy," "happiness," "anger," or "sorrow," helps us identify and see it deeply. Within a fraction of a second, many feelings can arise.

If our breathing is light and calm — a natural result of conscious breathing — our mind and body will slowly become light, calm, and clear, and our feelings also. Our feelings are not separate from us or caused just by something outside of us. Our feelings *are* us, and, for that moment, we *are* those feelings. We needn't be intoxicated or terrorized by them, nor do we need to reject them. The practice of not clinging to or rejecting feelings is an important part of meditation. If we face our feelings with care, affection, and nonviolence, we can transform them into a kind of energy that is healthy and nourishing. When a feeling arises, Right Mindfulness identifies it, simply recognizes what is there and whether it is pleasant, unpleasant, or neutral. Right Mindfulness is like a mother. When her child is sweet, she loves him, and when her child is crying, she still loves him. Everything that takes place in our body and our mind needs to be looked after equally. We don't fight. We say hello to our feeling so we can get to know each other better. Then, the next time that feeling arises, we will be able to greet it even more calmly.

We can embrace all of our feelings, even difficult ones like anger. Anger is a fire burning inside us, filling our whole being with smoke. When we are angry, we need to calm ourselves: "Breathing in, I calm my anger. Breathing out, I take care of my anger." As soon as a mother takes her crying baby into her arms, the baby already feels some relief. When we embrace our anger with Right Mindfulness, we suffer less right away.

We all have difficult emotions, but if we allow them to dominate us, we will become depleted. Emotions become strong when we do not know how to look after them. When our feelings are stronger than our mindfulness, we suffer. But if we practice conscious breathing day after day, mindfulness will become a habit. Don't wait to begin to practice until you are overwhelmed by a feeling. It may be too late.

The third establishment is mindfulness of the mind *(chitta) in the mind.* To be aware of the mind is to be aware of the mental formations *(chitta samskara).* "Formations" *(samskara)* is a technical term in Buddhism. Anything that is "formed," anything that is made of something else, is a formation. A flower is a formation. Our anger is a formation, a mental formation. Some mental formations are present all the time and are called "universal" (contact, attention, feeling, perception, and volition). Some arise only under particular circumstances (zeal, determination, mindfulness, concentration, and wisdom). Some are uplifting and help us transform our suffering (wholesome, or beneficial, mental formations), and others are heavy and imprison us in our suffering (unwholesome, or unbeneficial, mental formations).

There are mental formations that are sometimes wholesome and sometimes unwholesome, such as sleepiness, regret, initial thinking, and developing thought. When our body and mind need rest, sleep is wholesome. But if we sleep all the time, it can be unwholesome. If we hurt someone and regret it, that regret is wholesome. But if our regret leads to a guilt complex that colors whatever we do in the future, that regret can be called unwholesome. When our thinking helps us see clearly, it is beneficial. But if our mind is scattered in all directions, that thinking is unbeneficial.

There are many beautiful aspects of our consciousness, like faith, humility, self-respect, non-craving, non-anger, non-ignorance, diligence, ease, care, equanimity, and nonviolence. Unwholesome mental formations, on the other hand, are like a tangled ball of string. When we try to untangle it, we only wind it around ourselves until we cannot move. These mental formations are sometimes called afflictions (kleshas), because they bring pain to ourselves and others. Sometimes they are called obscurations because they confuse us and make us lose our way. Sometimes they are called leaks or set-backs (ashrava), because they are like a cracked vase. The basic unwholesome mental formations are greed, hatred, ignorance, pride, doubt, and views. The secondary unwhole-some mental formations, arising from the basic ones, are anger, malice, hypocrisy, malevolence, jealousy, selfishness, deception, guile, unwholesome excitement, the wish to harm, immodesty, arrogance, dullness, agitation, lack of faith, indolence, carelessness, forgetfulness, distraction, and lack of attention. According to the Vijñanavada School of Buddhism, altogether there are fifty-one kinds of mental formations, including feelings. Since feelings is, by itself, the second establishment of mindfulness, the other fifty fall into the category of the third establishment of mindfulness.

Every time a mental formation arises, we can practice mere recognition. When we are agitated, we just say, "I am agitated," and mindfulness is already there. Until we recognize agitation as agitation, it will push us around and we will not know what is going on or why. To practice mindfulness of the mind does not mean not to be agitated. It means that when we are agitated, we know that we are agitated. Our agitation has a good friend in us, and that is mindfulness.

Even before agitation manifests in our mind consciousness, it is already in our store consciousness in the form of a seed. All mental formations lie in our store consciousness in the form of seeds. Something someone does may water the seed of agitation, and then agitation manifests in our mind consciousness. Every mental formation that manifests needs to be recognized. If it is wholesome, mindfulness will cultivate it. If it is unwholesome, mindfulness will encourage it to return to our store consciousness and remain there, dormant.

We may think that our agitation is ours alone, but if we look carefully, we'll see that it is our inheritance from our whole society and many generations of our ancestors. Individual consciousness is made of the collective consciousness, and the collective consciousness is made of individual consciousnesses. They cannot be separated. Looking deeply into our individual consciousness, we touch the collective consciousness. Our ideas of beauty, goodness, and happiness, for example, are also the ideas of our society. Every winter, fashion designers show us the fashions for the coming spring, and we look at their creations through the lens of our collective consciousness. When we buy a fashionable dress, it is because we see with the eyes of the collective consciousness. Someone who lives deep in the upper Amazon would not spend that amount of money to buy such a dress. She would not see it as beautiful at all. When we produce a literary work, we produce it with both our collective consciousness and our individual consciousness.

We usually describe mind consciousness and store consciousness as two different things, but store consciousness is just mind consciousness at a deeper level. If we look carefully at our mental formations, we can see their roots in our store consciousness. Mindfulness helps us look deeply into the depths of our consciousness. Every time one of the fifty-one mental formations arises, we acknowledge its presence, look deeply into it, and see its nature of impermanence and interbeing. When we practice this, we are liberated from fear, sorrow, and the fires burning inside us. When mindfulness embraces our joy, our sadness, and all our other mental formations, sooner or later we will see their deep roots. With every mindful step and every mindful breath, we see the roots of our mental formations. Mindfulness shines its light upon them and helps them to transform.

The fourth establishment is mindfulness of phenomena *(dharmas) in phenomena.* "Phenomena" means "the objects of our mind." Each of our mental formations has to have an object. If you are angry, you have to be angry at someone or something, and that person or thing can be called the object of your mind. When you remember someone or something, that is the object of your mind. There are fifty-one kinds of mental formations, so there are fifty-one kinds of objects of mind.

When we are attentive to a bird singing, that sound is the object of our mind. When our eyes see the blue sky, this is the object of our mind. When we look at a candle, an idea or image of the candle arises in our mind. That object of perception is a sign *(lakshana).* In Chinese, the character for perception 想 is composed of the ideograms for sign and mind. A perception is a sign, an image in our mind.

"Investigation of dharmas" *(dharma-pravichaya)* is one of the Seven Factors of Awakening *(bodhyanga).*[6] When observing dharmas, five kinds of meditation can help us calm our minds: (1) counting the breath, (2) observing interdependent arising, (3) observing impurity, (4) observing with love and compassion,[7] and (5) observing the different realms.

What are the different realms? First, there are the Eighteen Elements *(dhatus):* eyes, forms (the objects of our vi-

---

[6] The Seven Factors of Awakening are mindfulness, investigation of phenomena, diligence, joy, ease, concentration, and letting go. See chap. 26.

[7] The Pure Land School replaces this meditation with contemplating Amida Buddha. In fact, when we contemplate Amida Buddha, we are observing with love and compassion, because any Buddha is an embodiment of love and compassion. What does *Buddhanusmriti,* "mindfulness of Buddha," mean? What does it mean to recite the name of the Buddha? It means to invite someone precious to come into our living room. Every moment that the Buddha seed is in our mind consciousness, it plants seeds of love and understanding. If we invite Mara in, it will not plant those seeds. Mindfulness means, above all, remembering the Buddha nature that is in us.

sion), and the consciousness that makes sight possible, which we can call eye-consciousness; ears, sound, and the consciousness connected with hearing; nose, smell, and the consciousness connected with smelling; tongue, taste, and the consciousness connected with tasting; body, touch, and the consciousness connected with touching; mind, the object of mind, and mind-consciousness. These Eighteen Elements make the existence of the universe possible. If we look deeply into the Eighteen Elements and see their substance and their source, we will be able to go beyond ignorance and fears.

In the *Discourse on the Many Realms (Bahudhatuka Sutta)*,[8] the Buddha taught that all our anxieties and difficulties come from our inability to see the true face, or true sign of things, which means that although we see their appearance, we fail to recognize their impermanent and interbeing nature. If we are afraid or insecure, at the root of our fear or insecurity is that we have not yet seen the true face of all dharmas. If we investigate and look deeply into the Eighteen Elements, we can transform our ignorance and overcome fear and insecurity.

One day during sitting meditation, the Venerable Ananda realized that all anxieties, fears, and misfortunes arise because we do not understand the true nature of physical and psychological phenomena. Later, he asked the Buddha if this was correct, and the Buddha said yes, first explaining the need to penetrate the Eighteen Elements.

Ananda then asked, "Is it possible to penetrate the Eighteen Elements in another way?" and the Buddha replied, "Yes, we can say that there are Six Elements." These are the Four Great Elements *(mahabhuta)* of earth, water, fire, and air, plus space and consciousness. All physical phenomena are made up of these Six Elements. If we observe these Six Elements inside us and around us, we see that we are not

---

[8] *Majjhima Nikaya* 115.

separate from the universe. This insight frees us from the idea of birth and death.

The Buddha then taught Ananda the Six Realms — happiness *(sukha)*, suffering (dukkha), joy *(mudita)*, anxiety (Pali: *domanassa)*, letting go *(upeksha)*, and ignorance *(avidya)*. Happiness can be true happiness or deception, so we have to look into its substance and go beyond attachment. True happiness will be of benefit and nourish ourselves and others. Deceptive happiness brings temporary pleasure and helps us forget our suffering, but is not of lasting benefit and can actually be harmful, like a cigarette or a glass of wine. When something causes us to suffer, if we look deeply into it, we may see that it is exactly what we need to restore our happiness. In fact, suffering is essential for happiness. We have to know the suffering of being too cold to enjoy and appreciate being warm. If we look deeply into the realm of joy, we can see whether it is authentic or whether it is just covering up our suffering and anxiety. Anxiety, the illness of our time, comes primarily from our inability to dwell in the present moment.

Letting go is an ongoing practice, one that can bring us a lot of happiness. When a Vietnamese woman who escaped her country by boat was robbed on the high seas of all her gold, she was so distraught that she contemplated suicide. But on shore, she met a man who had been robbed of even his clothes, and it helped her very much to see him smiling. He had truly let go. Letting go gives us freedom, and freedom is the only condition for happiness. If, in our heart, we still cling to anything — anger, anxiety, or possessions — we cannot be free.

The Buddha taught another list of Six Realms: craving *(kama)*, freedom from craving *(nekkhama)*,[9] anger *(vyapada)*,

---

[9] Nekkhama is Pali, and there is no Sanskrit equivalent for it. We do not know what word was used in the original Sanskrit texts, since they have been lost.

absence of anger *(avyapada)*, harming *(vihimsa)*, and non-harming *(avihimsa* or *ahimsa)*. If we look deeply into our craving, we see that we already have what we crave, because everything is already a part of everything else. This insight can take us from the realm of craving into the realm of freedom. The fire of anger burns in us day and night and causes us to suffer — even more than the one at whom we are angry. When anger is absent, we feel light and free. To live in the realm of non-harming is to love. Our world is full of hatred and violence, because we do not take the time to nourish the love and compassion that are already in our hearts. Non-harming is an important practice.

There are three further realms: the desire realm, the form realm, and the formless realm. The form and formless realms describe certain states of meditative concentration. In the form realm, material things are somewhat subtle. In the formless realm, they are very subtle. In the desire realm, material things are present in their grossest form, and human beings do not meditate there. These three realms are produced by our mind. If our mind has craving, anger, and harming, we are like a house on fire. If craving, anger, and harming are absent from our minds, we produce a cool, clear lotus lake.[10] Every time we practice Right Mindfulness, it is like jumping into that cool lake. If we are standing, we only have to know that we are standing. If we are sitting, we only have to know that we are sitting. We don't have to add or take away anything. We only need to be aware.

Finally, the Buddha taught the meditation on the Two Realms — the realm of the conditioned (samskrita) and the realm of the unconditioned (asamskrita). In the conditioned realm, there is birth, death, before, after, inner, outer, small,

---

[10] In the "Universal Door" chapter of the *Lotus Sutra*, it is said that the mindfulness of the Bodhisattva of Compassion can transform the fires that are about to burn us into a cool, clear lotus lake.

and large. In the world of the unconditioned, we are no longer subject to birth and death, coming or going, before or after. The conditioned realm belongs to the historical dimension. It is the wave. The unconditioned realm belongs to the ultimate dimension. It is the water. These two realms are not separate.

To arrive at liberation from narrow views and to obtain fearlessness and great compassion, practice the contemplations on interdependence, impermanence, and compassion. Sitting in meditation, direct your concentration onto the interdependent nature of certain objects. Remember that the subject of knowledge cannot exist independently from the object of knowledge. To see is to see something. To hear is to hear something. To be angry is to be angry about something. Hope is hope for something. Thinking is thinking about something. When the object of knowledge is not present, there can be no subject. Meditate and see the interbeing of the subject and the object. When you practice mindfulness of breathing, then the breathing *is* mind. When you practice mindfulness of the body, then your body is mind. When you practice mindfulness of objects outside yourself, these objects are mind. Therefore, the contemplation of the interbeing of subject and object is also the contemplation of the mind. Every object of the mind is itself mind. In Buddhism, we call the objects of mind the dharmas.

Contemplation on interdependence is a deep looking into all dharmas in order to pierce through to their real nature, in order to see them as part of the great body of reality and in order to see that the great body of reality is indivisible. It cannot be cut into pieces with separate existences of their own.

The object of our mind can be a mountain, a rose, the full moon, or the person standing in front of us. We believe these things exist outside of us as separate entities, but these objects of our perceptions *are* us. This includes our feeling.

When we hate someone, we also hate ourself. The object of our mindfulness is actually the whole cosmos. Mindfulness is mindfulness of the body, feelings, perceptions, any of the mental formations, and all of the seeds in our consciousness. The Four Establishments of Mindfulness contain everything in the cosmos. Everything in the cosmos is the object of our perception, and, as such, it does not exist only outside of us but also within us.

If we look deeply at the bud on the tree, we will see its nature. It may be very small, but it is also like the earth, because the leaf in the bud will become part of the earth. If we see the truth of one thing in the cosmos, we see the nature of the cosmos. Because of our mindfulness, our deep looking, the nature of the cosmos will reveal itself. It is not a matter of imposing our ideas on the nature of the cosmos.

श्र

Sitting and watching our breath is a wonderful practice, but it is not enough. For transformation to take place, we have to practice mindfulness all day long, not just on our meditation cushion. Mindfulness is the Buddha. Just as vegetation is sensitive to sunlight, mental formations are sensitive to mindfulness. Mindfulness is the energy that can embrace and transform all mental formations. Mindfulness helps us leave behind "upside-down perceptions," and wakes us up to what is happening. When Thich Quang Duc made himself into a human torch, people all over the world had to recognize that Vietnam was a land on fire, and they had to do something about it. When we practice mindfulness, we are in contact with life, and we can offer our love and compassion to lessen the suffering and bring about joy and happiness.

Do not lose yourself in the past. Do not lose yourself in the future. Do not get caught in your anger, worries, or fears. Come back to the present moment, and touch life deeply. This is mindfulness. We cannot be mindful of everything at the same time, so we have to choose what we find most interesting to be the object of our mindfulness. The blue sky is wonderful, but the beautiful face of a child is also wonderful. What is essential is to be alive and present to all the wonders of life that are available.

In many talks, the Buddha spoke about the Threefold Training of precepts, concentration, and insight. The practice of the precepts *(shila)* is the practice of Right Mindfulness. If we don't practice the precepts, we aren't practicing mindfulness. I know some Zen students who think that they can practice meditation without practicing precepts, but that is not correct. The heart of Buddhist meditation is the practice of mindfulness, and mindfulness is the practice of the precepts. You cannot meditate without practicing the precepts.[11]

When we practice mindfulness, we generate the energy of the Buddha within us and around us, and this is the energy that can save the world. A Buddha is someone who is mindful all day long. We are only part-time Buddhas. We breathe in and use our Buddha eyes to see with the energy of mindfulness. When we listen with our Buddha ears, we are able to restore communication and relieve a lot of suffering. When we put the energy of mindfulness into our hands, our Buddha hands will protect the safety and integrity of those we love.

Look deeply into your hand, and see if the Buddha eye is in it. In Tibetan, Chinese, Korean, Vietnamese, and Japanese temples, there is a bodhisattva with one thousand arms — it takes that many arms to help others — and in the palm of each hand there is an eye. The hand represents action, and the eye represents insight and understanding. Without understanding, our actions might cause others to suffer. We may be motivated by the desire to make others happy, but if

---

[11] See Thich Nhat Hanh, *For a Future To Be Possible.* See also chap. 13.

we do not have understanding, the more we do, the more trouble we may create. Unless our love is made of understanding, it is not true love. Mindfulness is the energy that brings the eyes of a Buddha into our hand. With mindfulness, we can change the world and bring happiness to many people. This is not abstract. It is possible for every one of us to generate the energy of mindfulness in each moment of our daily life.

CHAPTER TWELVE

Right Speech

"Aware of the suffering caused by unmindful speech and the inability to listen to others, I am committed to cultivating loving speech and deep listening in order to bring joy and happiness to others and relieve others of their suffering. Knowing that words can create happiness or suffering, I am determined to speak truthfully, with words that inspire self-confidence, joy, and hope. I will not spread news that I do not know to be certain and will not criticize or condemn things of which I am not sure. I will refrain from uttering words that can cause division or discord, or that can cause the family or the community to break. I am determined to make all efforts to reconcile and resolve all conflicts, however small." This is the Fourth Mindfulness Training,[1] and it offers a very good description of Right Speech *(samyag vac)*.

In our time, communication techniques have become very sophisticated. It takes no time at all to send news to the other side of the planet. But at the same time, communication between individuals has become very difficult. Fathers cannot talk to sons and daughters. Husbands cannot talk to wives, nor partners to partners. Communication is blocked. We are in a very difficult situation, not only between countries but person to person. Practicing the Fourth Mindfulness Training is very important.

The classical explanation of Right Speech is: (1) Speaking

---

[1] See Thich Nhat Hanh, *For a Future To Be Possible.* See also chap. 13.

truthfully. When something is green, we say it is green, and not purple. (2) Not speaking with a forked tongue. We don't say one thing to one person and something else to another. Of course, we can describe the truth in different ways to help different listeners understand our meaning, but we must always be loyal to the truth. (3) Not speaking cruelly. We don't shout, slander, curse, encourage suffering, or create hatred. Even those who have a good heart and don't want to hurt others sometimes allow toxic words to escape from their lips. In our mind are seeds of Buddha and also many fetters or internal formations *(samyojana)*. When we say something poisonous, it is usually because of our habit energies. Our words are very powerful. They can give someone a complex, take away their purpose in life, or even drive them to suicide. We must not forget this. (4) Not exaggerating or embellishing. We don't dramatize unnecessarily, making things sound better, worse, or more extreme than they actually are. If someone is a little irritated, we don't say that he is furious. The practice of Right Speech is to try to change our habits so that our speech arises from the seed of Buddha that is in us, and not from our unresolved, unwholesome seeds.[2]

Right Speech is based on Right Thinking. Speech is the way for our thinking to express itself aloud. Our thoughts are no longer our private possessions. We give earphones to others and allow them to hear the audiotape that is playing in our mind. Of course, there are things we think but do not want to say, and one part of our consciousness has to play the role of editor. If there is something we think we will be criticized for saying, the editor will censor it. Sometimes when a friend or a therapist asks us an unexpected question, we are provoked into telling the truth we wanted to hide.

Sometimes, when there are blocks of suffering in us, they

---

[2] See *Samyukta Agama* 785 and *Majjhima Nikaya* 117. See also Thich Nhat Hanh, *For a Future To Be Possible.*

may manifest as speech (or actions) without going through the medium of thought. Our suffering has built up and can no longer be repressed, especially when we have not been practicing Right Mindfulness. Expressing our suffering can harm us and other people as well, but when we don't practice Right Mindfulness, we may not know what is building up inside us. Then we say or write things we did not want to say, and we don't know where our words came from. We had no intention of saying something that could hurt others, yet we say such words. We have every intention of saying only words that bring about reconciliation and forgiveness, but then we say something very unkind. To water seeds of peace in ourselves, we have to practice Right Mindfulness while walking, sitting, standing, and so on. With Right Mindfulness, we see clearly all of our thoughts and feelings and know whether this or that thought is harming or helping us. When our thoughts leave our mind in the form of speech, if Right Mindfulness continues to accompany them, we know what we are saying and whether it is useful or creating problems.

Deep listening is at the foundation of Right Speech. If we cannot listen mindfully, we cannot practice Right Speech. No matter what we say, it will not be mindful, because we'll be speaking only our own ideas and not in response to the other person. In the *Lotus Sutra,* we are advised to look and listen with the eyes of compassion. Compassionate listening brings about healing. When someone listens to us this way, we feel some relief right away. A good therapist always practices deep, compassionate listening. We have to learn to do the same in order to heal the people we love and restore communication with them.

When communication is cut off, we all suffer. When no one listens to us or understands us, we become like a bomb ready to explode. Restoring communication is an urgent task. Sometimes only ten minutes of deep listening can transform us and bring a smile back to our lips. The Bodhisattva Kwan

Yin is the one who hears the cries of the world. She has the quality of listening deeply, without judging or reacting. When we listen with our whole being, we can defuse a lot of bombs. If the other person feels that we are critical of what they are saying, their suffering will not be relieved. When psychotherapists practice Right Listening, their patients have the courage to say things they have never been able to tell anyone before. Deep listening nourishes both speaker and listener.

Many of us have lost our capacity for listening and using loving speech in our families. It may be that no one is capable of listening to anyone else. So we feel very lonely even within our own families. That is why we have to go to a therapist, hoping that she is able to listen to us. But many therapists also have deep suffering within. Sometimes they cannot listen as deeply as they would like. So if you really love someone, train yourself to be a listener. Be a therapist. You may be the best therapist for the person you love if you know how to train yourself in the art of deep, compassionate listening. You must also use loving speech. We have lost our capacity to say things calmly. We get irritated too easily. Every time we open our mouths, our speech becomes sour or bitter. We know it's true. We have lost our capacity for speaking with kindness. This is the Fourth Mindfulness Training. This is so crucial to restoring peaceful and loving relationships. If you fail in this training, you cannot succeed in restoring harmony, love, and happiness. That is why practicing the Fourth Mindfulness Training is a great gift.

So many families, couples, and relationships have been broken because we have lost the capacity of listening to each other with calmness and compassion. We have lost the capacity of using calm and loving speech. The Fourth Mindfulness Training is very important to restore communication between us. Practicing the Fourth Training on the art of listening and the art of loving speech is a great gift. For example, a family member may suffer very much. No one in the family has been able to sit quietly and listen to him or her. If there is someone capable of sitting calmly and listening with his or her heart for one hour, the other person will feel a great relief from his suffering. If you suffer so much and no one has been able to listen to your suffering, your suffering will remain there. But if someone is able to listen to you and understand you, you will feel relief after one hour of being together.

In Buddhism, we speak of the Bodhisattva Avalokiteshvara, Kwan Yin, a person who has a great capacity of listening with compassion and true presence. "Kwan Yin" means the one who can listen and understand the sound of the world, the cries of suffering. Psychotherapists try to practice the same. They sit very quietly with a lot of compassion and listen to you. Listening like that is not to judge, criticize, condemn, or evaluate, but to listen with the single purpose of helping the other person suffer less. If they are able to listen like that to you for one hour, you feel much better. But psychotherapists have to practice so that they can always maintain compassion, concentration, and deep listening. Otherwise, their quality of listening will be very poor, and you will not feel better after one hour of listening.

You have to practice breathing mindfully in and out so that compassion always stays with you. "I am listening to him not only because I want to know what is inside him or to give him advice. I am listening to him just because I want to relieve his suffering." That is called compassionate listening. You have to listen in such a way that compassion remains with you the whole time you are listening. That is the art. If halfway through listening irritation or anger comes up, then you cannot continue to listen. You have to practice in such a way that every time the energy of irritation and anger comes up, you can breathe in and out mindfully and continue to hold compassion within you. It is with compassion that you can listen to another. No matter what he says, even if there is a lot of wrong information and injustice in his way of seeing things, even if he condemns or blames you, continue to sit very quietly breathing in and out. Maintain your compassion within you for one hour. That is called compassionate listening. If you can listen like that for one hour, the other person will feel much better.

If you don't feel that you can continue to listen in this way, ask your friend, "Dear one, can we continue in a few days? I need to renew myself. I need to practice so I can listen to you in the best way I can." If you are not in good shape, you are not going to listen the best way you can. You need to practice more walking meditation, more mindful breathing, more sitting meditation in order to restore your capacity for compassionate listening. That is the practice of the Fourth Mindfulness Training — training oneself to listen with compassion. That is very important, a great gift.

Sometimes we speak clumsily and create internal knots in others. Then we say, "I was just telling the truth." It may be the truth, but if our way of speaking causes unnecessary suffering, it is not Right Speech. The truth must be presented in ways that others can accept. Words that damage or destroy are not Right Speech. Before you speak, understand the person you are speaking to. Consider each word carefully before you say anything, so that your speech is "Right" in both form and content. The Fourth Mindfulness Training also has to do with loving speech. You have the right to tell another everything in your heart with the condition that you use only loving speech. If you are not able to speak calmly, then don't speak that day. "Sorry, my dear, allow me to tell you tomorrow or the next day. I am not at my best today. I'm afraid I'll say things that are unkind. Allow me to tell you about this another day." Open your mouth and speak only when you are sure you can use calm and loving speech. You have to train yourself to be able to do so.

In the *Lotus Sutra*, a bodhisattva named Wondrous Sound was able to speak to each person in his or her own language. For someone who needed the language of music, he used music. For those who understood the language of drugs, he spoke in terms of drugs. Every word the Bodhisattva Wondrous Sound said opened up communication and helped others transform. We can do the same, but it takes determination and skillfulness.

When two people are not getting along, we can go to one and speak in a positive way about the other, and then go to the other and speak constructively about the first. When person "A" knows that person "B" is suffering, A has a much better chance of understanding and appreciating B. The art of Right Speech needs Right View, Right Thought, and also correct practice.

Letter writing is a form of speech. A letter can sometimes be safer than speaking, because there is time for you to read what you have written before sending it. As you read your words, you can visualize the other person receiving your letter and decide if what you have written is skillful and appropriate. Your letter has to water the seeds of transformation in the other person and stir something in his heart if it is to be called Right Speech. If any phrase can be misunderstood or upsetting, rewrite it. Right Mindfulness tells you whether you are expressing the truth in the most skillful way. Once you have mailed your letter, you cannot get it back. So read it over carefully several times before sending it. Such a letter will benefit both of you.

Of course you have suffered, but the other person has suffered also. That is why writing is a very good practice. Writing is a practice of looking deeply. You send the letter only when you are sure that you have looked deeply. You don't need to blame anymore. You need to show that you have a deeper understanding. It is true that the other person suffers, and that

alone is worth your compassion. When you begin to understand the suffering of the other person, compassion will arise
in you, and the language you use will have the power of healing. Compassion is the only energy that can help us connect
with another person. The person who has no compassion in
him can never be happy. When you practice looking at the
person to whom you are going to write a letter, if you can begin to see his suffering, compassion will be born. The moment compassion is born in you, you feel better already, even
before you finish the letter. After sending the letter, you feel
even better, because you know the other person will also feel
better after reading your letter. Everyone needs understanding and acceptance. And now you have understanding to offer. By writing a letter like this, you restore communication.

Writing a book or an article can be done in the same way.
Writing is a deep practice. Even before we begin writing, during whatever we are doing — gardening or sweeping the floor
— our book or essay is being written deep in our consciousness. To write a book, we must write with our whole life, not
just during the moments we are sitting at our desk. When
writing a book or an article, we know that our words will af-
fect many other people. We do not have the right just to express our own suffering if it brings suffering to others. Many
books, poems, and songs take away our faith in life. Young
people today curl up in bed with their walkmen and listen to
unwholesome music, songs that water seeds of great sadness
and agitation in them. When we practice Right View and
Right Thinking, we will put all of our tapes and CDs that water only seeds of anguish into a box and not listen to them
anymore. Filmmakers, musicians, and writers need to practice
Right Speech to help our society move again in the direction
of peace, joy, and faith in the future.

Telephone meditation is another practice that can help us
cultivate Right Speech:

Words can travel thousands of miles.
May my words create mutual understanding and love.
May they be as beautiful as gems,
as lovely as flowers.[3]

You may like to write this gatha on a piece of paper and tape it near your telephone. Then, every time you are about to make a phone call, place your hand on the phone and recite these words. This gatha expresses the determination to practice Right Speech. Even as you say the words, your mind already becomes more peaceful and your insight more clear. The person you are calling will hear the freshness in your voice, and your words will bring her great happiness and not cause suffering.

As our meditation practice deepens, we are much less caught in words. Capable of practicing silence, we are free as a bird, in touch with the essence of things. The founder of one of the schools of Vietnamese Zen Buddhism wrote, "Don't ask me anything else. My essence is wordless."[4] To practice mindfulness of speech, sometimes we have to practice silence. Then we can look deeply to see what our views are and what internal knots give rise to our thinking. Silence is a time for looking deeply. There are times when silence is truth, and that is called "thundering silence." Confucius said, "The heavens do not say anything." That also means, the heavens tell us so much, but we don't know how to listen to them. If we listen out of the silence of our mind, every bird's song and every whistling of the pine trees in the wind will speak to us. In the *Sukhavati Sutra*, it is said that every time the wind blows through the jeweled trees, a miracle is produced. If we listen carefully to that sound, we will hear the

---

[3] Thich Nhat Hanh, *Present Moment Wonderful Moment: Mindfulness Verses for Daily Living* (Berkeley: Parallax Press, 1990), p. 69.

[4] Vô Ngôn Thông, d. 826.

Buddha teaching the Four Noble Truths and the Noble Eight-fold Path. Right Mindfulness helps us slow down and listen to each word from the birds, the trees, and our own mind and speech. Whether we say something kind or respond too hastily, we hear what we are saying.

Words and thoughts can kill. We cannot support acts of killing in our thinking or in our speech. If you have a job in which telling the truth is impossible, you may have to change jobs. If you have a job that allows you to speak the truth, please be grateful. To practice social justice and non-exploitation, we have to use Right Speech.

CHAPTER THIRTEEN

Right Action

Right Action *(samyak karmanta)* means Right Action of the body. It is the practice of touching love and preventing harm, the practice of nonviolence toward ourselves and others. The basis of Right Action is to do everything in mindfulness.

Right Action is closely linked with four (the first, second, third, and fifth) of the Five Mindfulness Trainings.[1] The First Training is about reverence for life: "Aware of the suffering caused by the destruction of life, I am committed to cultivating compassion and learning ways to protect the lives of people, animals, plants, and minerals. I am determined not to kill, not to let others kill, and not to support any act of killing in the world, in my thinking, and in my way of life." We may be killing every day by the way we eat, drink, and use the land, air, and water. We think that we don't kill, but we do. Mindfulness of action helps us be aware so we can stop the killing and begin saving and helping.

The Second Mindfulness Training is about generosity: "Aware of the suffering caused by exploitation, social injustice, stealing, and oppression, I am committed to cultivating loving kindness and learning ways to work for the well-being of people, animals, plants, and minerals. I will practice generosity by sharing my time, energy, and material resources with those who are in real need. I am determined not to steal and not to possess anything that should belong to others. I will re-

---

[1] The Fourth Mindfulness Training is about Right Speech. See chap. 12.

spect the property of others, but I will prevent others from profiting from human suffering or the suffering of other species on Earth." This training tells us not just to refrain from taking what is not ours or exploiting others. It also exhorts us to live in a way that brings about justice and well-being in society. We have to learn how to live simply so that we do not take more than our share. When we do something to promote social justice, that is Right Action.

The Third Mindfulness Training is about sexual responsibility: "Aware of the suffering caused by sexual misconduct, I am committed to cultivating responsibility and learning ways to protect the safety and integrity of individuals, couples, families, and society. I am determined not to engage in sexual relations without love and a long-term commitment. To preserve the happiness of myself and others, I am determined to respect my commitments and the commitments of others. I will do everything in my power to protect children from sexual abuse and to prevent couples and families from being broken by sexual misconduct."

Loneliness cannot be alleviated just by the coming together of two bodies, unless there is also good communication, understanding, and loving kindness. Right Mindfulness helps us protect ourselves and others, including children, from further suffering. Sexual misbehavior creates so much suffering. To protect the integrity of families and individuals, we do our best to behave responsibly and encourage others to do the same. Practicing this training, we not only protect ourselves and those dear to us, but we protect the whole human species, including children. When Right Mindfulness shines its light on our daily life, we are able to keep this training steadily.

Sexual misbehavior has broken so many families. There has been so much suffering because people do not practice sexual responsibility. A child who is sexually abused will suffer his or her whole life. Those who have been sexually abused have the capacity to become bodhisattvas, helping many children. Your mind of love can transform your own grief and pain, and you can share your insight with others. This is Right Action, and it frees you and those around you. When you practice to help others around you, at the same time, you are helping yourself.

The Fifth Mindfulness Training encourages mindful eating, drinking, and consuming. This is linked to the Four Noble Truths and all of the elements of the Noble Eightfold Path, but especially Right Action: "Aware of the suffering caused by unmindful consumption, I am committed to cultivating good health, both physical and mental, for myself, my family, and my society by practicing mindful eating, drinking, and consuming. I will ingest only items that preserve peace, well-being, and joy in my body, in my consciousness, and in the collective body and consciousness of my family and society. I am determined not to use alcohol or any other intoxicant or to ingest foods or other items that contain toxins, such as certain TV programs, magazines, books, films, and conversations. I am aware that to damage my body or my consciousness with these poisons is to betray my ancestors, my parents, my society, and future generations. I will work to transform violence, fear, anger, and confusion in myself and in society by practicing a diet for myself and for society. I understand that a proper diet is crucial for self-transformation and for the transformation of society." Right Action means bringing into our body and mind only the kinds of food that are safe and healthy. We practice mindful eating, mindful drinking, not eating things that create toxins in our body, not using alcohol or drugs, for ourselves, our family, and our society. We consume mindfully so that life will be possible for all of us. We practice mindful consumption to protect our body and our consciousness from ingesting toxins. Certain television programs, books, magazines, and conversations can bring into our consciousness violence, fear, and despair. We have to practice mindful consumption to protect our body and consciousness and the collective body and consciousness of our family and our society.

When we practice not drinking alcohol, we protect ourselves, and we also protect our family and our society. A woman in London told me, "I have been drinking two glasses of wine every week for the last twenty years, and it has done me no harm at all. Why should I give it up?" I said, "It's true that two glasses of wine do not harm you. But are you sure they do not harm your children? You may not have the seed of alcoholism in you, but who knows whether the seed of alcoholism is in your children. If you give up wine, you'll be doing it not only for yourself but also for your children and for your society." She understood, and the next morning she formally received the Five Mindfulness Trainings. That is the work of a bodhisattva, doing it not for herself alone but for everyone.

The Ministry of Health in France advises people not to drink too much. They advertise on television, "One glass is okay, but three glasses invite destruction." They want you to be moderate in drinking. But if the first glass were not there, how could there be a third glass? Not having the first glass of wine is the highest form of protection. If you refrain from having a first glass, you are protecting not only yourself, but all of us at the same time. When we consume mindfully, we protect our body, our consciousness, and the body and consciousness of our family and society. Without the Fifth Training, how can we transform the difficult situation of our society? The more we consume, the more we suffer, and the more we make our society suffer. Mindful consumption seems to be the only way out of this current situation, the only way to stop the course of destruction for our body, our consciousness, and the collective body and consciousness of our society.

Looking deeply, we can see the interbeing nature of the Five Mindfulness Trainings and the Eightfold Path. We apply Right Mindfulness to see whether our eating, drinking, and consuming is Right Action. Right View, Right Thinking, and Right Speech are all present when we put the Fifth Mindfulness Training into practice. The Five Mindfulness Trainings are interpenetrated by the elements of the Noble Eightfold Path, especially Right Action.

Right Action is based on Right View, Right Thinking, and Right Speech, and is very much linked to Right Livelihood. Those who earn their living by manufacturing weapons, depriving others of their chance to live, destroying the environment, exploiting nature and people, or producing items that bring us toxins may earn a lot of money, but they are practicing wrong livelihood. We have to be mindful to protect ourselves from their wrong action. If we don't have Right View and Right Thought and are not practicing Right Speech and Right Livelihood, even if we feel we are trying to go in the direction of peace and enlightenment, our effort may be wrong action.

A good teacher only needs to observe a student walking or inviting the bell to sound to know how long he has been in the practice. You look at his Right Action and see all the things that are contained in it. Looking this way into any of the elements of the path, you can measure the realization of that person as far as the whole path is concerned.

There are so many things we can do to practice Right Action. We can protect life, practice generosity, behave responsibly, and consume mindfully. The basis of Right Action is Right Mindfulness.

CHAPTER FOURTEEN

Right Diligence

Right Diligence *(samyak pradhana)*, or Right Effort, is the kind of energy that helps us realize the Noble Eightfold Path. If we are diligent for possessions, sex, or food, that is wrong diligence. If we work round-the-clock for profit or fame or to run away from our suffering, that is wrong diligence also. From outside, it may appear that we are diligent, but it is not Right Diligence. The same can be true of our meditation practice. We may appear diligent in our practice, but if it takes us farther from reality or from those we love, it is wrong diligence. When we practice sitting and walking meditation in ways that cause our body and mind to suffer, our effort is not Right Diligence and is not based on Right View. Our practice should be intelligent, based on Right Understanding of the teaching. It is not because we practice hard that we can say that we are practicing Right Diligence.

There was a monk in Tang Dynasty China who was practicing sitting meditation very hard, day and night. He thought he was practicing harder than anyone else, and he was very proud of this. He sat like a rock day and night, but his suffering was not transformed. One day a teacher[1] asked him, "Why are you sitting so hard?" and the monk replied, "To become a Buddha!" The teacher picked up a tile and began polishing it, and the monk asked, "Teacher, what are you doing?" His master replied, "I am making a mirror." The monk asked,

---

[1] Master Huairang (667–744).

"How can you make a tile into a mirror?" and his teacher replied, "How can you become a Buddha by sitting?"

The four practices usually associated with Right Diligence are: (1) preventing unwholesome seeds in our store consciousness that have not yet arisen from arising, (2) helping the unwholesome seeds that have already arisen to return to our store consciousness, (3) finding ways to water the wholesome seeds in our store consciousness that have not yet arisen and asking our friends to do the same, and (4) nourishing the wholesome seeds that have already arisen so that they will stay present in our mind consciousness and grow stronger. This is called the Fourfold Right Diligence.

"Unwholesome" means not conducive to liberation or the Path. In our store consciousness there are many seeds that are not beneficial for our transformation, and if those seeds are watered, they will grow stronger. When greed, hatred, ignorance, and wrong views arise, if we embrace them with Right Mindfulness, sooner or later they will lose their strength and return to our store consciousness.

When wholesome seeds have not yet arisen, we can water them and help them come into our conscious mind. These seeds of happiness, love, loyalty, and reconciliation need watering every day. If we water them, we will feel joyful, and this will encourage them to stay longer. Keeping wholesome mental formations in our mind consciousness is the fourth practice of Right Diligence.

The Fourfold Right Diligence is nourished by joy and interest. If your practice does not bring you joy, you are not practicing correctly. The Buddha asked the monk Sona, "Is it true that before you became a monk you were a musician?" Sona replied that it was so. The Buddha asked, "What happens if the string of your instrument is too loose?"

"When you pluck it, there will be no sound," Sona replied.

"What happens when the string is too taut?"

"It will break."

"The practice of the Way is the same," the Buddha said. "Maintain your health. Be joyful. Do not force yourself to do things you cannot do."[2] We need to know our physical and psychological limits. We shouldn't force ourselves to do ascetic practices or lose ourselves in sensual pleasures. Right Diligence lies in the Middle Way, between the extremes of austerity and sensual indulgence.

The teachings of the Seven Factors of Awakening[3] are also part of the practice of Right Diligence. Joy is a factor of awakening, and it is at the heart of Right Diligence. Ease, another Factor of Awakening, is also essential for Right Diligence. In fact, not only Right Diligence but also Right Mindfulness and Right Concentration need joy and ease. Right Diligence does not mean to force ourselves. If we have joy, ease, and interest, our effort will come naturally. When we hear the bell inviting us for walking or sitting meditation, we will have the energy to participate if we find meditation joyful and interesting. If we do not have the energy to practice sitting or walking meditation, it is because these practices do not bring us joy or transform us, or we do not yet see their benefit.

When I wanted to become a novice monk, my family thought that a monk's life would be too difficult for me. But I knew it was the only way I could be happy, and I persisted. Once I became a novice, I felt as happy and free as a bird in the sky. When it came time for chanting sutras, I felt as though I had been invited to a concert. Sometimes on moonlit nights, when the monks were chanting the sutras standing by the crescent pond, I thought I was in paradise listening to angels. When I could not attend morning chanting because I had another task, just hearing the words of the *Shurangama Sutra* coming from the Buddha Hall brought me happiness.

---

[2] *Vinaya Mahavagga Khuddaka Nikaya* 5.

[3] The Seven Factors of Awakening — mindfulness, investigating phenomena, diligence, joy, ease, concentration, and letting go. See chap. 26.

Everyone at Tu Hieu Pagoda practiced with interest, joy, and diligence. There was no forced effort, just the love and support of our teacher and brothers in the practice.

At Plum Village, children participate in sitting and walking meditation and silent meals. At first, they do it just to be with their friends who are already practicing, but after they taste the peace and joy of meditation, they continue on their own because they want to. Sometimes it takes adults four or five years of practicing the outer form before they taste the true joy of practice. Master Guishan said, "Time flies like an arrow. If we do not live deeply, we waste our life."[4] Someone who can devote her life to the practice, who has a chance to be near her teacher and friends in the practice, has a wonderful opportunity that can bring her great happiness. If we lack Right Diligence, it is because we have not found a way to practice that is true for us, or have not felt deeply the need to practice. A mindful life can be wonderful.

> *Waking up this morning, I smile.*
> *Twenty-four brand new hours are before me.*
> *I vow to live fully in each moment*
> *and to look at all beings with eyes of compassion.*[5]

Reciting this gatha can give us energy to live the day well. Twenty-four hours are a treasure-chest of jewels. If we waste these hours, we waste our life. The practice is to smile as soon as we wake up, recognizing this day as an opportunity for practicing. It is up to us not to waste it. When we look at all beings with eyes of love and compassion, we feel wonderful. With the energy of mindfulness, washing the dishes, sweeping

---

[4] From "Encouraging Words," in Thich Nhat Hanh, *Stepping into Freedom: An Introduction to Buddhist Monastic Training* (Berkeley: Parallax Press, 1997), pp. 89–97. Guishan (771–853) was one of the great Tang Dynasty meditation masters.

[5] Thich Nhat Hanh, *Present Moment Wonderful Moment*, p. 3.

the floor, or practicing sitting or walking meditation are all the more precious.

Suffering can propel us to practice. When we are anxious or sad and see that these practices bring us relief, we will want to continue. It takes energy to look into suffering and to see what has brought about that suffering. But this insight will lead us to see how to end our suffering, and the path needed to do so. When we embrace our suffering, we see its origins, and we see that it can end because there is a path. Our suffering is at the center. When we look into the compost, we see the flowers. When we look into the sea of fire, we see a lotus. The path that does not run away from but embraces our suffering is the path that will lead us to liberation.

It is not always necessary for us to deal directly with our suffering. Sometimes we can just allow it to lie dormant in our store consciousness, and we use the opportunity to touch the refreshing and healing elements within us and around us with our mindfulness. They will take care of our pain, like antibodies taking care of the foreign bodies that have entered our bloodstream. When unwholesome seeds have arisen, we have to take care of them. When unwholesome seeds are dormant, our job is to help them sleep peacefully and be transformed at the base.

With Right View, we see the way we need to go, and our seeing gives us faith and energy. If we feel better after practicing walking meditation for an hour, we will have the determination to continue the practice. When we see how walking meditation brings peace to others, we will have even more faith in practice. With patience, we can discover the joys of life that are all around us, and we will have more energy, interest, and diligence.

The practice of mindful living should be joyful and pleasant. If you breathe in and out and feel joy and peace, that is Right Diligence. If you suppress yourself, if you suffer during your practice, it probably is not Right Diligence. Examine your practice. See what brings you joy and happiness of a sustained kind. Try to spend time with a Sangha, brothers and sisters who are creating a field of mindful energy that can make your practice easy. Work together with a teacher and with a friend to transform your suffering into compassion, peace, and understanding, and do it with joy and ease. That is Right Diligence.

CHAPTER FIFTEEN

Right Concentration

The practice of Right Concentration *(samyak samadhi)* is to cultivate a mind that is one-pointed. The Chinese character for concentration means, literally, "maintaining evenness," neither too high nor too low, neither too excited nor too dull. Another Chinese term sometimes used for concentration means "the abode of true mind."

There are two kinds of concentration, active and selective. In active concentration, the mind dwells on whatever is happening in the present moment, even as it changes. This poem by a Buddhist monk[1] describes active concentration:

> *The wind whistles in the bamboo*
> *and the bamboo dances.*
> *When the wind stops,*
> *the bamboo grows still.*

The wind comes and the bamboo welcomes it. The wind goes, and the bamboo lets it go. The poem continues:

> *A silver bird*
> *flies over the autumn lake.*
> *When it has passed,*
> *the lake's surface does not try*
> *to hold on to the image of the bird.*

---

[1] Poem by Vietnamese Dhyana Master Huong Hai (Ocean of Fragrance),

As the bird flies over the lake, its reflection is lucid. After it is gone, the lake reflects the clouds and the sky just as clearly. When we practice active concentration, we welcome whatever comes along. We don't think about or long for anything else. We just dwell in the present moment with all our being. Whatever comes, comes. When the object of our concentration has passed, our mind remains clear, like a calm lake.

When we practice "selective concentration," we choose one object and hold onto it. During sitting and walking meditation, whether alone or with others, we practice. We know that the sky and the birds are there, but our attention is focused on our object. If the object of our concentration is a math problem, we don't watch TV or talk on the phone. We abandon everything else and focus on the object. When we are driving, the lives of the passengers in our car depend on our concentration.

We don't use concentration to run away from our suffering. We concentrate to make ourselves deeply present. When we walk, stand, or sit in concentration, people can see our stability and stillness. Living each moment deeply, sustained concentration comes naturally, and that, in turn, gives rise to insight.

Right Concentration leads to happiness, and it also leads to Right Action. The higher our degree of concentration, the greater the quality of our life. Vietnamese girls are often told by their mothers that if they concentrate, they will be more beautiful. This is the kind of beauty that comes from dwelling deeply in the present moment. When a young lady moves inattentively, she does not look as fresh or at ease. Her mother may not use these words, but she is encouraging her daughter to practice Right Concentration. It is a pity she does not encourage her son to do the same. Everyone needs concentration.

There are nine levels of meditative concentration. The first four are the Four Dhyanas. These are concentrations on the form realm. The next five levels belong to the formless realm. When practicing the first dhyana, you still think. At the other eight levels, thinking gives way to other energies. Formless concentrations are also practiced in other traditions, but when they are practiced outside of Buddhism, it is generally to escape from suffering rather than to realize the liberation that comes with insight into our suffering. When you use concentration to run away from yourself or your situation, it is wrong concentration. Sometimes we need to escape our problems for relief, but at some time we have to return to face them. Worldly concentration seeks to escape. Supramundane concentration aims at complete liberation.

To practice samadhi is to live deeply each moment that is given us to live. Samadhi means concentration. In order to be concentrated, we should be mindful, fully present and aware of what is going on. Mindfulness brings about concentration. When you are deeply concentrated, you are absorbed in the moment. You *become* the moment. That is why samadhi is sometimes translated as "absorption." Right Mindfulness and Right Concentration lift us above the realms of sensual pleasures and craving, and we find ourselves lighter and happier. Our world is no longer gross and heavy, the realm of desires *(karma dhatu)*. It is the realm of fine materiality, the realm of form *(rupa dhatu)*.

In the form realm, there are four levels of dhyana. Mindfulness, concentration, joy, happiness, peace, and equanimity continue to grow through these four levels. After the fourth dhyana, the practitioner enters a deeper experience of concentration — the four formless dhyanas — where he or she can see deeply into reality. Here, sensual desire and materiality reveal their illusory nature and are no longer obstacles. You begin to see the impermanent, nonself, and interbeing nature of the phenomenal world. Earth, water, air, fire, space, time, nothingness, and perceptions inter-are. Nothing can be by itself alone.

The object of the fifth level of concentration is limitless space. When we begin to practice this concentration, everything seems to be space. But as we practice more deeply, we see that space is composed of and exists only in "non-space elements," like earth, water, air, fire, and consciousness. Because space is only one of the six elements that make up all material things, we know space does not have a separate, independent existence. According to the teachings of the Buddha, nothing has a separate self. So space and everything else inter-are. Space inter-is with the other five elements.

The object of the sixth level of concentration is limitless consciousness. At first, we see only consciousness, but then we see that consciousness is also earth, water, air, fire, and space. What is true of space is also true of consciousness.

The object of the seventh level of concentration is nothingness. With normal perception, we see flowers, fruit, teapots, and tables, and we think they exist separately of one another. But when we look more deeply, we see that the fruit is in the flower, and that the flower, the cloud, and the earth are in the fruit. We go beyond outward appearances or signs and come to "signlessness." At first, we think that the members of our family are separate from one another, but afterwards we see that they contain each other. You are the way you are because I am the way I am. We see the intimate connection between people, and we go beyond signs. We used to think that the universe contains millions of separate entities. Now we understand "the nonexistence of signs."

The eighth level of concentration is that of neither perception nor non-perception. We recognize that everything is produced by our perceptions, which are, at least in part, erroneous. Therefore, we see that we cannot rely on our old way of perceiving, and we want to be in direct touch with reality. We cannot stop perceiving altogether, but at least now we know that perception is perception of a sign. Since we no longer believe in the reality of signs, our perception becomes wisdom. We go beyond signs ("no perception"), but we do not become perceptionless ("no non-perception").

The ninth level of concentration is called cessation. "Cessation" here means the cessation of ignorance in our feelings and perceptions, not the cessation of feelings and perceptions. From this concentration is born insight. The poet Nguyen Du said, "As soon as we see with our eyes and hear with our ears, we open ourselves to suffering." We long to be in a state of concentration where we cannot see or hear anything, in a world where there is no perception. We wish to become a pine tree with the wind singing in our branches, because we believe that a pine tree does not suffer. The search for a place of non-suffering is natural.

In the world of non-perception, the seventh *(manas)* and the eighth *(alaya)* consciousnesses continue to function as usual, and our ignorance and internal formations remain intact in our store consciousness, and they manifest in the seventh consciousness. The seventh consciousness is the energy of delusion that creates the belief in a self and distinguishes self from other. Since the non-perception concentration does not transform our habit energies, when people emerge from that concentration, their suffering is intact. But when the meditator reaches the ninth level of concentration, the stage of arhat, manas is transformed and the internal formations in the store consciousness are purified. The greatest internal formation is ignorance of the reality of impermanence and nonself. This ignorance gives rise to greed, hatred, confusion, pride, doubt, and views. Together, these afflictions produce a war of consciousness called manas, which always discriminates self from other.

When someone practices well, the ninth level of concentration shines light on the reality of things and transforms ignorance. The seeds that used to cause you to be caught in self and nonself are transformed, alaya is freed from the grip of manas, and manas no longer has the function of making a self. Manas becomes the Wisdom of Equality that can see the interbeing and interpenetrating nature of things. It can see that others' lives are as precious as our own, because there is no longer discrimination between self and other. When manas loses its grip on store consciousness, store consciousness becomes the Wisdom of the Great Mirror that reflects everything in the universe.

When the sixth consciousness *(manovijñana)* is transformed, it is called the Wisdom of Wonderful Observation. Mind consciousness continues to observe phenomena after it has been transformed into wisdom, but it observes them in a different way, because mind consciousness is aware of the interbeing nature of all that it observes — seeing the one in the many, all the manifestations of birth and death, coming and going, and so on — without being caught in ignorance. The first five consciousnesses become the Wisdom of Wonderful Realization. Our eyes, ears, nose, tongue, and body that previously caused us to suffer become miracles that bring us to the garden of suchness. Thus, the transformation of all levels of consciousness is realized as Four Wisdoms. Our wrong consciousness and wrong perceptions are transformed, thanks to the practice. At the ninth level of concentration, all eight consciousnesses are functioning. Perception and feeling are still there, but they are different from before, because they are free from ignorance.[2]

The Buddha taught many concentration practices. To practice the Concentration on Impermanence, every time you look at your beloved, see him as impermanent, and do your best to make him happy today. If you think he is permanent, you may believe that he will never improve. The insight into impermanence keeps you from getting caught in the suffering of craving, attachment, and despair. See and listen to everything with this insight.

---

[2] This is described in chap. 27.

To practice the Concentration on Nonself, touch the nature of interbeing in everything you contact. This will bring you a lot of peace and joy and prevent you from suffering. The practice of the Concentration on Nirvana helps you to touch the ultimate dimension of reality and establish yourself in the realms of no-birth and no-death. The Concentrations on Impermanence, Nonself, and Nirvana are enough for us to practice our whole lives. In fact, the three are one. If you touch the nature of impermanence deeply, you touch the nature of nonself (interbeing) and nirvana. One concentration contains all concentrations. You don't need to do everything.

In Mahayana Buddhism, there are hundreds of other concentrations, such as the *Shurangama Samadhi* (the Concentration of the Heroic March), the *Saddharmapundarika Samadhi,* and the *Avatamsaka Samadhi.* Each is wonderful and important. According to the *Lotus Sutra,* we have to live in the historical and ultimate dimensions of reality at the same time. We have to live deeply our life as a wave so we can touch the substance of water in us. We walk, look, breathe, and eat in a way that we touch the absolute dimension of reality. We transcend birth and death and the fears of being and nonbeing, one and many.

The Buddha is not found only on Gridhrakuta, the Vulture Peak. If you were to hear on the radio that the Buddha is going to reappear on Gridhrakuta Mountain and the public is invited to join him for walking meditation, all the seats on all the airplanes to India would be booked, and you might feel frustrated, because you want to go, also. Even if you were lucky enough to get a seat on that plane, it still might not be possible for you to enjoy practicing walking meditation with the Buddha. There would be *so* many people, most of whom don't know how to practice breathing in and out and dwelling in the present moment while walking. What is the use of going there?

Look deeply at your intention. Do you want to fly halfway

around the world so that later you can say you were with the Buddha? Many people want to do just that. They arrive at a place of pilgrimage, unable to be in the here and the now. After a few minutes of seeing the place, they rush to the next place. They take pictures to prove they were there, and they are eager to return home to show their friends. "I was there. I have proof. That is me standing beside the Buddha." That would be the desire of many of the people who would go there. They are not able to walk with the Buddha. They are not able to be in the here and the now. They only want to say, "I was there, and this is me standing beside the Buddha." But it is not true. They were not there. And that is not the Buddha. "Being there" is a concept, and the Buddha that you see is a mere appearance. You cannot photograph the real Buddha, even if you have a very expensive camera.

If you don't have the opportunity to fly to India, please practice walking at home, and you can really hold the hand of the Buddha while you walk. Just walk in peace and happiness, and the Buddha is there with you. The one who flies to India and returns with his photo taken with the Buddha has not seen the real Buddha. You have the reality; he has only a sign. Don't run around looking for photo opportunities. Touch the real Buddha. He is available. Take his hand and practice walking meditation. When you can touch the ultimate dimension, you walk with the Buddha. The wave does not need to die to become water. She is already water. This is the Concentration of the *Lotus Sutra*. Live every moment of your life deeply, and while walking, eating, drinking, and looking at the morning star, you touch the ultimate dimension.

CHAPTER SIXTEEN

Right Livelihood

To practice Right Livelihood *(samyag ajiva)*, you have to find a way to earn your living without transgressing your ideals of love and compassion. The way you support yourself can be an expression of your deepest self, or it can be a source of suffering for you and others.

The sutras usually define Right Livelihood as earning a living without needing to transgress any of the Five Mindfulness Trainings: not dealing in arms, in the slave trade, the meat trade, the sale of alcohol, drugs, or poisons; or making prophecies or telling fortunes. Monks and nuns must be careful not to make unreasonable demands on the laity for the four requisites of medicine, food, clothes, and lodging, and not to live with material requisites in excess of immediate needs. Bringing awareness to every moment, we try to have a vocation that is beneficial to humans, animals, plants, and the earth, or at least minimally harmful. We live in a society in which jobs are sometimes hard to find, but if it happens that our work involves harming life, we should try to find another job. Our vocation can nourish our understanding and compassion, or erode them. We should be awake to the consequences, far and near, of the way we earn our living. So many modern industries are harmful to humans and nature, even food production. Chemical pesticides and fertilizers can cause a lot of harm to the environment. Practicing Right Livelihood is difficult for farmers. If they do not use chemicals, it may be difficult for them to compete commercially. This is just one example. When you practice your profession or trade, observe the Five Mindfulness Trainings. A job that involves killing, stealing, sexual misconduct, lying, or selling drugs or alcohol is not Right Livelihood. If your company pollutes the rivers or the air, working there is not Right Livelihood. Making weapons or profiting from others' superstitions is also not Right Livelihood. People have superstitions, such as believing that their fate is sealed in the stars or in the palms of their hands. No one can be sure what will occur in the future. By practicing mindfulness, we can change the destiny astrologers have predicted for us. Moreover, prophecies can be self-fulfilling.

Composing or performing works of art can also be livelihood. A composer, writer, painter, or performer has an effect on the collective consciousness. Any work of art is, to a large extent, a product of the collective consciousness. Therefore, the individual artist needs to practice mindfulness so that his or her work of art helps those who touch it practice right attention. A young man wanted to learn how to draw lotus flowers, so he went to a master to apprentice with him. The master took him to a lotus pond and invited him to sit there. The young man saw flowers bloom when the sun was high, and he watched them return into buds when night fell. The next morning, he did the same. When one lotus flower wilted and its petals fell into the water, he just looked at the stalk, the stamen, and the rest of the flower, and then moved on to another lotus. He did that for ten days. On the eleventh day, the master asked him, "Are you ready?" and he replied, "I will try." The master gave him a brush, and although the young man's style was childlike, the lotus he drew was beautiful. He had *become* the lotus, and the painting came forth from him. You could see his naïveté concerning technique, but deep beauty was there.

Right Livelihood is not just a personal matter. It is our collective karma. Suppose I am a schoolteacher and I believe that nurturing love and understanding in children is a beautiful occupation. I would object if someone were to ask me to stop teaching and become, for example, a butcher. But when I meditate on the interrelatedness of things, I see that the butcher is not the only person responsible for killing animals. We may think the butcher's livelihood is wrong and ours is right, but if we didn't eat meat, he would not have to kill. Right Livelihood is a collective matter. The livelihood of each person affects everyone else. The butcher's children might benefit from my teaching, while my children, because they eat meat, share some responsibility for the butcher's livelihood. Suppose a farmer who sells his cattle as meat wants to receive the Five Mindfulness Trainings. He wants to know if he can, in light of the first training to protect life. He feels that he gives his cattle the best conditions for their well-being. He even operates his own slaughterhouse, so that there is no unnecessary cruelty inflicted on the animals when he puts an end to their lives. He inherited his farm from his father, and he has a family to support. This is a dilemma. What should he do? His intentions are good, but he has inherited his farm and his habit energies from his ancestors. Every time a cow is slaughtered, it leaves an impression on his consciousness, which will come back to him in dreams, during meditation, or at the moment of death. It is Right Livelihood to look after his cows so well while they are alive. He has the wish to be kind to his cows, and he also wants the security of regular income for himself and his family.

He should continue to look deeply and practice mindfulness with his local Sangha. As his insight deepens, the way out of the situation where he finds himself killing to make a living will present itself.

Everything we do contributes to our effort to practice Right Livelihood. It is more than just the way we earn our paycheck. We cannot succeed at having a Right Livelihood one hundred percent, but we can resolve to go in the direction of compassion and reducing suffering. And we can resolve to help create a society in which there is more Right Livelihood and less wrong livelihood.

Millions of people, for example, make their living in the arms industry, helping directly or indirectly to manufacture conventional and nuclear weapons. The U.S., Russia, France, Britain, China, and Germany are the primary suppliers of these weapons. Weapons are then sold to Third World countries, where the people do not need guns; they need food. To manufacture or sell weapons is not Right Livelihood, but the responsibility for this situation lies with all of us — politicians, economists, and consumers. We have not yet organized a compelling national debate on this problem. We have to discuss this further, and we have to keep creating new jobs so that no one has to live on the profits from weapons' manufacture. If you are able to work in a profession that helps realize your ideal of compassion, be grateful. And please try to help create proper jobs for others by living mindfully, simply, and sanely. Use all of your energy to try to improve the situation.

To practice Right Livelihood means to practice Right Mindfulness. Every time the telephone rings, hear it as a bell of mindfulness. Stop what you are doing, breathe in and out consciously, and then proceed to the telephone. The way you answer the phone will embody Right Livelihood. We need to discuss among ourselves how to practice mindfulness in the workplace, how to practice Right Livelihood. Do we breathe when we hear the telephone ringing and before we pick up the phone to make a call? Do we smile while we take care of others? Do we walk mindfully from meeting to meeting? Do we practice Right Speech? Do we practice deep and total relaxation after hours of hard work? Do we live in ways that encourage everyone to be peaceful and happy and to have a job that is in the direction of peace and happiness? These are very practical and important questions. To work in a way that encourages this kind of thinking and acting, in a way that encourages our ideal of compassion, is to practice Right Livelihood.

If someone has a profession that causes living beings to suffer and oppresses others, it will infect their own consciousness, just as when we pollute the air that we ourselves have to breathe. Many people get rich by means of wrong livelihood. Then they go to their temple or church and make donations. These donations come from feelings of fear and guilt rather than the wish to bring happiness to others and relieve others of suffering. When a temple or church receives large donations, those responsible for receiving the funds must understand this; they should do their best to help the donor transform by showing him or her a way out of that wrong livelihood. Such persons need, more than anything, the teachings of the Buddha.

۶

As we study and practice the Noble Eightfold Path, we see that each element of the path is contained within all the other seven elements. We also see that each element of the path contains the Noble Truths of suffering, the making of suffering, and the ending of suffering.

Practicing the First Noble Truth, we recognize our suffering and call it by its name — depression, anxiety, fear, or insecurity. Then we look directly into that suffering to discover its basis, and that is practicing the Second Noble Truth. These two practices contain the first two elements of the Noble Eightfold Path, namely, Right View and Right Thinking. All of us have a tendency to run away from suffering, but now with the practice of the Noble Eightfold Path we have the courage to face our suffering directly. We use Right Mindfulness and Right Concentration to look courageously at our suffering. The looking deeply that shows us clearly the basis of our suffering is Right View. Right View will not show one reason for our suffering, but layers upon layers of causes and conditions: seeds we have inherited from our parents, grandparents, and ancestors; seeds in us that have been watered by our friends and the economic and political situations of our country; and so many other causes and conditions.

Now the time has come to do something to lessen our suffering. Once we know what is feeding our suffering, we find a way to cease ingesting that nutriment, whether it is edible food, the food of sense-impression, the food we receive from our intentions, or the food from our consciousness. We do this by practicing Right Speech, Right Action, and Right Livelihood, remembering that Right Speech is also listening deeply. To practice these three aspects, we take the Mindfulness Trainings as our guide. Practicing according to the Mindfulness Trainings, we see that when we speak, act, or earn our living, we do it with Right Mindfulness. Right Mindfulness lets us know when we say something that is not Right Speech or do something that is not Right Action. Once Right Mindfulness is practiced along with Right Diligence, Right Concentration will follow easily and give rise to insight or Right View. In fact, it is not possible to practice one element of the Noble Eightfold Path without practicing all seven other elements. This is the nature of interbeing, and it is true for all of the teachings offered by the Buddha.

PART THREE

Other Basic Buddhist Teachings

CHAPTER SEVENTEEN

The Two Truths

According to Buddhism, there are two kinds of truth, relative or worldly truth *(samvriti satya)* and absolute truth *(paramartha satya)*. We enter the door of practice through relative truth. We recognize the presence of happiness and the presence of suffering, and we try to go in the direction of increased happiness. Every day we go a little further in that direction, and one day we realize that suffering and happiness are "not two."

A Vietnamese poem says:

> *People talk endlessly about their suffering and their joy.*
> *But what is there to suffer or be joyful about?*
> *Joy from sensual pleasure always leads to pain,*
> *and suffering while practicing the Way always brings joy.*
> *Wherever there is joy, there is suffering.*
> *If you want to have no-suffering, you must accept no-joy.*

The poet is trying to leap into absolute truth without walking the path of relative truth. Many people think that in order to avoid suffering, they have to give up joy, and they call this "transcending joy and suffering." This is not correct. If you recognize and accept your pain without running away from it, you will discover that although pain exists, joy also exists. Without experiencing relative joy, you will not know what to do when you are face-to-face with absolute joy. Don't get caught in theories or ideas, such as saying that suffering is an illusion or that we have to "transcend" both suffering and joy. Just stay in touch with what is actually going on, and you will touch the true nature of suffering *and* the true nature of joy. When you have a headache, it would not be correct to call your headache illusory. To help it go away, you have to acknowledge its existence and understand its causes.

We enter the path of practice through the door of knowledge, perhaps from a Dharma talk or a book. We continue along the path, and our suffering lessens, little by little. But at some point, all of our concepts and ideas must yield to our actual experience. Words and ideas are only useful if they are put into practice. When we stop discussing things and begin to realize the teachings in our own life, a moment comes when we realize that our life *is* the path, and we no longer rely merely on the forms of practice. Our action becomes "non-action," and our practice becomes "non-practice." The boundary has been crossed, and our practice cannot be set back. We do not have to transcend the "world of dust" *(saha)* in order to go to some dust-free world called nirvana. Suffering and nirvana are of the same substance. If we throw away the world of dust, we will have no nirvana.

In the *Discourse on Turning the Wheel of the Dharma,* the Buddha taught the Four Noble Truths of suffering, the cause of suffering, the cessation of suffering, and the path. But in the *Heart Sutra,* the Bodhisattva Avalokiteshvara tells us that there is no suffering, no cause of suffering, no cessation of suffering, and no path.[1] Is this a contradiction? No. The Buddha is speaking in terms of relative truth, and Avalokiteshvara is teaching in terms of absolute truth. When Avalokiteshvara says there is no suffering, he means that suffering is made entirely of things that are not suffering.[2]

---

[1] See Thich Nhat Hanh, *The Heart of Understanding: Commentaries on the Prajñaparamita Heart Sutra* (Berkeley: Parallax Press, 1988).

[2] See pp. 126-127 for a fuller explication of this sentence. See also pp. 135-137.

Whether you suffer or not depends on many circumstances. The cold air can be painful if you are not wearing warm enough clothes, but with proper clothing, cold air can be a source of joy. Suffering is not objective. It depends largely on the way you perceive. There are things that cause you to suffer but do not cause others to suffer. There are things that bring you joy but do not bring others joy. The Four Noble Truths were presented by the Buddha as relative truth to help you enter the door of practice, but they are not his deepest teaching.

With the eyes of interbeing, we can always reconcile the Two Truths. When we see, comprehend, and touch the nature of interbeing, we see the Buddha.

> *All conditioned things are impermanent.*
> *They are phenomena, subject to birth and death.*
> *When birth and death no longer are,*
> *the complete silencing is joy.*[3]

This verse *(gatha)* was spoken by the Buddha shortly before his death. The first two lines express relative truth, while the third and fourth lines express absolute truth. "All conditioned things" includes physical, physiological, and psychological phenomena.[4] "Complete silencing" means nirvana, the extinction of all concepts. When the Buddha says, "The complete silencing is joy," he means that thinking, conceptualizing, and speaking have come to an end. This is the Third Noble Truth in absolute terms.

The Buddha recommends that we recite the "Five Remembrances" every day:

-----

[3] *Ekottara Agama* 18.

[4] "Form-conditioned things" *(rupa-samskara)*, like a teapot or a flower, can be seen with our eyes. "Mind-conditioned things" *(chitta-samskara)*, such as anger or sadness, are psychological.

(1) I am of the nature to grow old. There is no way to escape growing old.

(2) I am of the nature to have ill-health. There is no way to escape having ill-health.

(3) I am of the nature to die. There is no way to escape death.

(4) All that is dear to me and everyone I love are of the nature to change. There is no way to escape being separated from them.

(5) My actions are my only true belongings. I cannot escape the consequences of my actions. My actions are the ground on which I stand.

The Five Remembrances help us make friends with our fears of growing old, getting sick, being abandoned, and dying. They are also a bell of mindfulness that can help us appreciate deeply the wonders of life that are available here and now. But in the *Heart Sutra,* Avalokiteshvara teaches that there is no birth and no death. Why would the Buddha tell us that we are of the nature to die if there is no birth and no death? Because in the Five Remembrances, the Buddha is using the tool of relative truth. He is well aware that in terms of absolute truth, there is no birth and no death.

When we look at the ocean, we see that each wave has a beginning and an end. A wave can be compared with other waves, and we can call it more or less beautiful, higher or lower, longer lasting or less long lasting. But if we look more deeply, we see that a wave is made of water. While living the life of a wave, it also lives the life of water. It would be sad if the wave did not know that it is water. It would think, Some day, I will have to die. This period of time is my life span, and when I arrive at the shore, I will return to nonbeing. These notions will cause the wave fear and anguish. We have to help it remove the notions of self, person, living being, and life span if we want the wave to be free and happy.

A wave can recognized by signs — high or low, beginning or ending, beautiful or ugly. But in the world of the water, there are no signs. In the world of relative truth, the wave feels happy as she swells, and she feels sad when she falls. She may think, "I am high," or "I am low," and develop a superiority or inferiority complex. But when the wave touches her true nature — which is water — all her complexes will cease, and she will transcend birth and death.

We become arrogant when things go well, and we are afraid of falling, or being low or inadequate. But these are relative ideas, and when they end, a feeling of completeness and satisfaction arises. Liberation is the ability to go from the world of signs to the world of true nature. We need the relative world of the wave, but we also need to touch the water, the ground of our being, to have real peace and joy. We shouldn't allow relative truth to imprison us and keep us from touching absolute truth. Looking deeply into relative truth, we penetrate the absolute. Relative and absolute truths inter-embrace. Both truths, relative and absolute, have a value.

Sitting in the northern hemisphere, we think we know which direction is above and which is below. But someone sitting in Australia will not agree. Above and below are relative truths. Above what? Below what? There is no absolute truth of above and below, old age and youth, etc. For me, old age is fine. It is nice to be old! There are things young people cannot experience. Young people are like a source of water from the top of the mountain, always trying to go as quickly as possible. But when you become a river going through the lowland, you are much more peaceful. You reflect many clouds and the beautiful blue sky. Being old has its own joys. You can be very happy being an old person. When I sit with young monks and nuns, I feel that they are my continuation. I have done my best, and now they are continuing my being. This is interbeing, nonself.

This morning, before giving a Dharma talk, I was having breakfast with my attendant, a lovely novice monk. I paused and said to him, "Dear one, do you see the cow on the hillside? She is eating grass in order to make my yogurt, and I am now eating the yogurt to make a Dharma talk." Somehow, the cow will offer today's Dharma talk. As I drank the cow's milk, I was a child of the cow. The Buddha recommends we live our daily life in this way, seeing everything in the light of interbeing. Then we will not be caught in our small self. We will see our joy and our suffering everywhere. We will be free, and we won't see dying as a problem. Why should we say that dying is suffering? We continue with the next generations. What is essential is to be our best while we are here. Then we continue to be through our children and grandchildren. Motivated by love, we invest ourselves in the next generations. Whether birth and death are suffering depends on our insight. With insight, we can look at all these things and smile to them. We are not affected in the same way anymore. We ride on the wave of birth and death, and we are free from birth and death. This insight liberates us.

All "formations" (samskara) are impermanent. This sheet of paper is a physical formation formed by many elements. A rose, a mountain, and cloud are formations. Your anger is a mental formation. Your love and the idea of nonself are mental formations. My fingers and my liver are physiological formations.

Look into the self and discover that it is made only of nonself elements. A human being is made up of only non-human elements. To protect humans, we have to protect the non-human elements — the air, the water, the forest, the river, the mountains, and the animals. The *Diamond Sutra* is the most ancient text about how to respect all forms of life on earth, the animals, vegetation, and also minerals. We have to remove the notion of human as something that can survive by itself alone. Humans can survive only with the survival of other species. This is exactly the teaching of the Buddha, and also the teaching of deep ecology.

When we look deeply into living beings, we find out that they are made of non-living-being elements. So-called inanimate things are alive also. Our notions about living beings and inanimate things should be removed for us to touch reality.

The fourth notion to be removed is life span. We think that we exist only from this point in time until this point in time, and we suffer because of that notion. If we look deeply, we will know that we have never been born and we will never die. A wave is born and dies, is higher or lower, more or less beautiful. But you cannot apply these notions to water. When we see this, our fear will suddenly vanish.

Within us, we carry the world of no-birth and no-death. But we never touch it, because we live only with our notions. The practice is to remove these notions and touch the ultimate dimension — nirvana, God, the world of no-birth and no-death. Because of the notions we carry, we are unable to touch it, and we live in constant fear and suffering. When the wave lives her life as a wave deeply, she touches the dimension of water that is within her, and suddenly her fears and notions vanish, and she is truly happy. Before that, her happiness was just a kind of band-aid. The greatest relief is to touch nirvana, the world of no-birth and no-death.

The Third Holy Truth is about relative well-being, which is impermanent. Your toothache is impermanent, but your non-toothache is also impermanent. When you practice deep Buddhism, you remove all these notions and touch the world of no-birth and no-death. With that insight, you look at birth, death, old-age, ups and downs, suffering, and happiness with the eyes of a sage, and you don't suffer anymore. You smile, no longer afraid.

The Fourth Noble Truth is the cessation of the causes of suffering. When we put an end to our suffering, we feel relative joy. But when all of our concepts of suffering and not suffering cease, we taste absolute joy. Imagine two hens about to be slaughtered, but they do not know it. One hen says to the other, "The rice is much tastier than the corn. The corn is slightly off." She is talking about relative joy. She does not realize that the real joy of this moment is the joy of not being slaughtered, the joy of being alive.

When we practice the Four Holy Truths in the dimension of relative truth, we obtain some relief. We are able to transform our suffering and restore our well-being. But we are still in the historical dimension of reality. The deeper level of practice is to lead our daily life in a way that we touch both the absolute and the relative truth. In the dimension of relative truth, the Buddha passed away many years ago. But in the realm of absolute truth, we can take his hand and join him for walking meditation every day.

Practice in a way that gives you the greatest relief. The wave is already water. To enter the heart of the Buddha, use your Buddha eyes, which means your insight into interbeing. Approach the heart of the Buddha in the realm of absolute truth, and the Buddha will be there with you. When you hear the sound of the bell, listen with your ears, and also listen with the ears of your ancestors, your children, and their children. Listen in the relative and absolute dimensions at the same time. You don't have to die to enter nirvana or the Kingdom of God. You only have to dwell deeply in the present moment, right now.

The *Avatamsaka Sutra* says that all dharmas (phenomena) enter one dharma, and one dharma enters all dharmas. If you go deeply into any one of the teachings of the Buddha, you will find all of the other teachings in it. If you practice looking deeply into the First Holy Truth, you can see the Noble Eightfold Path revealed. Outside of the First Holy Truth, there cannot be any path, holy or unholy. That is why you have to embrace your suffering, hold it close to your chest, and look deeply into it. The way out of your suffering depends on how you look into it. That is why suffering is called a Holy Truth. Look deeply into the nature of the path, using your Buddha eyes. The truth of the path is one with the truth of suffering. Every second I am on the path that leads out of suffering, suffering is there to guide me. That is why it is a holy path.

This book began with the sentence, "Buddha was not a god. He was a human being...." What does this mean? What is a human being? If the trees and the rivers were not there, could human beings be alive? If animals and all other species were not there, how could we be? A human being is made entirely of non-human elements. We must free ourselves of our ideas of Buddha and of human beings. Our ideas may be the obstacles that prevent us from seeing the Buddha.

"Dear Buddha, are you a living being?" We want the Buddha to confirm the notion we have of him. But he looks at us, smiles, and says, "A human being is not a human being. That is why we can say that he is a human being." These are the dialectics of the *Diamond Sutra.* "A is not A. That is why it is truly A." A flower is not a flower. It is made only of non-flower elements — sunshine, clouds, time, space, earth, minerals, gardeners, and so on. A true flower contains the whole universe. If we return any one of these non-flower elements to its source, there will be no flower. That is why we can say, "A rose is not a rose. That is why it is an authentic rose." We have to remove our concept of rose if we want to touch the real rose.

Nirvana means extinction — first of all, the extinction of all concepts and notions. Our concepts about things prevent us from really touching them. We have to destroy our notions if we want to touch the real rose. When we ask, "Dear Buddha, are you a human being?" it means we have a concept about what a human being is. So the Buddha just smiles at us. It is his way of encouraging us to transcend our concepts and touch the real being that he is. A real being is quite different from a concept.

If you have been to Paris, you have a concept of Paris. But your concept is quite different from Paris itself. Even if you've lived in Paris for ten years, your idea of Paris still does not coincide with the reality. You may have lived with someone for ten years and think that you know her perfectly, but you are living only with your concept. You have a concept of yourself, but have you touched your true self? Look deeply to try to overcome the gap between your concept of reality and reality itself. Meditation helps us remove concepts.

The Buddhist teaching of the Two Truths is also a concept. But if we know how to use it, it can help us penetrate reality itself.

CHAPTER EIGHTEEN

The Three Dharma Seals

The Three Dharma Seals *(Dharma mudra)* are impermanence *(anitya)*, nonself *(anatman)*, and nirvana. Any teaching that does not bear these Three Seals cannot be said to be a teaching of the Buddha.[1]

The First Dharma Seal is impermanence. The Buddha taught that everything is impermanent — flowers, tables, mountains, political regimes, bodies, feelings, perceptions, mental formations, and consciousness. We cannot find anything that is permanent. Flowers decompose, but knowing this does not prevent us from loving flowers. In fact, we are able to love them more because we know how to treasure them while they are still alive. If we learn to look at a flower in a way that impermanence is revealed to us, when it dies, we will not suffer. Impermanence is more than an idea. It is a practice to help us touch reality.

When we study impermanence, we have to ask, "Is there anything in this teaching that has to do with my daily life, my daily difficulties, my suffering?" If we see impermanence as merely a philosophy, it is not the Buddha's teaching. Every time we look or listen, the object of our perception can re-

---

[1] In the Southern Transmission, the Three Dharma Seals are often said to be impermanence, suffering *(dukkha)*, and nonself. But in the *Samyukta Agama,* the Buddha taught impermanence, nonself, and nirvana as the Three Dharma Seals. See chaps. 4 and 5 for a fuller explication of why the author has chosen to include nirvana rather than dukkha as a Dharma Seal.

veal to us the nature of impermanence. We have to nourish our insight into impermanence all day long.

When we look deeply into impermanence, we see that things change because causes and conditions change. When we look deeply into nonself, we see that the existence of every single thing is possible only because of the existence of everything else. We see that everything else is the cause and condition for its existence. We see that everything else is in it.

From the point of view of time, we say "impermanence," and from the point of view of space, we say "nonself." Things cannot remain themselves for two consecutive moments, therefore, there is nothing that can be called a permanent "self." Before you entered this room, you were different physically and mentally. Looking deeply at impermanence, you see nonself. Looking deeply at nonself, you see impermanence. We cannot say, "I can accept impermanence, but nonself is too difficult." They are the same.

Understanding impermanence can give us confidence, peace, and joy. Impermanence does not necessarily lead to suffering. Without impermanence, life could not be. Without impermanence, your daughter could not grow up into a beautiful young lady. Without impermanence, oppressive political regimes would never change. We think impermanence makes us suffer. The Buddha gave the example of a dog that was hit by a stone and got angry at the stone. It is not impermanence that makes us suffer. What makes us suffer is wanting things to be permanent when they are not.

We need to learn to appreciate the value of impermanence. If we are in good health and are aware of impermanence, we will take good care of ourselves. When we know that the person we love is impermanent, we will cherish our beloved all the more. Impermanence teaches us to respect and value every moment and all the precious things around us and inside of us. When we practice mindfulness of impermanence, we become fresher and more loving.

Looking deeply can become a way of life. We can practice conscious breathing to help us be in touch with things and to look deeply at their impermanent nature. This practice will keep us from complaining that everything is impermanent and therefore not worth living for. Impermanence is what makes transformation possible. We should learn to say, "Long live impermanence." Thanks to impermanence, we can change suffering into joy.

If we practice the art of mindful living, when things change, we won't have any regrets. We can smile, because we have done our best to enjoy every moment of our life and to make others happy. When you get into an argument with someone you love, please close your eyes and visualize your-selves three hundred years from now. When you open your eyes, you will only want to take each other in your arms and acknowledge how precious each of you is. The teaching of impermanence helps us appreciate fully what is there, with-out attachment or forgetfulness.

We have to nourish our insight into impermanence every day. If we do, we will live more deeply, suffer less, and enjoy life much more. Living deeply, we will touch the foundation of reality, nirvana, the world of no-birth and no-death. Touching impermanence deeply, we touch the world beyond permanence and impermanence. We touch the ground of being and see that which we have called being and nonbeing are just notions. Nothing is ever lost. Nothing is ever gained.

The Second Dharma Seal is nonself. Nothing has a sepa-rate existence or a separate self. Everything has to inter-be with everything else.

The first time I tasted peanut butter cookies, I was at Tassajara Zen Mountain Center in California, and I loved them! I learned that to make peanut butter cookies, you mix the ingredients to prepare the batter, and then you put each cookie onto a cookie sheet using a spoon. I imagined that the moment each cookie leaves the bowl of dough and is placed onto the tray, it begins to think of itself as separate. You, the creator of the cookies, know better, and you have a lot of compassion for them. You know that they are originally all one, and that even now, the happiness of each cookie is still the happiness of all the other cookies. But they have developed "discriminative perception" *(vikalpa)*, and suddenly they set up barriers between themselves. When you put them in the oven, they begin to talk to each other: "Get out of my way. I want to be in the middle." "I am brown and beautiful, and you are ugly!" "Can't you please spread a little in that direction?" We have the tendency to behave this way also, and it causes a lot of suffering. If we know how to touch our nondiscriminating mind, our happiness and the happiness of others will increase manifold.

We all have the capacity of living with nondiscriminating wisdom, but we have to train ourselves to see in that way, to see that the flower is us, the mountain is us, our parents and our children are all us. When we see that everyone and everything belongs to the same stream of life, our suffering will vanish. Nonself is not a doctrine or a philosophy. It is an insight that can help us live life more deeply, suffer less, and enjoy life much more. We need to live the insight of nonself.

Tolstoy wrote a story about two enemies. "A" suffered greatly because of "B," and his only motive in life was to eradicate "B." Every time he heard the name of B, every time he thought about B's image, he became enraged. Then one day A visited the hut of a sage. After listening to A deeply, the sage offered him a glass of refreshing water, and then he poured the same water onto A's head and washed him. When they sat down for tea, the sage told him, "Now you are B."

A was astonished! "That is the last thing I want to be! I am A, and he is B! There cannot be any connection."

"But you are B, whether you believe it or not," the sage said. Then he brought him a mirror, and sure enough when A looked in it, he saw B! Every time he moved, B in the mirror did exactly the same. The sound of A's voice became the sound of B's. He began to have B's feelings and perceptions. A tried to come back to himself, but he couldn't. What a wonderful story!

We should practice so that we can see Muslims as Hindus and Hindus as Muslims. We should practice so that we can see Israelis as Palestinians and Palistinians as Israelis. We should practice until we can see that each person is us, that we are not separate from others. This will greatly reduce our suffering. We are like the cookies, thinking we are separate and opposing each other, when actually we are all of the same reality. We *are* what we perceive. This is the teaching of nonself, of interbeing.

When Avalokiteshvara declared that eyes, ears, nose, tongue, body, and mind are empty, he meant that they cannot be by themselves alone.[2] They have to inter-be with everything else. Our eyes would not be possible without non-eye elements. That is why he can say that our eyes have no separate existence. We have to see the nature of interbeing to really understand. It takes some training to look at things this way.

Nonself means that you are made of elements which are not you. During the past hour, different elements have entered you and other elements have flown out of you. Your happiness, in fact your existence, comes from things that are not you. Your mother is happy because you are happy. And you are happy because she is happy. Happiness is not an individual matter. The daughter should practice in a way that she can understand her mother better and her mother can understand her better. The daughter cannot find happiness by running away from home, because she carries her family in her. There is nothing she can leave behind. There is nothing she can get rid of, even if she runs away and tells no one

---

[2] See Thich Nhat Hanh, *The Heart of Understanding.*

where she is going. Her store consciousness carries all the seeds. She cannot get rid of a single one.

The teachings of impermanence and nonself were offered by the Buddha as keys to unlock the door of reality. We have to train ourselves to look in a way that we know that when we touch one thing, we touch everything. We have to see that the one is in the all and the all is in the one. We touch not only the phenomenal aspects of reality but the ground of being. Things are impermanent and without self. They have to undergo birth and death. But if we touch them very deeply, we touch the ground of being that is free from birth and death, free from permanence and impermanence, self and nonself.

Nirvana, the Third Dharma Seal, is the ground of being, the substance of all that is. A wave does not have to die in order to become water. Water is the substance of the wave. The wave is already water. We are also like that. We carry in us the ground of interbeing, nirvana, the world of no-birth and no-death, no permanence and no impermanence, no self and no nonself. Nirvana is the complete silencing of concepts. The notions of impermanence and nonself were offered by the Buddha as instruments of practice, not as doctrines to worship, fight, or die for. "My dear friends," the Buddha said. "The Dharma I offer you is only a raft to help you to cross over to the other shore." The raft is not to be held onto as an object of worship. It is an instrument for crossing over to the shore of well-being. If you are caught in the Dharma, it is no longer the Dharma. Impermanence and nonself belong to the world of phenomena, like the waves. Nirvana is the ground of all that is. The waves do not exist outside the water. If you know how to touch the waves, you touch the water at the same time. Nirvana does not exist separate of impermanence and nonself. If you know how to use the tools of impermanence and nonself to touch reality, you touch nirvana in the here and the now.

Nirvana is the extinction of all notions. Birth is a notion. Death is a notion. Being is a notion. Nonbeing is a notion. In our daily lives, we have to deal with these relative realities. But if we touch life more deeply, reality will reveal itself in a different way.

We think that being born means from nothing we become something, from no one we become someone, from nonbeing we become being. We think that to die means we suddenly go from something to nothing, from someone to no one, from being to nonbeing. But the Buddha said, "There is no birth and no death, no being and no nonbeing," and he offered us impermanence, nonself, interbeing, and emptiness to discover the true nature of reality. In the *Heart Sutra,* we repeat over and over that there is no birth and no death. But reciting is not enough. The *Heart Sutra* is an instrument to investigate the true nature of ourselves and the world.

When you look at this sheet of paper, you think it belongs to the realm of being. There was a time that it came into existence, a moment in the factory it became a sheet of paper. But before the sheet of paper was born, was it nothing? Can nothing become something? Before it was recognizable as a sheet of paper, it must have been something else — a tree, a branch, sunshine, clouds, the earth. In its former life, the sheet of paper was all these things. If you ask the sheet of paper, "Tell me about all your adventures," she will tell you, "Talk to a flower, a tree, or a cloud and listen to their stories."

The paper's story is much like our own. We, too, have many wonderful things to tell. Before we were born, we were also already in our mother, our father, and our ancestors. The koan, "What was your face before your parents were born?" is an invitation to look deeply, to identify ourselves in time and space. We usually think we did not exist before the time of our parents, that we only began to exist at the moment of our birth. But we were already here in many forms.

The day of our birth was only a day of continuation. Instead of singing "Happy Birthday" every year, we should sing "Happy Continuation."

"Nothing is born, nothing dies" was a statement made by the French scientist Lavoisier. He was not a Buddhist. He did not know the *Heart Sutra*. But his words are exactly the same. If I burn this sheet of paper, will I reduce it to nonbeing? No, it will just be transformed into smoke, heat, and ash. If we put the "continuation" of this sheet of paper into the garden, later, while practicing walking meditation, we may see a little flower and recognize it as the rebirth of the sheet of paper. The smoke will become part of a cloud in the sky, also to continue the adventure. After tomorrow, a little rain may fall on your head, and you will recognize the sheet of paper saying, "Hello." The heat produced by the burning will penetrate into your body and the cosmos. With a sophisticated enough instrument, you will be able to measure how much of this energy penetrates you. The sheet of paper clearly continues, even after it is burned. The moment of its so-called dying is actually a moment of continuation.

When a cloud is about to become rain, she is not afraid. She may even be excited. Being a cloud floating in the blue sky is wonderful, but being rain falling on the fields, the ocean, or the mountains is also wonderful. As she falls down as rain, the cloud will sing. Looking deeply, we see that birth is just a notion and death is a notion. Nothing can be born from nothing. When we touch the sheet of paper deeply, when we touch the cloud deeply, when we touch our grandmother deeply, we touch the nature of no birth and no death, and we are free from sorrow. We already recognize them in many other forms. This is the insight that helped the Buddha become serene, peaceful, and fearless. This teaching of the Buddha can help us touch deeply the nature of our being, the ground of our being, so that we can touch the world of no-birth and no-death. This is the insight that liberates us from fear and sorrow.

Nirvana means extinction, above all the extinction of ideas — the ideas of birth and death, existence and nonexistence, coming and going, self and other, one and many. All these ideas cause us to suffer. We are afraid of death because ignorance gives us an illusory idea about what death is. We are disturbed by ideas of existence and nonexistence because we have not understood the true nature of impermanence and nonself. We worry about our own future, but we fail to worry about the future of the other because we think that our happiness has nothing to do with the happiness of the other. This idea of self and other gives rise to immeasurable suffering. In order to extinguish these ideas, we have to practice. Nirvana is a fan that helps us extinquish the fire of all our ideas, including ideas of permanence and self. That fan is our practice of looking deeply every day.

In Buddhism we talk about the Eight Concepts: birth, death, permanence, dissolution, coming, going, one, and many. The practice to end attachment to these eight ideas is called the Eight No's of the Middle Way — no birth and no death, no permanence and no dissolution, no coming and no going, no one and no many. In the thirteenth century in Vietnam, someone asked Master Tue Trung a question following a Dharma talk, and he replied, "Having offered complete release from the Eight Concepts, what further explanation could I possibly give?"

Once these eight ideas have been destroyed, we touch nirvana. Nirvana is release from the Eight Concepts, and also from their opposites — impermanence, nonself, Interdependent Co-Arising, emptiness, and the Middle Way. If we hold onto the Three Seals as fixed ideas, these ideas also have to be destroyed. The best way to do this is by putting these teachings into practice in our daily lives. Experience always goes beyond ideas.

Tenth-century Vietnamese master Thiên Hôi told his students, "Be diligent in order to attain the state of no-birth and no-death." One student asked, "Where can we touch the world of no-birth and no-death?" and he responded, "Right here in the world of birth and death." To touch the water, you have to touch the waves. If you touch birth and death deeply, you touch the world of no birth and no death.

Impermanence, nonself, Interdependent Co-Arising, and the Middle Way are all keys to open the door of reality. There is no point in leaving them in your pocket. You have to use them. When you understand impermanence and nonself, you are already free of much suffering and in touch with nirvana, the Third Dharma Seal. Nirvana is not something to look for in the future. As a Dharma Seal, it is present in every one of the Buddha's teachings. The nirvana-nature of the candle, the table, and the flower are revealed in the teachings, just as their impermanent and nonself nature are.

Imagine a meeting in which everyone is stating his own opinions and disagreeing with everyone else's. After the meeting is over, you are exhausted by all these ideas and discussions. You open the door and go out into the garden, where the air is fresh, the birds are singing, and the wind is whistling in the trees. Life out here is quite different from the meeting with its words and anger. In the garden, there are still sounds and images, but they are refreshing and healing. Nirvana is not the absence of life. *Drishtadharma nirvana* means "nirvana in this very life." Nirvana means pacifying, silencing, or extinguishing the fire of suffering. Nirvana teaches that we already are what we want to become. We don't have to run after anything anymore. We only need to return to ourselves and touch our true nature. When we do, we have real peace and joy.

This morning, I wake up and discover
that I've been using the sutras as my pillow.

I hear the excited buzzing of the diligent bees
preparing to rebuild the universe.
Dear ones, the work of rebuilding
may take thousands of lifetimes,
but it has already been completed
just that long ago.[3]

In the *Sutra of Forty-Two Chapters*, the Buddha says, "My practice is non-action, non-practice, and non-realization."[4] It means that what we seek does not lie outside of ourselves.

Any teaching that does not bear the mark of the Three Dharma Seals, the Four Holy Truths, and the Noble Eight-fold Path is not authentically Buddhist. But sometimes only Two Dharma Seals are taught — suffering and nirvana. Sometimes Four Dharma Seals are taught — impermanence, nonself, nirvana, and suffering. But suffering is not a basic element of existence. It is a feeling. When we insist on something that is impermanent and without self being permanent and having a self, we suffer. The Buddha taught that when suffering is present, we have to identify it and take the necessary steps to transform it. He did not teach that suffering is always present. In Mahayana Buddhism, there is also the teaching of One Dharma Seal — the seal of the True Mark. The teachings of one, two, and four Dharma Seals were all introduced after the Buddha passed away.

We practice the Three Dharma Seals to realize liberation. If you memorize a 5,000-page book on the Three Dharma Seals but do not apply the teachings during your daily life, that book is of no use. Only by using your intelligence and putting the teachings into practice can they bring you happiness. Please base your practice on your own life and your own

---

[3] From Thich Nhat Hanh, "Butterflies over the Golden Mustard Fields," in *Call Me By My True Names*, p. 75.

[4] *Sutra of Forty-Two Chapters. Taisho* 789.

experiences — your successes and your failures. The Buddha's teachings are jewels, but we have to dig deep in order to touch them fully.

There are other criteria that can help us navigate the sutras and determine whether a teaching represents a correct understanding of the Dharma. These include the Two Relevances, the Four Standards of Truth, and the Four Reliances.

The first of the Two Relevances is "Relevance to the Essence." The essence is the Three Dharma Seals. If someone teaches the Dharma, what he or she says must be in accord with the Buddha's teachings on impermanence, nonself, and nirvana. When you understand the Three Dharma Seals deeply, you will bring them into every situation of your daily life.

The Second Relevance is "Relevance to the Circumstance." When someone shares the Dharma, what she says must fit the situation and the mentality of those she is addressing so that the teaching is appropriate. If it is not appropriate, it is not the true Dharma, even if it sounds like the Dharma. She mustn't just repeat some words of the Buddha. If she acts like a tape player and just pops in a cassette, that is not speaking in accord with the Relevance to the Circumstance. She must ask, To whom am I speaking? On what stage is their life set? What are their beliefs, concerns, and aspirations? Looking deeply this way will bring love and compassion into whatever she says. One cannot offer the right medicine without knowing the patient's illness.

When you are in a Dharma discussion, each word you say should be Relevant to the Essence and to the Circumstance. Please speak in accord with the teachings of impermanence, nonself, and nirvana; and speak directly to those present, taking into account their experience, their knowledge, and their insight. There may be things you consider important but cannot say to this particular group. The Two Relevances require you to speak with skillfulness, tolerance, and care.

꒐

The Four Standards of Truth (siddhanta) are another guide to help us understand the Buddha's teachings. The First Standard is "the worldly." The teaching is offered in the language of the world so that those in the world will be able to understand. We have to take into account the contemporary cosmologies, arts, philosophies, metaphysics, and so forth and deal with them. For example, we call the days of the week Monday, Tuesday, Wednesday, etc. We divide time into days, months, and years to express truth relatively, for our convenience. When the Buddha tells us that he was born in Lumbini, it is in accord with the First Standard.

The Second Standard is "the person." We must remember as we read the Buddha's discourses that his words varied according to the needs and aspirations of his listeners. When the Buddha taught, he was deeply aware of the particular assembly, and what he said was specifically addressed to them.

The Third Standard is "healing." When the Buddha spoke, it was always to cure the particular illness of those he was addressing. Everyone has some illness that needs to be healed. When you speak to express healing, what you say will always be helpful.

The Fourth Standard is "the absolute." The Buddha expressed absolute truth directly and unequivocally. He said there is no self even when people did not believe or agree with him. He said it because he knew it was true. Fifteenth-century explorers said the world was round even when the community threatened to imprison them for saying so. We can use these Four Standards of Truth to understand the sutras as we read them.

လ

A third list to help us study the Dharma is called the Four Reliances. It was formulated by later teachers, not by the Buddha. The First Reliance is that we should rely on the teaching and not the person. It means we can learn even from a teacher who does not practice everything he teaches. My fifth grade teacher, Miss Liên, often wore high-heeled shoes. One day she wrote on the blackboard, "Never wear high-heeled shoes. You might twist your ankle." I couldn't understand why she did not apply that teaching to herself. Another teacher who was a heavy smoker taught us about the health hazards of smoking, even sixty years ago! The class laughed, and he replied, "Do as I say, not as I do." Later, when I attended the Institute of Buddhist Studies, we were told that if a precious jewel is in a garbage can, you have to dirty your hands. Remember the monk who had memorized all the sutras. He was not an easy person or a good practitioner, but the other monks had to put up with him and encourage him to recite the sutras so they could write them down.

To me, the relationship between a teacher and a student is based on the trust that the teacher has practiced and continues to practice what he teaches. This is teaching by example, by the way we live. Perhaps the ancestral teachers thought it was so rare to find someone who could teach by his or her life's example that if we just wait for someone like that to come along, we might miss the chance to benefit from the teachings that are available now.

The Second Reliance is to rely only on discourses where the Buddha taught in terms of absolute truth and not on those whose means are relative truth. I feel uneasy about this standard also, because it does not show us how discourses that explain by means of absolute truth are related to those that explain by means of relative truth. In fact, sutras that teach absolute truth can be better understood in the light of sutras that teach relative truth. We should not think that discourses about practical matters like the Five Mindfulness Trainings[5] are not worthy of our attention and that we only should study the *Avatamsaka* and *Lotus Sutras*.[6] We need to know how to go from down-to-earth sutras to less down-to-earth sutras. When we train ourselves in understanding the most basic discourses, we will be able to grasp more easily those that are more esoteric.

The Third Reliance is that we should rely on the meaning and not on the words. When we have an overall view of the way the Buddha teaches and understand the context and circumstances of a particular teaching, we will not extrapolate inappropriately or use the Buddha's words out of context. Then, when there is an error due to inaccurate transmission, we can rectify it by ourselves.

The Fourth Reliance is that we should rely on the insight of looking deeply *(jñana)* rather than on differentiation and discrimination (vijñana). However, it is important to be able to discriminate when we are reading the sutras so that we know according to which of the Four Standards of Truth the Buddha is teaching. We can rely on discriminative as well as nondiscriminative wisdom.

The teachings of the Two Truths, Three Dharma Seals, Two Relevances, Four Standards of Truth, and Three Doors of Liberation are important guides to help us understand the language the Buddha used when he taught. Without understanding the Buddha's language, we cannot understand the Buddha.

---

[5] *The Discourse on the White-Clad Disciple (Upasaka Sutra), Madhyama Agama* 128, *Anguttara Nikaya* III, 211. See Thich Nhat Hanh, *For a Future To Be Possible,* pp. 199–247.

[6] See Thich Nhat Hanh, *Cultivating the Mind of Love.*

CHAPTER NINETEEN

The Three Doors of Liberation

The Three Dharma Seals[1] are the keys we can use to enter the Three Doors of Liberation — emptiness *(shunyata)*, signlessness *(animitta),* and aimlessness *(apranihita).* All schools of Buddhism accept the teaching of the Three Doors of Liberation.[2] These Three Doors are sometimes called the Three Concentrations.[3] When we enter these doors, we dwell in concentration and are liberated from fear, confusion, and sadness.

The First Door of Liberation is emptiness, shunyata. Emptiness always means empty of something. A cup is empty of water. A bowl is empty of soup. We are empty of a separate, independent self. We cannot be by ourselves alone. We can only inter-be with everything else in the cosmos. The practice is to nourish the insight into emptiness all day long. Wherever we go, we touch the nature of emptiness in everything we contact. We look deeply at the table, the blue sky, our friend, the mountain, the river, our anger, and our happiness and see that these are all empty of a separate self. When we touch these things deeply, we see the interbeing and interpenetrating nature of all that is. Emptiness does not mean nonexistence. It means Interdependent Co-Arising, impermanence, and nonself.

---

[1] Impermanence, nonself, and nirvana (see chap. 18).

[2] The Theravada School does not emphasize this wonderful teaching, but it is there.

[3] See chap. 15, on Right Concentration.

When we first hear about emptiness, we feel a little frightened. But after practicing for a while, we see that things do exist, only in a different way than we'd thought. Emptiness is the Middle Way between existent and nonexistent. The beautiful flower does not *become* empty when it fades and dies. It is already empty, in its essence. Looking deeply, we see that the flower is made of non-flower elements — light, space, clouds, earth, and consciousness. It is empty of a separate, independent self. In the *Diamond Sutra*, we are taught that a human being is not independent of other species, so to protect humans, we have to protect the non-human species. If we pollute the water and air, the vegetables and minerals, we destroy ourselves. We have to learn to see ourselves in things that we thought were outside of ourselves in order to dissolve false boundaries.

In Vietnam, we say that if one horse is sick, all the horses in the stable will refuse to eat. Our happiness and suffering are the happiness and suffering of others. When we act based on nonself, our actions will be in accord with reality, and we will know what to do and what not to do. When we maintain awareness that we are all linked to each other, this is the Concentration on Emptiness *(shunyata samadhi).* Reality goes beyond notions of being and nonbeing. To say that the flower exists is not exactly correct, but to say that it does not exist is also not correct. True emptiness is called "wondrous being," because it goes beyond existence and nonexistence.

When we eat, we need to practice the Door of Liberation called emptiness. "I am this food. This food is me." One day in Canada, I was eating lunch with the Sangha, and a student looked up at me and said, "I am nourishing you." He was practicing the concentration on emptiness. Every time we look at our plate of food, we can contemplate the impermanent, nonself nature of food. This is deep practice, because it can help us see Interdependent Co-Arising. The one who eats and the food that is eaten are both, by nature, empty.

That is why the communication between them is perfect. When we practice walking meditation in a relaxed, peaceful way, it is the same. We step not just for ourselves, but for the world. When we look at others, we see how their happiness and suffering are linked to our happiness and suffering. "Peace begins with me."

Everyone we cherish will, someday, get sick and die. If we do not practice the meditation on emptiness, when it happens, we will be overwhelmed. The Concentration on Emptiness is a way of staying in touch with life as it is, but it has to be practiced and not just talked about. We observe our body and see all the causes and conditions that have brought it to be — our parents, our country, the air, and even future generations. We go beyond time and space, me and mine, and taste true liberation. If we only study emptiness as a philosophy, it will not be a Door of Liberation. Emptiness is a Door of Liberation when we penetrate it deeply and we realize Interdependent Co-Arising and the interbeing nature of everything that is.

The Second Door of Liberation is signlessness, animitta. "Sign" here means an appearance or the object of our perception. When we see something, a sign or image appears to us, and that is what is meant by "lakshana." If water, for example, is in a square container, its sign is "squareness." If in a round container, its sign is "roundness." When we open the freezer and take out some ice, the sign of that water is solid. Chemists call water "H_2O." The snow on the mountain and the steam rising from the kettle are also H_2O. Whether H_2O is round or square, liquid, gaseous, or solid depends on circumstances. Signs are instruments for our use, but they are not absolute truth, and they can mislead us. The *Diamond Sutra* says, "Wherever there is a sign, there is deception, illusion." Perceptions often tell us as much about the perceiver as the object of perception. Appearances can deceive.

Practicing the Concentration on Signlessness is necessary

for us to free ourselves. Until we can break through the signs, we cannot touch reality. As long as we are caught by signs — round, square, solid, liquid, gas — we will suffer. Nothing can be described in terms of just one sign. But without signs, we feel anxious. Our fear and attachment come from our being caught in signs. Until we touch the signless nature of things, we will continue to be afraid and to suffer. Before we can touch H_2O, we have to let go of signs like squareness, roundness, hardness, heaviness, lightness, up, and down. Water is, in itself, neither square nor round nor solid. When we free ourselves from signs, we can enter the heart of reality. But until we can see the ocean in the sky, we are still caught by signs.

The greatest relief is when we break through the barriers of sign and touch the world of signlessness, nirvana. Where should we look to find the world of no signs? Right here in the world of signs. If we throw away the water, there is no way for us to touch the suchness of water. We touch the water when we break through the signs of the water and see its true nature of interbeing. There are three phases — water, not water, true water. True water is the suchness of water. Its ground of being is free from birth and death. When we can touch that, we will not be afraid of anything.

"If you see the signlessness of signs, you see the Tathagata." This is a sentence from the *Diamond Sutra*. *Tathagata* means "the wondrous nature of reality."[4] To see the wondrous nature of water, you need to look beyond the sign (appearance) of the water, and see that it is made of non-water elements. If you think that water is only water, that it cannot be the sun, the earth, or the flower, you are not correct. When you can see that the water *is* the sun, the earth, and the flower, that just by looking at the sun or the earth you can see the water, this is "the signlessness of signs." An or-

---

[4] See also definition in footnote 3, p. 158.

ganic gardener who looks at a banana peel, dead leaves, or rotting branches can see flowers, fruit, and vegetables in them. She is able to see the nonself nature of flowers, fruit, and garbage. When she can apply this insight to all other spheres, she will realize complete awakening.

Politicians, economists, and educators need to practice signlessness. We put many young men in jail. But if we meditate on signlessness, we will discover where their violence comes from. What is our society like? How are our families organized? What is taught at our schools? Why should we lay all the blame at the feet of the young people? Why can't we acknowledge our own co-responsibility? Young people harm themselves and others because life has no meaning for them. If we continue to live the way we do and organize society the way we do, we will continue to produce so many thousands of young people who will need to be imprisoned.

Signlessness is not just an idea. When we look deeply into our children, we see all the elements that have produced them. They are the way they are because our culture, economy, society, and we ourselves are the way we are. We can't simply blame our children when things go wrong. Many causes and conditions have contributed. When we know how to transform ourselves and our society, our children will transform also.

Our children learn reading, writing, math, science, and other subjects in school that can help them earn a living. But very few school programs teach young people how to live — how to deal with anger, how to reconcile conflicts, how to breathe, smile, and transform internal formations. There needs to be a revolution in education. We must encourage schools to train our students in the art of living in peace and harmony. It isn't easy to learn to read, write, or solve math problems, but children manage to do it. Learning how to breathe, smile, and transform anger can also be difficult, but I have seen many young people succeed. If we teach children properly, by the time they are around twelve, they will know how to live harmoniously with others.

When we go beyond signs, we enter the world of no-fear and no-blame. We can see the flower, the water, and our child beyond time and space. We know that our ancestors are present in us, right here and right now. We see that the Buddha, Jesus, and all of our other spiritual ancestors have not died. The Buddha cannot be confined to 2,600 years ago. The flower cannot be limited to its brief manifestation. Everything manifests by means of signs. If we get caught by the signs, we become afraid of losing that particular manifestation.

When an eight-year-old boy who had lived at Plum Village suddenly died, I asked his father to be fully aware of the presence of his son in the air he was breathing and in the blades of grass beneath his feet, and he was able to do this. When a well-known Vietnamese meditation teacher passed away, his disciple wrote this poem:

> *Dharma brothers, do not be attached to the sign.*
> *The mountains and rivers around us are our teacher.*[5]

The *Diamond Sutra* enumerates four signs — self, person, living being, and life span. We get caught in the sign "self," because we think there are things that are not self. But when we look deeply, we see that there is no separate, independent self, and we become free of the sign of self. We see that to protect ourselves, we have to protect everything that is not ourselves.

We get caught in the sign "person." We separate humans from animals, trees, and rocks, and feel that non-humans — the fish, the cows, the vegetation, the earth, the air, and the

---

[5] The disciple was a court official in the Ly Era (1010–1225). His name was Doan Van Kham.

seas — are there for our exploitation. Other species also hunt for food, but not in such an exploitative way. When we look deeply at our own species, we can see the non-human elements in it, and when we look deeply at the animal, vegetal, and mineral realms, we see the human element in them. When we practice the Concentration on Signlessness, we live in harmony with all other species.

The third sign is "living being." We think that sentient beings are different from insentient beings. But living or sentient beings are made of non-living or non-sentient species. When we pollute the so-called non-living species, like the air or the rivers, we pollute living beings as well. If we look deeply into the interbeing of living and non-living beings, we will stop acting this way.

The fourth sign is "life span," the period of time between our birth and our death. We think we are alive for a specific period of time that has a beginning and an end. But when we look deeply, we see that we have never been born and we will never die, and our fear dissolves. With mindfulness, concentration, and the Three Dharma Seals, we can unlock the Door of Liberation called signlessness and obtain the greatest relief.

The Third Door of Liberation is aimlessness, apranihita. There is nothing to do, nothing to realize, no program, no agenda. This is the Buddhist teaching about eschatology. Does the rose have to do something? No, the purpose of a rose is to be a rose. Your purpose is to be yourself. You don't have to run anywhere to become someone else. You are wonderful just as you are. This teaching of the Buddha allows us to enjoy ourselves, the blue sky, and everything that is refreshing and healing in the present moment.

There is no need to put anything in front of us and run after it. We already have everything we are looking for, everything we want to become. We are already a Buddha so why not just take the hand of another Buddha and practice walking meditation? This is the teaching of the *Avatamsaka Sutra*. Be yourself. Life is precious as it is. All the elements for your happiness are already here. There is no need to run, strive, search, or struggle. Just be. Just being in the moment in this place is the deepest practice of meditation. Most people cannot believe that just walking as though you have nowhere to go is enough. They think that striving and competing are normal and necessary. Try practicing aimlessness for just five minutes, and you will see how happy you are during those five minutes.

The *Heart Sutra* says that there is "nothing to attain." We meditate not to attain enlightenment, because enlightenment is already in us. We don't have to search anywhere. We don't need a purpose or a goal. We don't practice in order to obtain some high position. In aimlessness, we see that we do not lack anything, that we already are what we want to become, and our striving just comes to a halt. We are at peace in the present moment, just seeing the sunlight streaming through our window or hearing the sound of the rain. We don't have to run after anything. We can enjoy every moment. People talk about entering nirvana, but we are already there. Aimlessness and nirvana are one.

> *Waking up this morning, I smile.*
> *Twenty-four brand new hours are before me.*
> *I vow to live fully in each moment*
> *and to look at all beings with the eyes of love.*[6]

These twenty-four hours are a precious gift, a gift we can only receive fully when we have opened the Third Door of Liberation, aimlessness. If we think we have twenty-four hours to achieve a certain purpose, today will become a means to attain an end. The moment of chopping wood and

---

[6] Thich Nhat Hanh, *Present Moment Wonderful Moment*, p. 3.

carrying water *is* the moment of happiness. We do not need to wait for these chores to be done to be happy. To have happiness in this moment is the spirit of aimlessness. Otherwise, we will run in circles for the rest of our life. We have everything we need to make the present moment the happiest in our life, even if we have a cold or a headache. We don't have to wait until we get over our cold to be happy. Having a cold is a part of life.

Someone asked me, "Aren't you worried about the state of the world?" I allowed myself to breathe and then I said, "What is most important is not to allow your anxiety about what happens in the world to fill your heart. If your heart is filled with anxiety, you will get sick, and you will not be able to help." There are wars — big and small — in many places, and that can cause us to lose our peace. Anxiety is the illness of our age. We worry about ourselves, our family, our friends, our work, and the state of the world. If we allow worry to fill our hearts, sooner or later we will get sick.

Yes, there is tremendous suffering all over the world, but knowing this need not paralyze us. If we practice mindful breathing, mindful walking, mindful sitting, and working in mindfulness, we try our best to help, and we can have peace in our heart. Worrying does not accomplish anything. Even if you worry twenty times more, it will not change the situation of the world. In fact, your anxiety will only make things worse. Even though things are not as we would like, we can still be content, knowing we are trying our best and will continue to do so. If we don't know how to breathe, smile, and live every moment of our life deeply, we will never be able to help anyone. I am happy in the present moment. I do not ask for anything else. I do not expect any additional happiness or conditions that will bring about more happiness. The most important practice is aimlessness, not running after things, not grasping.

We who have been fortunate enough to encounter the

practice of mindfulness have a responsibility to bring peace and joy into our own lives, even though not everything in our body, mind, or environment is exactly as we would like. Without happiness we cannot be a refuge for others. Ask yourself, What am I waiting for to make me happy? Why am I not happy right now?

My only desire is to help you see this. How can we bring the practice of mindfulness to the widest spectrum of society? How can we give birth to the greatest number of people who are happy and who know how to teach the art of mindful living to others? The number of people who create violence is very great, while the number of people who know how to breathe and create happiness is very small. Every day gives us a wonderful opportunity to be happy ourselves and to become a place of refuge for others.

We don't need to become anything else. We don't need to perform some particular act. We only need to be happy in the present moment, and we can be of service to those we love and to our whole society. Aimlessness is stopping and realizing the happiness that is already available. If someone asks us how long he has to practice in order to be happy, we can tell him that he can be happy right now! The practice of apranihita, aimlessness, is the practice of freedom.

CHAPTER TWENTY

The Three Bodies of Buddha

It is natural for human beings to want to personify qualities like love, freedom, and understanding. It was in this spirit that the Buddha came to be represented as having "three bodies": Dharmakaya, the source of enlightenment and happiness; Sambhogakaya, the body of bliss or enjoyment; and Nirmanakaya, the historical embodiment of the Buddha viewed as one of the many transformation bodies sent forth by the Dharmakaya. *Kaya* means "body."

When he was about to pass away, the Buddha told his disciples, "Dear friends, my physical body will not be here tomorrow, but my teaching body (Dharmakaya) will always be with you. Consider it to be the teacher who never leaves you. Be islands unto yourselves, and take refuge in the Dharma. Use the Dharma as your lamp, your island." The Buddha meant that in order to have nirvana available to us in every moment, we have to practice the Dharma, the Way of Understanding and Love. That is the birth of Dharmakaya, the body of the teaching, the body of the Way, the source of enlightenment and happiness. The original meaning of Dharmakaya was quite simple — the way to realize understanding and love.

The Dharmakaya is the embodiment of the Dharma, always shining, always enlightening everything. Anything that can help us wake up is part of the Dharmakaya — trees, grass, birds, human beings, and so on. When I hear a bird sing, if I return deeply to myself and breathe and smile, that bird reveals the Buddha's Dharma body. People who are awake can hear the Dharma being preached in a pebble, a bamboo, or the cry of a baby. Anything can be the voice of the Dharma if you are awake. Every morning, when you open the window and see the light streaming in, know that it, too, is part of the Dharmakaya.

> *Opening the window,*
> *I look out onto the Dharmakaya.*
> *How wondrous is life!*
> *Attentive to each moment,*
> *my mind is clear like a calm river.*[1]

The living Dharma is not just a library of sutra books or audio or video cassettes of inspiring Dharma talks. It is mindfulness manifesting in your daily life. When I see you walking mindfully in peace and joy, a deep presence is also awakened in me. When you walk like this, the sun of the Dharmakaya in both of us shines brightly. When you take good care of yourself, your brothers, and your sisters, I recognize the living Dharma. When you are really there, the Dharmakaya is easy to touch.

Dharmakaya is expressed not only through words and actions, but also through non-action. Look at the tree in the garden. An oak tree is an oak tree, and that is all it has to do. Every time we look at it, we feel stable and confident. It offers us air to breathe and shade to protect us during the summertime. If an oak tree is less than an oak tree, we will all be in trouble. We can learn the Dharma from an oak tree, so we can say that it is part of the Dharmakaya. Each pebble, each leaf, and each flower is preaching the *Saddharmapundarika Sutra*.[2] The Buddha has his Dharma body, and we Buddhas-

---

[1] Thich Nhat Hanh, *Present Moment Wonderful Moment*, p. 4.

[2] See Thich Nhat Hanh, "Beckoning," in *Call Me By My True Names*, p. 107.

to-be must express the Dharma through our own Dharma bodies. When someone says something challenging, if we can smile and return to our breathing, our Dharma will be a living Dharma, and others will be able to touch it. Sometimes, through non-action, we can help more than if we do a lot. Like a calm person on a small boat during a storm, just by being there, we can change the situation.

The Dharma body is the Buddha that is everlasting. Mahayana Buddhists later began to call the Dharmakaya *Vairochana*, the ontological Buddha, the soul of the Buddha, the spirit of the Buddha, the true Buddha, the ground of all being, the ground of enlightenment. Finally, Dharmakaya became equivalent to suchness, nirvana, and *Tathagatagarbha* ("the womb of the tathagata").[3] This is a natural development. But if we spend too much time talking about these things, it will be less valuable than learning how to touch our own Dharma body through dwelling in peace and mindfulness. When you touch the Dharmakaya, you touch the Buddha. The Buddha said very clearly that his Dharma body is even more important than his physical body. For his Dharmakaya to continue, the Buddha relies on us, on our practice.

The Sambhogakaya is the Buddha's body of bliss, enjoyment, celebration, results, or rewards. Because the Buddha practices deeply, he experiences boundless peace, joy, and happiness; and Sambhogakaya is the fruit of his practice. When we practice mindfulness, we, too, can enjoy this fruit. Breathing in and looking at the blue sky, drinking our tea in mindfulness, we can feel happy just being alive. This is our body of enjoyment, Sambhogakaya.

I once read a story about a Christian man whose faith in God was not firm. He was hunting in the jungles of Africa

---

[3] Tathagata is a title of the Buddha meaning "he or she who has come from the world of suchness (ultimate reality)."

when he lost his way. After some time, still lost, he decided to pray for help, but because his faith was weak, he prayed weakly. "God, if you exist, please come and save me now." As soon as he finished speaking, an African man appeared. The man showed him the way to a village, and he was saved. But then he wrote in his diary, "I called upon God, but only a Negro appeared." In fact, the man who saved him was God himself, but because he was ignorant, he failed to see that. We can say that the man who saved him was the Sambhogakaya Buddha. Buddha and God appear in many forms. The Buddha is not only in the cloud. He is in our hearts, and in the hearts of many others.

Every time we touch something beautiful, in harmony and peace, we touch the Sambhogakaya Buddha. This is called "self-enjoyment." When we feel happy and peaceful, our happiness and peace radiate around us, and others can enjoy it as well. This is called "the enjoyment of others of our body of bliss." When we do this, many Sambhogakayas are born into the world. Each of us has the capacity to bring joy to others and to help relieve them of their suffering, if we know how to cultivate the seeds of awakening within ourselves. Like the Dharmakaya, the Sambhogakaya body of the Buddha is available, if we know how to touch it.

Shakyamuni, the historical Buddha, is the Nirmanakaya, a beam of light sent into the world by the sun of the Dharmakaya to help relieve the suffering of living beings. Shakyamuni Buddha was a real human being, and the Dharmakaya was embodied by his presence. The living Buddha is still available to us as an embodiment, as a ray of the sun of the Dharmakaya. If that ray is not apparent to you, don't worry. There are many other rays, or transformation bodies, expounding the Dharma — the trees, the birds, the violet bamboo, and the yellow chrysanthemum. Shakyamuni is just one of these transformation bodies. You can be in touch with the Nirmanakaya through him or through any of these others.

Each of us has three bodies — a Dharma body, an enjoyment body, and a physical body. Please discover your own Dharma body, your own body of bliss, and your own body of transformation. These bodies are deep within you; it is only a matter of discovery. When you practice walking meditation and release some of your sorrow and your anger, when you look deeply into things and shed some of your misperceptions, cravings, and attachments, you discover the body of the Dharma, the body of bliss, and the body of transformation within you. When you touch these three bodies of yourself and of the Buddha, you will suffer less. The Dharmakaya, Sambhogakaya, and Nirmanakaya are available. Allow yourself to be struck by the beams of light emanated by the Buddha and to be transformed. When we know how to discover the seeds of enlightenment within ourselves, we realize our capacity to transform many others as well. The Buddha depends on us to live mindfully, to enjoy the practice, and to transform ourselves, so we can share the body of the Dharma with many other living beings.

CHAPTER TWENTY-ONE

The Three Jewels

I take refuge in the Buddha,
the one who shows me the way in this life.

I take refuge in the Dharma,
the way of understanding and love.

I take refuge in the Sangha,
the community that lives in harmony and awareness.

Taking refuge in Buddha, Dharma, and Sangha is a fundamental practice in Buddhism. These are universal values that transcend sectarian and cultural boundaries. When we were in our mother's womb, we felt secure, protected from heat, cold, hunger, and other difficulties. To seek for refuge means to look for a place like that that is safe, a place we can rely on.

Faith *(shraddha),* in Buddhism, does not mean accepting a theory that we have not personally verified. The Buddha encouraged us to see for ourselves. Taking refuge in the Three Jewels is not blind faith; it is the fruit of our practice. At first, our Buddha may be a book we've read, our Dharma a few encouraging words we've heard, and our Sangha a community we've visited once or twice. But as we continue to practice, the Buddha, the Dharma, and the Sangha reveal themselves to us more fully.

Faith is important for all religions. Some people say, "If we believe in God and it turns out that He does exist, we'll be safe. And if He doesn't, we won't have lost anything." Theologians speak of a "leap of faith," like a child jumping off the table into the arms of his father. The child is not one hundred percent sure his father will catch him, but he has enough faith to jump. In Buddhism, our faith is concrete, not blind, not a leap. It is formed by our own insight and experience. When we take refuge in the Buddha, we express trust in our capacity to walk in the direction of beauty, truth, and deep understanding, based on our experience of the efficacy of the practice. When we take refuge in the Dharma, we enter the path of transformation, the path to end suffering. When we take refuge in the Sangha, we focus our energies on building a community that dwells in mindfulness, harmony, and peace. When we touch these Three Jewels directly and experience their capacity to bring about transformation and peace, our faith is strengthened even further. The Three Jewels are not notions. They are our life.

In Chinese and Vietnamese, practitioners always say, "I go back and rely on the Buddha in myself." Adding "in myself" makes it clear that we ourselves are the Buddha. When we take refuge in Buddha, we must also understand, "The Buddha takes refuge in me." Without the second part, the first is not complete. There is a verse we can recite when planting trees and other plants:

> *I entrust myself to Earth,*
> *Earth entrusts herself to me.*
> *I entrust myself to Buddha,*
> *Buddha entrusts herself to me.*

To plant a seed or a seedling is to entrust it to the earth. The plant will live or die because of the earth. But the earth also entrusts herself to the plant. Each leaf that falls down and decomposes will help the soil be alive. When we take refuge in the Buddha, we entrust ourselves to the soil of understanding. And the Buddha entrusts himself or herself to us for understanding, love, and compassion to be alive in the world. Whenever I hear someone recite, "I take refuge in the Buddha," I also hear, "The Buddha takes refuge in me."

> *Going back, taking refuge in the Buddha in myself,*
> *I vow, together with all beings, to realize the Great Way in*
> *order to give rise to the highest mind (bodhichitta).*

> *Going back, taking refuge in the Dharma in myself,*
> *I vow, together with all beings, to realize understanding and*
> *wisdom as immense as the ocean.*

> *Going back, taking refuge in the Sangha in myself,*
> *I vow, together with all beings, to help build a Sangha*
> *without obstacles.*

During the Buddha's last months, he always taught, "Take refuge in yourselves, not in anything else. In you are Buddha, Dharma, and Sangha. Don't look for things that are far away. Everything is in your own heart. Be an island unto yourself." Whenever you feel confused, angry, or lost, if you practice mindful breathing and return to your island of self, you will be in a safe place filled with warm sunlight, cool shade trees, and beautiful birds and flowers. Buddha is our mindfulness. Dharma is our conscious breathing. Sangha is our Five Aggregates[1] working in harmony.

If I am ever in an airplane and the pilot announces that the plane is about to crash, I will practice mindful breathing while reciting the Three Refuges. When you receive bad

---

[1] For an explanation of the Five Aggregates (skandhas), the components of our "self," see chap. 23.

news, I hope you will do the same. But don't wait until a critical moment to go back to your island of self. Go back each day by living mindfully. If the practice becomes a habit, when difficulties arise, it will be easy for you to touch the Three Jewels in yourself. Walking, breathing, sitting, and eating mindfully are all ways to take refuge. This is not blind faith. It is faith based on your real experience.

Dharma books and tapes are valuable, but the true Dharma is revealed through our life and our practice. Whenever the Four Noble Truths and the Noble Eightfold Path are practiced, the living Dharma is there. There are said to be 84,000 Dharma doors. Sitting meditation is one door, and walking meditation is another. To take refuge in the Dharma is to choose the doors that are most appropriate for us. Dharma is great compassion, understanding, and love.[2] To realize these qualities, we need a Sangha.

Sangha is the fourfold community of monks, nuns, laymen, and laywomen, as well as the other elements that support our practice — our cushion, our walking meditation path, the trees, the sky, and the flowers. In my country, we say that when a tiger leaves his mountain and goes to the lowlands, he will be caught by humans and killed. When a practitioner leaves her Sangha, she may abandon her practice and "die" as a practitioner. Practicing with a Sangha is essential. Even if we have a deep appreciation for the practice, it can be difficult to continue without the support of friends.

It is well worth investing in a Sangha. If you sow seeds in arid land, few seeds will sprout. But if you select a fertile field and invest your wonderful seeds in it, the harvest will be bountiful. Building a Sangha, supporting a Sangha, being with a Sangha, receiving the support and guidance of a Sangha is the practice. We have individual eyes and Sangha

---

[2] For a further explication of the Second Jewel, Dharma, see chap. 20, "The Three Bodies of Buddha."

eyes. When a Sangha shines its light on our personal views, we see more clearly. In the Sangha, we won't fall into negative habit patterns. Stick to your Sangha. Take refuge in the Sangha, and you'll have the wisdom and support you need.

When members of a Sangha live in harmony, their Sangha is holy. Don't think that holiness is only for the Pope or the Dalai Lama. Holiness is also within you and within your Sangha. When a community sits, breathes, walks, and eats together in mindfulness, holiness is there. When you build a Sangha that has happiness, joy, and peace, you'll see the element of holiness in the Sangha. King Prasenajit, a close friend and disciple of the Buddha, told the Lord, "When I look at the Sangha, I have faith in the Buddha and the Dharma." Looking at the monks and nuns who were calm, peaceful, joyful, and free, who walked, stood, and sat in mindfulness, he saw the Buddha and the Dharma in them. Dharma and Sangha are the doors through which we enter the heart of the Buddha.

One day, the Buddha went with Ananda to a monastery in Koshala. All the monks had gone out on alms round except one monk who had dysentery. He was lying exhausted, his robes and bedding covered in filth. When the Buddha saw this, he asked, "Where have the other monks gone? Why is no one looking after you?" The unwell monk replied, "Lord, all my brothers have gone out on alms round. At first, they looked after me, but when I was getting no better, I told them I would look after myself." The Buddha and Ananda bathed the monk, cleaned his room, washed his robes, and gave him a fresh robe to wear. When the monks returned, the Buddha said, "Friends, if we do not look after each other, who will look after us? When you look after each other, you are looking after the Tathagata."[3]

---

[3] See p. 158, n. 3.

There are true jewels and jewels that are not authentic. If someone gives spiritual teachings that contradict the Three Seals of impermanence, nonself, and nirvana, that is not authentic Dharma. When a community has mindfulness, peace, joy, and liberation, it is a true Sangha. A Sangha that does not practice mindfulness and is not free, peaceful, or joyful cannot be called a true Sangha. The Buddha also can be true or false. In the *Diamond Sutra,* the Buddha says, "If you look for me in forms and sounds, you will never see the Tathagata."

Looking into any of the Three Jewels, you see the other two. Buddha, Dharma, and Sangha inter-are. If you look after the Sangha, you are looking after the Buddha. When your Sangha is happy and advancing in the practice, the holiness of the Sangha increases, and the presence of the true Buddha and true Dharma become clearer. When you walk in mindfulness, you are taking good care of the Dharma. When you make peace with another member of your Sangha, you are looking after the Buddha. Going into the meditation hall, offering incense, and tidying the altar are not the only ways to look after the Buddha. Taking someone's hand or comforting someone who suffers is also to look after the Buddha. When you touch the true Sangha, you touch the Buddha and the Dharma. The Dharma cannot exist without a Buddha and a Sangha. How could the Dharma exist if there were no practitioners? A Buddha is a Buddha when the Dharma is in him or her. Each jewel contains the other two. When you take refuge in one jewel, you take refuge in all three. This can be realized in every moment of our life.

Traditionally, we chant the Three Refuges three times. During the first recitation, we turn in the direction of greater mindfulness, understanding, and love. During the second recitation, we begin to embody the Three Jewels. When we recite the third time, we vow to help others realize the Way of Understanding and Love and become a source of peace.

Our problems today are no longer as simple as those encountered by the Buddha. In the twenty-first century, we will have to practice meditation collectively — as a family, a city, a nation, and a community of nations. The Buddha of the twenty-first century — Maitreya, the Buddha of Love — may well be a community rather than an individual. Sanghas that practice loving kindness and compassion are the Buddha we need. We can prepare the ground for bringing that Buddha to life, for our sake and for the sake of countless others, by transforming our own suffering and cultivating the art of Sangha-building. It is the most important work we can do.

Buddha is the teacher showing the way,
the perfectly awakened one,
beautifully seated, peaceful and smiling,
the living source of understanding and compassion.

Dharma is the clear path
leading us out of ignorance
bringing us back
to an awakened life.

Sangha is the beautiful community
that practices joy,
realizing liberation,
bringing peace and happiness to life.

∽

I take refuge in the Buddha, the one who shows me the way in
  this life.
I take refuge in the Dharma, the way of understanding and of
  love.
I take refuge in the Sangha, the community that lives in
  harmony and awareness.

*Dwelling in the refuge of Buddha, I see clearly the path of
light and beauty in the world.*
*Dwelling in the refuge of Dharma, I learn to open many doors
on the path of transformation.*
*Dwelling in the refuge of Sangha, I am supported by its
shining light that keeps my practice free of obstacles.*

*Taking refuge in the Buddha in myself, I aspire to help all
people recognize their own awakened nature and realize the
mind of love.*
*Taking refuge in the Dharma in myself, I aspire to help all
people grasp the way of practice and walk together on the
path of liberation.*
*Taking refuge in the Sangha in myself, I aspire to help all
people build fourfold communities and encourage the
transformation of all beings.*

CHAPTER TWENTY-TWO

The Four Immeasurable Minds

During the Buddha's lifetime, those of the Brahmanic faith prayed that after death they would go to Heaven to dwell eternally with Brahma, the universal God. One day a Brahman man asked the Buddha, "What can I do to be sure that I will be with Brahma after I die?" and the Buddha replied, "As Brahma is the source of Love, to dwell with him you must practice the 'Brahma Abodes,' *(Brahmaviharas)* or Four Immeasurable Minds — love, compassion, joy, and equanimity." Love in Sanskrit is *maitri;* in Pali it is *metta.* Compassion is *karuna* in both languages. Joy is mudita. Equanimity is upeksha in Sanskrit and *upekkha* in Pali. A *vihara* is an abode or a dwelling place. The Four Brahmaviharas are the abodes of true love. This address is much greater than a four-star hotel. It is a 1,000-star dwelling. The Four Brahmaviharas are called "immeasurable," because if you practice them, they will grow in you every day until they embrace the whole world. You will become happier, and everyone around you will become happier, also.

The Buddha respected people's desire to practice their own faith, so that is why he encouraged the Brahman man in his own language. If you enjoy walking meditation, practice walking meditation. If you enjoy sitting meditation, practice sitting meditation. But preserve your Jewish, Christian, or Muslim roots. That is the best way to realize the Buddha's spirit. If you are cut off from your roots, you cannot be happy.

If you learn to practice love, compassion, joy, and equanimity, you will know how to heal the illnesses of anger, sorrow, insecurity, sadness, hatred, loneliness, and unhealthy attachments.

Some sutra commentators have said that the Brahmaviharas are not the highest teaching of the Buddha, that they cannot put an end to all suffering and afflictions, but that is not correct. One time the Buddha said to Ananda, "Teach these Four Immeasurable Minds to the young monks, and they will feel secure, strong, and joyful, without afflictions of body or mind. For the whole of their lives, they will be well equipped to practice the pure way of a monk."[1] On another occasion, a group of the Buddha's disciples visited the monastery of a nearby sect, and the monks there asked, "We have heard that your teacher Gautama teaches the Four Immeasurable Minds of love, compassion, joy, and equanimity. Our master teaches this also. What is the difference?" The Buddha's disciples did not know how to respond. When they returned to their monastery, the Buddha told them, "Whoever practices the Four Immeasurable Minds together with the Seven Factors of Awakening, the Four Noble Truths, and the Noble Eightfold Path will arrive deeply at enlightenment."[2] Love, compassion, joy, and equanimity are the very nature of an enlightened person. They are the four aspects of true love within ourselves and within everyone and everything.

The first aspect of true love is maitri, the intention and capacity to offer joy and happiness. To develop that capacity, we have to practice looking and listening deeply so that we know what to do and what not to do to make others happy. If you offer your beloved something she does not need, that is not

---

[1] *Madhyama Agama* 86, *Taisho* 26.

[2] *Samyukta Agama* 744, *Taisho* 99.

maitri. You have to see her real situation or what you offer might bring her unhappiness.

In Southeast Asia, many people are extremely fond of a large, thorny fruit called durian. You could even say they are addicted to it. Its smell is extremely strong, and when some people finish eating the fruit, they put the skin under their bed so they can continue to smell it. To me, the smell of durian is horrible. One day when I was practicing chanting in my temple in Vietnam, there was a durian on the altar that had been offered to the Buddha. I was trying to recite the *Lotus Sutra,* using a wooden drum and a large bowl-shaped bell for accompaniment, but I could not concentrate at all. I finally carried the bell to the altar and turned it upside down to imprison the durian, so I could chant the sutra. After I finished, I bowed to the Buddha and liberated the durian. If you were to say to me, "Thây, I love you so much I would like you to eat some of this durian," I would suffer. You love me, you want me to be happy, but you force me to eat durian. That is an example of love without understanding. Your intention is good, but you don't have the correct understanding.

Without understanding, your love is not true love. You must look deeply in order to see and understand the needs, aspirations, and suffering of the one you love. We all need love. Love brings us joy and well-being. It is as natural as the air. We are loved by the air; we need fresh air to be happy and well. We are loved by trees. We need trees to be healthy. In order to be loved, we have to love, which means we have to understand. For our love to continue, we have to take the appropriate action or non-action to protect the air, the trees, and our beloved.

Maitri can be translated as "love" or "loving kindness." Some Buddhist teachers prefer "loving kindness," as they find the word "love" too dangerous. But I prefer "love." Words sometimes get sick and we have to heal them. We have been using the word "love" to mean appetite or desire, as in "I love hamburgers." We have to use language more carefully. "Love" is a beautiful word; we have to restore its meaning. The word "maitri" has roots in the word *mitra,* which means friend. In Buddhism, the primary meaning of love is friendship.

We all have the seeds of love in us. We can develop this wonderful source of energy, nurturing the unconditional love that does not expect anything in return. When we understand someone deeply, even someone who has done us harm, we cannot resist loving him or her. Shakyamuni Buddha declared that the Buddha of the next eon will be named "Maitreya, the Buddha of Love."

The second aspect of true love is karuna, the intention and capacity to relieve and transform suffering and lighten sorrows. Karuna is usually translated as "compassion," but that is not exactly correct. "Compassion" is composed of *com* ("together with") and *passion* ("to suffer"). But we do not need to suffer to remove suffering from another person. Doctors, for instance, can relieve their patients' suffering without experiencing the same disease in themselves. If we suffer too much, we may be crushed and unable to help. Still, until we find a better word, let us use "compassion" to translate karuna.

To develop compassion in ourselves, we need to practice mindful breathing, deep listening, and deep looking. The *Lotus Sutra* describes Avalokiteshvara as the bodhisattva who practices "looking with the eyes of compassion and listening deeply to the cries of the world." Compassion contains deep concern. You know the other person is suffering, so you sit close to her. You look and listen deeply to her to be able to touch her pain. You are in deep communication, deep communion with her, and that alone brings some relief.

One compassionate word, action, or thought can reduce

another person's suffering and bring him joy. One word can give comfort and confidence, destroy doubt, help someone avoid a mistake, reconcile a conflict, or open the door to liberation. One action can save a person's life or help him take advantage of a rare opportunity. One thought can do the same, because thoughts always lead to words and actions. With compassion in our heart, every thought, word, and deed can bring about a miracle.

When I was a novice, I could not understand why, if the world is filled with suffering, the Buddha has such a beautiful smile. Why isn't he disturbed by all the suffering? Later I discovered that the Buddha has enough understanding, calmness, and strength; that is why the suffering does not overwhelm him. He is able to smile to suffering because he knows how to take care of it and to help transform it. We need to be aware of the suffering, but retain our clarity, calmness, and strength so we can help transform the situation. The ocean of tears cannot drown us if karuna is there. That is why the Buddha's smile is possible.

The third element of true love is mudita, joy. True love always brings joy to ourselves and to the one we love. If our love does not bring joy to both of us, it is not true love.

Commentators explain that happiness relates to both body and mind, whereas joy relates primarily to mind. This example is often given: Someone traveling in the desert sees a stream of cool water and experiences joy. On drinking the water, he experiences happiness. Drishta dharma sukha viharin means "dwelling happily in the present moment." We don't rush to the future; we know that everything is here in the present moment. Many small things can bring us tremendous joy, such as the awareness that we have eyes in good condition. We just have to open our eyes and we can see the blue sky, the violet flowers, the children, the trees, and so many other kinds of forms and colors. Dwelling in mindfulness, we can touch these wondrous and refreshing things, and our mind of joy arises naturally. Joy contains happiness and happiness contains joy.

Some commentators have said that mudita means "sympathetic joy" or "altruistic joy," the happiness we feel when others are happy. But that is too limited. It discriminates between self and others. A deeper definition of mudita is a joy that is filled with peace and contentment. We rejoice when we see others happy, but we rejoice in our own well-being as well. How can we feel joy for another person when we do not feel joy for ourselves? Joy is for everyone.

The fourth element of true love is upeksha, which means equanimity, nonattachment, nondiscrimination, even-mindedness, or letting go. *Upa* means "over," and *iksh* means "to look." You climb the mountain to be able to look over the whole situation, not bound by one side or the other. If your love has attachment, discrimination, prejudice, or clinging in it, it is not true love. People who do not understand Buddhism sometimes think upeksha means indifference, but true equanimity is neither cold nor indifferent. If you have more than one child, they are all your children. Upeksha does not mean that you don't love. You love in a way that all your children receive your love, without discrimination.

Upeksha has the mark called *samatajñana*, "the wisdom of equality," the ability to see everyone as equal, not discriminating between ourselves and others. In a conflict, even though we are deeply concerned, we remain impartial, able to love and to understand both sides. We shed all discrimination and prejudice, and remove all boundaries between ourselves and others. As long as we see ourselves as the one who loves and the other as the one who is loved, as long as we value ourselves more than others or see ourselves as different from others, we do not have true equanimity. We have to put ourselves "into the other person's skin" and become one with him if we want to understand and truly love him. When that happens, there is no "self" and no "other."

Without upeksha, your love may become possessive. A summer breeze can be very refreshing; but if we try to put it in a tin can so we can have it entirely for ourselves, the breeze will die. Our beloved is the same. He is like a cloud, a breeze, a flower. If you imprison him in a tin can, he will die. Yet many people do just that. They rob their loved one of his liberty, until he can no longer be himself. They live to satisfy themselves and use their loved one to help them fulfill that. That is not loving; it is destroying. You say you love him, but if you do not understand his aspirations, his needs, his difficulties, he is in a prison called love. True love allows you to preserve your freedom and the freedom of your beloved. That is upeksha.

For love to be true love, it must contain compassion, joy, and equanimity. For compassion to be true compassion, it has to have love, joy, and equanimity in it. True joy has to contain love, compassion, and equanimity. And true equanimity has to have love, compassion, and joy in it. This is the interbeing nature of the Four Immeasurable Minds. When the Buddha told the Brahman man to practice the Four Immeasurable Minds, he was offering all of us a very important teaching. But we must look deeply and practice them for ourselves to bring these four aspects of love into our own lives and into the lives of those we love. In many sutras, the Buddha says that if you practice the Four Immeasurable Minds along with the Four Noble Truths and the Noble Eightfold Path, you will never again descend into the realms of suffering.[3]

---

[3] For a full explication on the Four Immeasurable Minds and related teachings, see Thich Nhat Hanh, *Teachings on Love* (Berkeley: Parallax Press, 1997).

CHAPTER TWENTY-THREE

The Five Aggregates

According to Buddhism, a human being is composed of Five Aggregates (skandhas): form, feelings, perceptions, mental formations, and consciousness. The Five Aggregates contain everything — both inside us and outside of us, in nature and in society.

Form *(rupa)* means our body, including our five sense organs and our nervous system. To practice mindfulness of the body, you might like to lie down and practice total relaxation. Allow your body to rest, and then be mindful of your forehead. "Breathing in, I am aware of my forehead. Breathing out, I smile to my forehead." Use the energy of mindfulness to embrace your forehead, your brain, your eyes, your ears, and your nose. Every time you breathe in, become aware of one part of your body, and every time you breathe out, smile to that part of your body. Use the energies of mindfulness and love to embrace each part. Embrace your heart, your lungs, and your stomach. "Breathing in, I am aware of my heart. Breathing out, I embrace my heart." Practice scanning your body with the light of mindfulness and smiling to each part of your body with compassion and concern. When you finish scanning in this way, you will feel wonderful. It takes only half an hour, and your body will rest deeply during those thirty minutes. Please take good care of your body, allowing it to rest and embracing it with tenderness, compassion, mindfulness, and love.

Learn to look at your body as a river in which every cell is a drop of water. In every moment, cells are born and cells die. Birth and death support each other. To practice mindfulness of the body, follow your breathing and focus your attention on each part of the body, from the hair on your head to the soles of your feet. Breathe mindfully and embrace each part of the body with the energy of mindfulness, smiling to it with recognition and love. The Buddha said that there are thirty-two parts of the body to recognize and embrace. Identify the form elements in your body: earth, water, air, and heat. See the connection of these four elements inside and outside of your body. See the living presence of your ancestors and future generations, as well as the presence of all other beings in the animal, vegetal, and mineral realms. Become aware of the positions of your body (standing, sitting, walking, lying down) and its movements (bending, stretching, taking a shower, getting dressed, eating, working, etc.). When you master this practice, you will be able to be aware of your feelings and your perceptions as they arise, and you will be able to practice looking deeply into them.

See your body's nature of impermanence and interbeing. Observe that your body has no permanent entity, and you will no longer identify yourself solely with your body or consider it to be a "self." See the body as a formation, empty of any substance that might be called "self." See your body as an ocean filled with hidden waves and sea monsters. The ocean might be calm at times, but at other times you can be caught in a storm. Learn to calm the waves and master the monsters without allowing yourself to be carried away or caught by them. With deep looking, the body ceases to be an aggregate of grasping *(upadana skandha),* and you dwell in freedom, no longer caught by fear.

༅

The Second Aggregate is feelings (vedana). There is a river of feelings within us, and every drop of water in that river is a feeling. To observe our feelings, we sit on the bank of the river and identify each feeling as it flows by. It may be pleasant, unpleasant, or neutral. One feeling lasts for a while, and then another comes. Meditation is to be aware of each feeling. Recognize it, smile to it, look deeply into it, and embrace it with all our heart. If we continue to look deeply, we discover the true nature of that feeling, and we are no longer afraid, even of a painful feeling. We know we are more than our feelings, and we are able to embrace each feeling and take good care of it.

Looking deeply into each feeling, we identify its roots as being in our body, our perceptions, or our deep consciousness. Understanding a feeling is the beginning of its transformation. We learn to embrace even our strong emotions with the energy of mindfulness until they are calmed down. We practice mindful breathing, focusing our attention on the rise and fall of our abdomen and take good care of our emotions just as we would take good care of our baby brother or sister. We practice looking deeply into our feelings and emotions and identify the nutriments that have brought them into being.[1] We know that if we are able to offer ourselves nutriments that are more wholesome, we can transform our feelings and emotions. Our feelings are formations, impermanent and without substance. We learn not to identify ourselves with our feelings, not to consider them as a self, not to seek refuge in them, not to die because of them. This practice helps us cultivate non-fear, and it frees us from the habit of clinging, even clinging to suffering.

৵

The Third Aggregate is perceptions (samjña). In us there is a river of perceptions. Perceptions arise, stay for a period of

---

[1] See chap. 7, pp. 31-39.

time, and cease to be. The aggregate of perception includes noticing, naming, and conceptualizing, as well as the perceiver and the perceived. When we perceive, we often distort, which brings about many painful feelings. Our perceptions are often erroneous, and we suffer. It is very helpful to look deeply into the nature of our perceptions, without being too sure of anything. When we are too sure, we suffer. "Am I sure?" is a very good question. If we ask this, we'll have a good chance to look again and see if our perception is incorrect. The perceiver and the perceived are inseparable. When the perceiver perceives wrongly, the things perceived are also incorrect.

A man was rowing his boat upstream when, suddenly, he saw another boat coming toward him. He shouted, "Be careful! Be careful!" but the boat plowed right into him, nearly sinking his boat. The man became angry and began to shout, but when he looked closely, he saw that there was no one in the other boat. The boat had drifted downstream by itself. He laughed out loud. When our perceptions are correct, we feel better, but when our perceptions are not correct, they can cause us a lot of unpleasant feelings. We have to look deeply into things so we will not be led into suffering and difficult feelings. Perceptions are very important for our well-being.

Our perceptions are conditioned by the many afflictions that are present in us: ignorance, craving, hatred, anger, jealousy, fear, habit energies, etc. We perceive phenomena on the basis of our lack of insight into the nature of impermanence and interbeing. Practicing mindfulness, concentration, and deep looking, we can discover the errors of our perceptions and free ourselves from fear and clinging. All suffering is born from wrong perceptions. Understanding, the fruit of meditation, can dissolve our wrong perceptions and liberate us. We have to be alert always and never seek refuge in our perceptions. The *Diamond Sutra* reminds us,

"Where there is perception, there is deception." We should be able to substitute perceptions with *prajña,* true vision, true knowledge.[2]

⇛

The Fourth Aggregate is mental formations (samskara). Anything made from another element is a "formation." A flower is a formation, because it is made from sunshine, clouds, seeds, soil, minerals, gardeners, and so on. Fear is also a formation, a mental formation. Our body is a formation, a physical formation. Feelings and perceptions are mental formations, but because they are so important, they have their own categories. According to the Vijñanavada School of the Northern Transmission, there are fifty-one categories of mental formations.

This Fourth Aggregate consists of forty-nine of these mental formations (excluding feelings and perceptions). All fifty-one mental formations are present in the depths of our store consciousness in the form of seeds *(bijas).* Every time a seed is touched, it manifests on the upper level of our consciousness (mind consciousness) as a mental formation. Our practice is to be aware of the manifestation and the presence of mental formations and to look deeply into them in order to see their true nature. Since we know that all mental formations are impermanent and without real substance, we do not identify ourselves with them or seek refuge in them. With daily practice, we are able to nourish and develop wholesome mental formations and transform unwholesome ones. Freedom, non-fear, and peace are the result of this practice.

⇛

The Fifth Aggregate is consciousness (vijñana). Consciousness here means store consciousness, which is at the base of

---

[2] For more on perceptions, see pp. 52-54.

everything we are, the ground of all of our mental formations. When mental formations are not manifesting, they re-
side in our store consciousness in the form of seeds — seeds
of joy, peace, understanding, compassion, forgetfulness, jealousy, fear, despair, and so on. Just as there are fifty-one categories of mental formations, there are fifty-one kinds of
seeds buried deep in our consciousness. Every time we water
one of them or allow it to be watered by someone else, that
seed will manifest and become a mental formation. We have
to be careful about which seeds we and others water. If we let
the negative seeds in us be watered, we can be overwhelmed.
The Fifth Aggregate, consciousness, contains all the other aggregates and is the basis of their existence.

Consciousness is, at the same time, both collective and individual. The collective is made of the individual, and the individual is made of the collective. Our consciousness can be
transformed at its base through the practice of mindful consuming, mindfully guarding our senses, and looking deeply.
The practice should aim at transforming both the individual
and the collective aspects of our consciousness. It is essential
to practice with a Sangha to produce such a transformation.
When the afflictions within us are transformed, our consciousness becomes wisdom, shining near and far and showing the way to liberation to both individuals and the whole
society.

꒜

These Five Aggregates inter-are. When you have a painful
feeling, look into your body, your perceptions, your mental
formations, and your consciousness to see what has brought
about this feeling. If you have a headache, your painful feeling comes from the First Aggregate. Painful feelings can also
come from mental formations or from perceptions. You
might, for example, think someone hates you who actually
loves you.

Look deeply into the five rivers of yourself and see how each river contains the other four. Look at the river of form. In the beginning you may think that form is just physical and not mental. But every cell in your body contains all aspects of yourself. It is now possible to take one cell of your body and duplicate your whole body. It is called "cloning." The one contains the all. One cell of your body contains your entire body. It also contains all of your feelings, perceptions, mental formations, and consciousness, and not only yours, but also your parents' and your ancestors'. Each aggregate contains all the other aggregates. Each feeling contains all perceptions, mental formations, and consciousness. Looking into one feeling, you can discover everything. Look in the light of interbeing, and you will see the all in the one and the one in the all. Don't think that form exists outside of feelings or that feelings exist outside of form.

In the *Turning the Wheel Sutra,* the Buddha said, "The Five Aggregates, when grasped at, are suffering." He did not say that the Five Aggregates are, in themselves, suffering. There is a helpful image in the *Ratnakuta Sutra.* A man throws a clod of earth at a dog. The dog looks at the clod and barks at it furiously. The dog does not realize that it is the man and not the clod of earth that is responsible. The sutra goes on to say, "In the same way, an ordinary person caught in dualistic conceptions thinks that the Five Aggregates are the cause of his suffering, but in fact the root of his suffering is his lack of understanding about the impermanent, nonself, and interdependent nature of the Five Aggregates."[3] It is not the Five Aggregates that make us suffer, but the way we relate to them. When we observe the impermanent, nonself, and interdependent nature of all that is, we will not feel aversion for life. In fact, this knowing will help us see the preciousness of all life.

---

[3] *Ratnakuta Sutra,* chap. 23. *Taisho* 310.

When we do not understand correctly, we become attached to things and get caught by them. In the *Ratnakuta Sutra,* the terms "aggregate" (skandha) and "aggregate of clinging" (upadana skandha) are used. Skandhas are the Five Aggregates that give rise to life. Upadana skandhas are the same Five Aggregates as the objects of our grasping. The root of our suffering is not the aggregates but our grasping. There are people who, because of their incorrect understanding of what the root of suffering is, instead of dealing with their attachments, fear the six sense objects and feel aversion for the Five Aggregates. A Buddha is someone who lives in peace, joy, and freedom, neither afraid of nor attached to anything.

When we breathe in and out and harmonize the Five Aggregates within us, this is true practice. But to practice is not to confine ourselves to the Five Aggregates within ourselves. We are also aware that the Five Aggregates in us have their roots in society, in nature, and in the people with whom we live. Meditate on the assembly of the Five Aggregates in yourself until you are able to see the oneness of your own self and the universe. When the Bodhisattva Avalokita looked deeply into the reality of the Five Aggregates, he saw the emptiness of self, and he was liberated from suffering. If we contemplate the Five Aggregates in a diligent way, we, too, will be liberated from suffering. If the Five Aggregates return to their sources, the self no longer exists. To see the one in the all is to break through the attachment to the false view of self, the belief in the self as an unchanging entity that can exist on its own. To break through this false view is to be liberated from every form of suffering.

CHAPTER TWENTY-FOUR

The Five Powers

As children growing up in central Vietnam, my brothers, sisters, and I used to run out to the yard every time it rained. It was our way of taking a shower. We were so happy! Sometime later, our mother would call us and serve us a bowl of rice with pickled bean sprouts or salty fish. We'd take our bowls and sit in the doorway, eating and continuing to watch the falling rain. We were free of all worries and anxieties, not thinking about the past, the future, or anything at all. We just enjoyed ourselves, our food, and each other. On New Year's Day, Mother served us special cakes, and we went outside and ate the cakes while playing with the cat and the dog. Sometimes our New Year's clothes were so starchy that they squeaked as we walked. We thought we were in paradise.

Growing up, we began to worry about homework, the right clothes, a good job, and supporting our family, not to mention war, social injustice, and so many other difficulties. We thought our paradise was lost, but it was not. We only had to remember how to water the seeds of paradise in ourselves, and we were able to produce true happiness again. Even today, you and I can return to our own paradise every time we breathe in and out mindfully. Our true home was not only in the past. It is present now. Mindfulness is the energy we can produce in our daily lives to bring our paradise back.

The Five Faculties, or Bases *(indriyani)*, are the power plants that can help us generate this energy in ourselves. The Five Powers *(balani)* are that energy in action. The Five Faculties and Powers are faith, energy, mindfulness, concentration, and insight. When practiced as bases, they are like factories that produce electricity. When practiced as powers, they have the capacity to bring about all the elements of the Eightfold Path, just as electricity manifests as light or heat.

The first of the five is faith (shraddha). When we have faith, a great energy in us is unleashed. If our faith is in something unreliable or false, not informed by insight, sooner or later it will lead us to a state of doubt and suspicion. But when our faith is made of insight and understanding, we will touch the things that are good, beautiful, and reliable. Faith is the confidence we receive when we put into practice a teaching that helps us overcome difficulties and obtain some transformation. It is like the confidence a farmer has in his way of growing crops. It is not blind. It is not some belief in a set of ideas or dogmas.[1]

The second power is diligence *(virya)*, the energy that brings joy into our practice. Faith gives birth to diligence, and this diligence continues to strengthen our faith. Animated with diligent energy, we become truly alive. Our eyes shine, and our steps are solid.[2]

The third power is mindfulness (smriti). To look deeply, to have deep insight, we use the energy of Right Mindfulness. Meditation is a power plant for mindfulness. When we sit, eat a meal, or wash the dishes, we can learn to be mindful. Mindfulness allows us to look deeply and see what is going on. Mindfulness is the plow, the hoe, and the irrigation source that waters insight. We are the gardener — plowing, sowing, and watering our beneficial seeds.[3]

---

[1] See chap. 21, pp. 161–162, for more on faith.

[2] See chap. 14 and also chap. 26, pp. 216–217, for more on virya, diligence.

[3] See chap. 11 for more on mindfulness.

The fourth power is concentration *(samadhi)*. To look deeply and see clearly, we need concentration. When we eat, wash dishes, walk, stand, sit, lie down, breathe, or work in mindfulness, we develop concentration. Mindfulness leads to concentration, and concentration leads to insight and to faith. With these four qualities, our life is filled with joy and the energy of being alive, which is the second power.[4]

The fifth power is insight, or wisdom (prajña), the ability to look deeply and see clearly, and also the understanding that results from this practice. When we can see clearly, we abandon what is false, and our faith becomes Right Faith.[5]

When all five power plants are working, producing electricity, they are no longer just faculties. They become the Five Powers. There is a difference between producing something and having the power that it has generated. If there is not enough energy in our body and mind, our five power plants need repair. When our power plants function well, we are able to produce the energy we need for our practice and for our happiness.

Our store consciousness contains the seeds of all of these energies. When joy or anger is not present in our mind consciousness, we may say, "I don't have that," but we do. It's below, in our store consciousness. Under the right conditions, that seed will manifest. We may say, "I'm not angry. I don't have anger in me," but anger is still there in our unconscious mind. Everyone has a seed of anger lying dormant, below, in our store consciousness. When we practice, our effort is to water positive seeds and let the negative seeds remain dormant. We don't say, "Until I've gotten rid of all my bad seeds, I can't practice." If you get rid of all your unwholesome seeds, you won't have anything to practice. We need to practice now with all the unwholesome seeds in us. If we don't,

---

[4] See chap. 15 for more on concentration.

[5] See chap. 25, pp. 210–212, for more on prajña.

the negative seeds will grow and cause a great deal of suffering.

Practicing the Five Powers is a matter of cultivating the earth of our store consciousness and sowing and watering good seeds. Then, when they arise into our mind consciousness and become flowers and fruits, they will scatter more good seeds throughout our store consciousness. If you want wholesome seeds to be in your mind consciousness, you need the condition of continuity. "Fruits of the same nature" will resow wholesome seeds in you.[6]

The *Lotus Sutra* says, "All sentient beings have the Buddha nature *(Buddhata).*" With the right conditions, the seed of Buddha nature in us will grow. We could also call that seed the seed of Right Mindfulness or the seed of insight, wisdom, or right faith. These are, in fact, one seed. To practice means to help that wonderful seed manifest. When we are mindful, concentration is already there. When we are concentrated, there is insight and wisdom. When we have faith, there is energy. Mindfulness is the seed of Buddha in us. Concentration is, therefore, already present in this seed of mindfulness in us.

The appellation "Buddha" comes from the root of the verb *budh* — which means to wake up, to understand, to know what is happening in a very deep way. In knowing, understanding, and waking up to reality, there is mindfulness, because mindfulness means seeing and knowing what is happening. Whether our seeing is deep or superficial depends on our degree of awakening. In each of us, the seed of Buddha, the capacity to wake up and understand, is called Buddha nature. It is the seed of mindfulness, the awareness of what is happening in the present moment. If I say, "A lotus for you, a Buddha to be," it means, "I see clearly the Buddha nature in you." It may be difficult for you to accept that the

---

[6] See chap. 27, pp. 224–225.

seed of Buddha is in you, but we all have the capacity for faith, awakening, understanding, and awareness, and that is what is meant by Buddha nature. There is no one who does not have the capacity to be a Buddha.

But the treasure we are looking for remains hidden to us. Stop being like the man in the *Lotus Sutra*, who looked all over the world for the gem that was already in his pocket. Come back and receive your true inheritance. Don't look outside yourself for happiness. Let go of the idea that you don't have it. It is available within you.

The Bodhisattva Never-Despising could not dislike anyone, because he knew that each of us has the capacity to become a Buddha. He would bow to every child and adult and say, "I do not dare to underestimate you. You are a future Buddha." Some people felt so joyful upon hearing this that faith arose in them. But others, thinking that he was making fun of them, shouted and hurled stones at him. He continued this practice for his whole life, reminding others they had the capacity to wake up. Why wander all over the world looking for something you already have? You are already the richest person on Earth.

How can we help someone who feels she cannot love herself? How can we help her be in touch with the seed of love already in her, so it can manifest as a flower and she can smile? As a good friend, we have to learn to look deeply into our own consciousness and into the consciousness of others. We can help our friend cultivate that seed and realize her capacity to love.

There is a sixth power called "capacity" or "inclusiveness" *(kshanti)*. The capacity to be happy is very precious. Someone who is able to be happy even when confronted with difficulties, has the capacity to offer light and a sense of joy to herself and to those around her. When we are near someone like this, we feel happy, also. Even when she enters hell, she will lighten up hell with the sound of her laughter. There is a bodhisattva named Kshitigarbha whose practice is to go into the places of deepest suffering and bring light and laughter to others. If your Sangha has one person like that, someone who can smile, be happy, and have faith in all circumstances, it is a good Sangha.

Ask yourself, "Am I like that?" At first glance, you might think not. You might have an inferiority complex, which is the second kind of pride.[7] Please follow the advice of Never-Despising Bodhisattva and look deeply into your store consciousness to accept that the seed of happiness, the capacity to love and to be happy, is there. Practice joy. You may think that washing dishes is menial work, but when you roll up your sleeves, turn on the water, and pour in the soap, you can be very happy. Washing the dishes mindfully, you see how wonderful life is. Every moment is an opportunity to water the seeds of happiness in yourself. If you develop the capacity to be happy in any surroundings, you will be able to share your happiness with others.

Otherwise you might think, This is an unhappy situation. I must go somewhere else. And you'll go from place to place wandering like the prodigal son. When you realize your own capacity to be happy anywhere, you can put down roots in the present moment. You can take whatever the conditions of the present moment are and make them the foundation of your life and your happiness. When the sun is shining, you are happy. When it is raining, you are also happy. You don't need to go anywhere else. You don't need to travel into the future or return to the past. Everything in the present moment belongs to your true home. All the conditions for happiness are here. You only have to touch the seeds of happiness that are already in you.

When you enter a well-tended garden and see a fresh,

---

[7] The Three Kinds of Pride are: (1) thinking I am better than the other(s); (2) thinking I am worse than the other(s); and (3) thinking I am just as good as the other(s).

beautiful rose, you want to pick it. But to do so, you have to touch some thorns. The rose is there, but the brambles are also there. You have to find a way to understand the thorns so you can pick the rose. Our practice is the same. Don't say that because there are thorns you cannot be happy. Don't say that because there is still anger or sadness in your heart, you cannot enjoy anything at all. You have to know how to deal with your anger and sadness so you don't lose the flowers of joy.

When our internal formations (samyojana) and suffering are dormant in our store consciousness, it is a good time to practice watering the positive seeds. When feelings of pain come into our conscious mind, we have to breathe mindfully and practice walking meditation in order to deal with those feelings. Don't lose the opportunity to water the seeds of happiness, so that more seeds of happiness will enter your store consciousness.

When the Buddha was about to pass away, his attendant Ananda cried and cried. The Buddha comforted him, saying, "Buddhas in the past had good attendants, but none were as good as you, Ananda." He was watering the seeds of happiness in Ananda, because Ananda had looked after Buddha with all his heart. He said, "Ananda, have you seen the wonderful fields of golden rice stretching out to the horizon? They are very beautiful." Ananda replied, "Yes, Lord, they are very beautiful." The Buddha was always reminding Ananda to notice the things that are beautiful. Ananda was anxious about taking care of the Buddha well, and he wasn't able to pick the rose of his daily life. When you see a cloud in the sky, ask your friend, "Do you see that cloud? Isn't it splendid?" How can we live so that the seeds of happiness in us are watered every day? That is the cultivation of joy, the practice of love. We can practice these things easily when we have the energy of mindfulness. But without mindfulness, how can we see the beautiful rice fields? How can we feel the delightful rain? Breathing in, I know the rain is falling. Breathing out, I smile to the rain. Breathing in, I know that rain is a necessary part of life. Breathing out, I smile again. Mindfulness helps us regain the paradise we thought we had lost.

We want to return to our true home, but we are in the habit of running away. We want to sit on a lotus flower, but instead we sit on burning charcoal, and we want to jump off. If we sit firmly in the present moment, it is as though we are sitting on a lotus. The Buddha is always represented as sitting peacefully on a lotus flower, because he was always at home. He didn't need to run anymore. To enjoy sitting in the present moment is called "just sitting" or "non-action." Venerable Thich Quang Duc was able to sit peacefully even while fire was blazing all around him. He was burning, but he was still sitting on a lotus. That is the ultimate capacity to sit peacefully in any circumstance, knowing that nothing is lost.

The capacity to feel at peace anywhere is a positive seed. The energy to run away is not. If we practice mindfulness, whenever the energy of wanting to run away arises, we can smile at it and say, "Hello, my old friend, I recognize you." The moment we recognize any habit energy, it loses a little of its power. Every time Mara appeared, the Buddha said, "I know you, my old friend," and Mara fled.

In the *Samiddhi Sutra*, we are taught to practice so that our happiness is present here and now. It isn't necessary to run away or abandon our present home and look for an illusory home, a so-called paradise that is really just a shadow of happiness. When we produce faith, energy, mindfulness, concentration, and insight in our power plants, we realize that our true home is already filled with light and power.

CHAPTER TWENTY-FIVE

The Six Paramitas

The Six Paramitas are a teaching of Mahayana Buddhism. *Paramita* can be translated as "perfection" or "perfect realization." The Chinese character used for paramita 度 means "crossing over to the other shore," which is the shore of peace, non-fear, and liberation. The practice of the paramitas can be the practice of our daily lives. We are on the shore of suffering, anger, and depression, and we want to cross over to the shore of well-being. To cross over, we have to do something, and that is called paramita. We return to ourselves and practice mindful breathing, looking at our suffering, anger, and depression, and smile. Doing this, we overcome our pain and cross over. We can practice "perfection" every day.

Every time you take one mindful step, you have a chance to go from the land of sorrow to the land of joy. The Pure Land is available right here and now. The Kingdom of God is a seed in us. If we know how to plant that seed in moist soil, it will become a tree, and birds will come and take refuge. Please practice crossing over to the other shore whenever you feel the need. The Buddha said, "Don't just hope for the other shore to come to you. If you want to cross over to the other shore, the shore of safety, well-being, non-fear, and non-anger, you have to swim or row across. You have to make an effort." This effort is the practice of the Six Paramitas.

The Six Paramitas

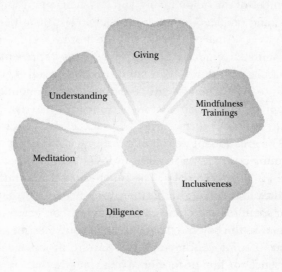

Figure Four

(1) *dana paramita* – giving, offering, generosity.

(2) *shila paramita* – precepts or mindfulness trainings.

(3) *kshanti paramita* – inclusiveness, the capacity to receive, bear, and transform the pain inflicted on you by your enemies and also by those who love you.

(4) *virya paramita* – diligence, energy, perseverance.

(5) *dhyana paramita* – meditation.

(6) *prajña paramita* – wisdom, insight, understanding.

Practicing the Six Paramitas helps us to reach the other shore — the shore of freedom, harmony, and good relationships.

ॐ

The first practice of crossing over is the perfection of giving, dana paramita. To give means first of all to offer joy, happiness, and love. There is a plant, well-known in Asia — it is a member of the onion family, and it is delicious in soup, fried rice, and omelets — that grows back in less than twenty-four hours every time you cut it. And the more you cut it, the bigger and stronger it grows. This plant represents dana paramita. We don't keep anything for ourselves. We only want to give. When we give, the other person might become happy, but it is certain that we become happy. In many stories of the Buddha's former lives, he practices dana paramita.[1]

The greatest gift we can offer anyone is our true presence. A young boy I know was asked by his father, "What would you like for your birthday?" The boy hesitated. His father was wealthy and could give him anything he wanted. But his father spent so much time making money that he was rarely at home. So the boy said, "Daddy, I want you!" The message was clear. If you love someone, you have to produce your true presence for him or for her. When you give that gift, you receive, at the same time, the gift of joy. Learn how to produce your true presence by practicing meditation. Breathing mindfully, you bring body and mind together. "Darling, I am here for you" is a mantra you can say when you practice this paramita.

What else can we give? Our stability. "Breathing in, I see myself as a mountain. Breathing out, I feel solid." The person we love needs us to be solid and stable. We can cultivate our stability by breathing in and out, practicing mindful walking, mindful sitting, and enjoy living deeply in every moment. Solidity is one of the characteristics of nirvana.

What else can we offer? Our freedom. Happiness is not possible unless we are free from afflictions — craving, anger, jealousy, despair, fear, and wrong perceptions. Freedom is one of the characteristics of nirvana. Some kinds of happiness actually destroy our body, our mind, and our relation-

---

[1] See any of the translations of the *Jataka Tales*.

ships. Freedom from craving is an important practice. Look deeply into the nature of what you think will bring you happiness and see whether it is, in fact, causing those you love to suffer. You have to know this if you want to be truly free. Come back to the present moment, and touch the wonders of life that are available. There are so many wholesome things that can make us happy right now, like the beautiful sunrise, the blue sky, the mountains, the rivers, and all the lovely faces around us.

What else can we give? Our freshness. "Breathing in, I see myself as a flower. Breathing out, I feel fresh." You can breathe in and out three times and restore your flowerness right away. What a gift!

What else can we offer? Peace. It is wonderful to sit near someone who is peaceful. We benefit from her peace. "Breathing in, I see myself as still water. Breathing out, I reflect things as they are." We can offer those we love our peace and lucidity.

What else can we offer? Space. The person we love needs space in order to be happy. In a flower arrangement, each flower needs space around it in order to radiate its true beauty. A person is like a flower. Without space within and around her, she cannot be happy. We cannot buy these gifts at the market. We have to produce them through our practice. And the more we offer, the more we have. When the person we love is happy, happiness comes back to us right away. We give to her, but we are giving to ourselves at the same time.

Giving is a wonderful practice. The Buddha said that when you are angry at someone, if you have tried everything and still feel angry, practice dana paramita. When we are angry, our tendency is to punish the other person. But when we do, there is only an escalation of the suffering. The Buddha proposed that instead, you send her a gift. When you feel angry, you won't want to go out and buy a gift, so take the opportunity now to prepare the gift while you are not angry. Then, when all else fails, go and mail that gift to her, and amazingly, you'll feel better right away. The same is true for nations. For Israel to have peace and security, the Israelis have to find ways to ensure peace and security for the Palestinians. And for the Palestinians to have peace and security, they also have to find ways to ensure peace and security for the Israelis. You get what you offer. Instead of trying to punish the other person, offer him exactly what he needs. The practice of giving can bring you to the shore of well-being very quickly.

When another person makes you suffer, it is because he suffers deeply within himself, and his suffering is spilling over. He does not need punishment; he needs help. That is the message he is sending. If you are able to see that, offer him what he needs — relief. Happiness and safety are not an individual matter. His happiness and safety are crucial for your happiness and safety. Wholeheartedly wish him happiness and safety, and you will be happy and safe also.

What else can we offer? Understanding. Understanding is the flower of practice. Focus your concentrated attention on one object, look deeply into it, and you'll have insight and understanding. When you offer others your understanding, they will stop suffering right away.

The first petal of the flower of the paramitas is dana paramita, the practice of giving. What you give is what you receive, more quickly than the signals sent by satellite. Whether you give your presence, your stability, your freshness, your solidity, your freedom, or your understanding, your gift can work a miracle. Dana paramita is the practice of love.

꒜

The second practice is the perfection of the precepts, or mindfulness trainings, shila paramita. The Five Mindfulness Trainings help protect our body, mind, family, and society.

The First Mindfulness Training is about protecting the lives of human beings, animals, vegetables, and minerals. To protect other beings is to protect ourselves. The second is to prevent the exploitation by humans of other living beings and of nature. It is also the practice of generosity. The third is to protect children and adults from sexual abuse, to preserve the happiness of individuals and families. Too many families have been broken by sexual misconduct. When you practice the Third Mindfulness Training, you protect yourself and you protect families and couples. You help other people feel safe. The Fourth Mindfulness Training is to practice deep listening and loving speech. The Fifth Mindfulness Training is about mindful consumption.[2]

The practice of the Five Mindfulness Trainings is a form of love, and a form of giving. It assures the good health and protection of our family and society. Shila paramita is a great gift that we can make to our society, our family, and to those we love. The most precious gift we can offer our society is to practice the Five Mindfulness Trainings. If we live according to the Five Mindfulness Trainings, we protect ourselves and the people we love. When we practice shila paramita, we offer the precious gift of life.

Let us look deeply together into the causes of our suffering, individually and collectively. If we do, I am confident we will see that the Five Mindfulness Trainings are the correct medicine for the malaise of our times. Every tradition has the equivalent of the Five Mindfulness Trainings. Every time I see someone receive and practice the Five Mindfulness Trainings, I feel so happy — for him, his family, and also for myself — because I know that the Five Mindfulness Trainings are the most concrete way to practice mindfulness. We need a Sangha around us in order to practice them deeply.

---

[2] For more on the Five Mindfulness Trainings, see chaps. 12 and 13 on Right Speech and Right Action. See also Thich Nhat Hanh, *For a Future To Be Possible*.

જ

The third petal of the flower is inclusiveness, kshanti paramita. Inclusiveness is the capacity to receive, embrace, and transform. Kshanti is often translated as patience or forbearance, but I believe "inclusiveness" better conveys the Buddha's teaching. When we practice inclusiveness, we don't have to suffer or forbear, even when we have to embrace suffering and injustice. The other person says or does something that makes us angry. He inflicts on us some kind of injustice. But if our heart is large enough, we don't suffer.

The Buddha offered this wonderful image. If you take a handful of salt and pour it into a small bowl of water, the water in the bowl will be too salty to drink. But if you pour the same amount of salt into a large river, people will still be able to drink the river's water. (Remember, this teaching was offered 2,600 years ago, when it was still possible to drink from rivers!) Because of its immensity, the river has the capacity to receive and transform. The river doesn't suffer at all because of a handful of salt. If your heart is small, one unjust word or act will make you suffer. But if your heart is large, if you have understanding and compassion, that word or deed will not have the power to make you suffer. You will be able to receive, embrace, and transform it in an instant. What counts here is your capacity. To transform your suffering, your heart has to be as big as the ocean. Someone else might suffer. But if a bodhisattva receives the same unkind words, she won't suffer at all. It depends on your way of receiving, embracing, and transforming. If you keep your pain for too long, it is because you have not yet learned the practice of inclusiveness.

When Rahula, the Buddha's son, was eighteen, the Buddha delivered to him a wonderful Dharma talk on how to practice inclusiveness. Sariputra, Rahula's tutor, was there, and he listened and absorbed that teaching, also. Then, twelve years later, Sariputra had the chance to repeat this teaching to the full assembly of monks and nuns. It was the day after the completion of the three-month rainy-season re-treat, and every monk was getting ready to leave the com-pound and go off in the ten directions to offer the teachings to others. At that time, one monk reported to the Buddha, "My Lord, this morning as Venerable Shariputra was leaving, I asked him where he was heading, and instead of answering my question, he pushed me to the ground and did not even say, 'I'm sorry.'"

The Buddha asked Ananda, "Has Shariputra gone far yet?" and Ananda said, "No, Lord, he left just an hour ago." So the Buddha asked a novice to find Shariputra and invite him to come back. When the novice brought Shariputra back, Ananda summoned all the monks who were still there to gather. Then, the Buddha stepped into the hall and asked Shariputra formally, "Shariputra, is it true that this morning when you were going out of the monastery, a brother of yours wanted to ask you a question and you did not answer him? Is it true that instead you pushed him to the ground and didn't even say you were sorry?" Thereupon, Shariputra answered the Buddha, in front of all his fellow monks and nuns:[3]

"Lord, I remember the discourse you gave twelve years ago to Bhikshu Rahula, when he was eighteen years old. You taught him to contemplate the nature of earth, water, fire, and air in order to nourish and develop the virtues of love, compassion, joy, and equanimity.[4] Although your teaching was directed to Rahula, I also learned from it, and I have tried to observe and practice that teaching.

"Lord, I have tried to practice like the earth. The earth is

---

[3] *Shariputra's Lion's Roar, Anguttara Nikaya* IX, 11. Also, *Mahaparinirvana Sutra.*

[4] The Buddha also taught the Four Immeasurable Minds — love, compassion, joy, and equanimity — to help us make our hearts bigger, so we don't have to suffer every time others inflict pain and injustice upon us. See chap. 22. See also Thich Nhat Hanh, *Teachings on Love.*

wide and open and has the capacity to receive, embrace, and transform. Whether people toss pure and fragrant substances such as flowers, perfume, or fresh milk upon the earth, or toss unclean and foul-smelling substances like excrement, urine, blood, mucus, and spit upon the earth, the earth receives them all equally, without grasping or aversion. No matter what you throw into the earth, the earth has the power to receive, embrace, and transform it. I try my best to practice like earth, to receive without resisting, complaining, or suffering.

"Lord, I practice mindfulness and loving kindness. A monk who does not practice mindfulness of the body in the body, of the actions of the body in the actions of the body, could knock down a fellow monk and leave him lying there without apologizing. But it is not my way to be rude to a fellow monk, to push him to the ground and walk on without apologizing.

"Lord, I have learned the lesson you offered to Rahula to practice like the water. Whether someone pours a fragrant substance or an unclean substance into the water, the water receives them all equally without grasping or aversion. Water is immense and flowing and has the capacity to receive, contain, transform, and purify all these things. I have tried my best to practice like water. A monk who does not practice mindfulness, who does not practice becoming like water, might push a fellow monk to the ground and go on his way without saying 'I'm sorry.' I am not such a monk.

"My Lord, I have practiced to be more like fire. Fire burns everything, the pure as well as the impure, the beautiful as well as the distasteful, without grasping or aversion. If you throw flowers or silk into it, it burns. If you throw old cloth and other foul-smelling things into it, the fire will accept and burn everything. It does not discriminate. Why? Because fire can receive, consume, and burn everything offered to it. I have tried to practice like fire. I am able to burn the things that are negative in order to transform them. A monk who does not practice mindfulness of looking, listening, and contemplating might push a fellow monk to the ground and go on without apologizing. Lord, I am not such a monk.

"Lord, I have tried to practice to be more like air. The air carries all smells, good and bad, without grasping or aversion. The air has the capacity to transform, purify, and release. Lord Buddha, I have contemplated the body in the body, the movement of the body in the movement of the body, the positions of the body in the positions of the body, the feelings in the feelings, and the mind in the mind. A monk who does not practice mindfulness might push a fellow monk to the ground and go on without apologizing. I am not such a monk.

"My Lord, I am like an untouchable child with nothing to wear, with no title or any medal to put on my tattered cloth. I have tried to practice humility, because I know that humility has the power to transform. I have tried to learn every day. A monk who does not practice mindfulness can push a fellow monk to the ground and go on without apologizing. My Lord, I am not such a monk."

Shariputra continued to deliver his "Lion's Roar," but the other monk could stand it no longer, and he bared his right shoulder, knelt down, and begged for forgiveness. "Lord, I have transgressed the *Vinaya* (rules of monastic discipline). Out of anger and jealousy, I told a lie to discredit my elder brother in the Dharma. I beg the community to allow me to practice Beginning Anew." In front of the Buddha and the whole Sangha, he prostrated three times to Shariputra. When Shariputra saw his brother prostrating, he bowed and said, "I have not been skillful enough, and that is why I have created misunderstanding. I am co-responsible for this, and I beg my brother monk to forgive me." Then he prostrated three times to the other monk, and they reconciled. Ananda asked Shariputra to stay for a cup of tea before starting off on his journey again.

To suppress our pain is not the teaching of inclusiveness. We have to receive it, embrace it, and transform it. The only way to do this is to make our heart big. We look deeply in order to understand and forgive. Otherwise we will be caught in anger and hatred, and think that we will feel better only after we punish the other person. Revenge is an unwholesome nutriment. The intention to help others is a wholesome nutriment.

To practice kshanti paramita, we need the other paramitas. If our practice of inclusiveness does not bear the marks of understanding, giving, and meditation, we are just trying to suppress our pain and drive it down to the bottom of our consciousness. This is dangerous. That kind of energy will blow up later and destroy ourselves and others. If you practice deep looking, your heart will grow without limits, and you will suffer less.

The first disciple I ordained was a monk named Thich Nhât Tri. Brother Nhât Tri went with Sister Chân Không and me on many missions to rescue flood victims in central Vietnam, and he spent many months in a poor hamlet because I had asked him to. We were setting up the School of Youth for Social Service, and we needed to learn the real situation of the people in the rural areas. We wanted to find ways to apply nonviolence and loving kindness to help poor people improve their standard of living. It was a beautiful movement for social improvement. Eventually, we had 10,000 workers. The communists said our Buddhist movement was proAmerican, and the mass media said that we Buddhist monks were disguised communists trying to arrange a communist takeover. We were just trying to be ourselves, not aligned with any warring party. In 1967, Brother Nhât Tri and seven other social workers were kidnapped by a group on the extreme right, and he has not been heard from since then.

One day, Nhât Tri was walking on the streets of Saigon, when an American soldier standing on a military truck spit on his head. Brother Nhât Tri came home and cried and cried. Being a young man, he was tempted to fight back, and so I held him in my arms for half an hour in order to transform that feeling of being deeply hurt. I said, "My child, you were not born to hold a gun. You were born to be a monk, and your power is the power of understanding and love. The American soldier considered you to be his enemy. That was a wrong perception of his. We need 'soldiers' who can go to the front armed only with understanding and love." He stayed on with the School of Youth for Social Service. Then he was kidnapped and probably killed. Thich Nhât Tri is a big brother of the monks and nuns at Plum Village. His handwriting looked almost exactly like mine. And he wrote beautiful songs for buffalo boys to sing in the countryside.

How can we wash away that kind of injustice? How can we transform the injustice received by whole nations? Cambodians, Bosnians, Palestinians, Israelis, Tibetans, all of us suffer from injustice and intolerance. Instead of being brothers and sisters to each other, we aim guns at each other. When we are overtaken by anger, we think that the only response is to punish the other person. The fire of anger continues to burn in us, and it continues to burn our brothers and sisters. This is the situation of the world, and it is why deep looking is needed to help us understand that all of us are victims.

I told Brother Nhât Tri, "If you were born into a family along the coast of New Jersey or California and if you read the kinds of newspapers and magazine articles that those soldiers read, you would also believe that all Buddhist monks are communists, and you would spit on the head of a monk, too." I told him that American G.I.s were trained to look on all Vietnamese as enemies. They were sent here to kill or be killed. They are victims, just like the Vietnamese soldiers and Vietnamese civilians. The ones who hold the guns and shoot at us, the one who spit at you, they are not the makers of the war. The war makers are in comfortable offices in Beijing, Moscow, and Washington, D.C. It was a wrong policy born of a wrong understanding. When I went to Washington in 1966, I met with Robert McNamara, and what I told him about the nature of war was entirely true. Half a year later, he resigned as Secretary of Defense, and recently he wrote a book and confessed that the war in Vietnam was a terrible mistake. Perhaps I helped plant some seeds of understanding in him.

A wrong perception was responsible for a wrong policy, and a wrong policy was responsible for the deaths of many thousands of American and Vietnamese soldiers, and several million Vietnamese civilians. The people in the countryside could not understand why they had to die like that, why the bombs had to fall on them day and night. I was sleeping in my room close to the Buddha Hall on the School of Youth for Social Service campus when a rocket was fired into that hall. I could have been killed. If you nourish your hatred and your anger, you burn yourself. Understanding is the only way out. If you understand, you will suffer less, and you will know how to get to the root of injustice. The Buddha said that if one arrow strikes you, you'll suffer. But if a second arrow hits you in the same spot, you'll suffer one hundred times more.[5] When you are a victim of injustice, if you get angry, you will suffer one hundred times more. When you have some pain in your body, breathe in and out and say to yourself, "It is only a physical pain." If you imagine that it is cancer and that you will die very soon, your pain will be one hundred times worse. Fear or hatred, born of ignorance, amplifies your

---

[5] *Samyutta Nikaya* V, 210.

pain. Prajña paramita is the savior. If you know how to see things as themselves and not more than that, you can survive.

I love the Vietnamese people, and I tried my best to help them during the war. But I also saw the American boys in Vietnam as victims. I did not look at them with rancor, and I suffered much less. This is the kind of suffering many of us have overcome, and the teaching is born out of that suffering, not from academic studies. I survived for Brother Nhât Tri and for so many others who died in order to bring the message of forgiveness, love, and understanding. I share this so they will not have died in vain.

Please practice deep looking, and you will suffer much less from disease, injustice, or the small pains within you. Deep looking leads to understanding, and understanding always leads to love and acceptance. When your baby is sick, of course you do your best to help him. But you also know that a baby has to be sick a number of times in order to get the immunity he needs. You know that you can survive, too, because you have developed antibodies. Don't worry. "Perfect health" is just an idea. Learn to live in peace with whatever ailments you have. Try to transform them, but don't suffer too much.

During his lifetime, the Buddha suffered too. There were plots to compete with him and even to kill him. One time, when he had a wound in his leg and people tried to help him, he said it was only a small wound, and he did his best to minimize the pain. Another time, five hundred of his monks went off to set up an alternative Sangha, and he took it very much in stride. Finally, the difficulties were overcome.

The Buddha gave very concrete teachings on how to develop inclusiveness — maitri (love), karuna (compassion), mudita (joy), and upeksha (equanimity).[6] If you practice these Four Immeasurable Minds, you will have a huge heart.

---

[6] See chap. 22 on the Four Immeasurable Minds.

Because bodhisattvas have great compassion, they have the capacity of receiving, embracing, and transforming. Because they have great understanding, they don't have to suffer. This is a great gift for the world and for the people we love.

～

The fourth petal of the flower is virya paramita, the perfection of diligence, energy, or continuous practice. The Buddha said that in the depth of our store consciousness, alayavijñana, there are all kinds of positive and negative seeds — seeds of anger, delusion, and fear, and seeds of understanding, compassion, and forgiveness. Many of these seeds have been transmitted to us by our ancestors. We should learn to recognize every one of these seeds in us in order to practice diligence. If it is a negative seed, the seed of an affliction like anger, fear, jealousy, or discrimination, we should refrain from allowing it to be watered in our daily life. Every time such a seed is watered, it will manifest on the upper level of our consciousness, and we will suffer and make the people we love suffer at the same time. The practice is to refrain from watering the negative seeds in us.

We also recognize the negative seeds in the people we love and try our best not to water them. If we do, they will be very unhappy, and we will be unhappy, also. This is the practice of "selective watering." If you want to be happy, avoid watering your own negative seeds and ask others not to water those seeds in you. Also, avoid watering the negative seeds in others.

We also try to recognize the positive seeds that are in us and to live our daily life in a way that we can touch them and help them manifest on the upper level of our consciousness, manovijñana. Every time they manifest and stay on the upper level of our consciousness for a while, they grow stronger. If the positive seeds in us grow stronger day and night, we will be happy and we will make the people we love happy. Recognize the positive seeds in the person you love, water those seeds, and he will become much happier. In Plum Village, we practice "flower watering," recognizing the best seeds in others and watering them. Whenever you have time, please water the seeds that need to be watered. It is a wonderful and very pleasant practice of diligence, and it brings immediate results.

Imagine a circle divided in two. Below is the store consciousness and above is mind consciousness. All mental formations lie deep down in our store consciousness. Every seed in our store consciousness can be touched and manifests itself on the upper level, namely our mind consciousness. Continued practice means trying our best not to allow the negative seeds in our store consciousness to be touched in our daily life, not to give them a chance to manifest themselves. The seeds of anger, discrimination, despair, jealousy, and craving are all there. We do what we can to prevent them from coming up. We tell the people we live with, "If you truly love me, don't water these seeds in me. It is not good for my health or yours." We have to recognize the kinds of seeds not to be watered. If it happens that a negative seed, the seed of an affliction, is watered and manifests itself, we do everything in our power to embrace it with our mindfulness and help it return to where it came from. The longer such seeds stay in our mind consciousness, the stronger they become.

The Buddha suggested a practice called "changing the peg." When a peg of wood is not the right size or is rotting or in disrepair, a carpenter will replace it by putting another peg on exactly the same spot and driving the new peg into the old one. If you have a mental formation arising that you consider to be unwholesome, one way to practice is to invite another mental formation to replace it. Many seeds in your store consciousness are wholesome and beautiful. Just

Seeds of Mindfulness

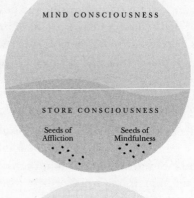

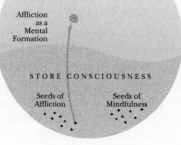

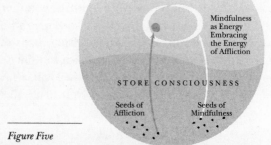

Figure Five

breathe in and out and invite one of them to come up, and the other seed will go down. This is called "changing the peg."

The third practice is to touch as many positive seeds in your store consciousness as you can so that they will manifest in your mind consciousness. On a television set, if you want a certain program, you push the button to bring you that program. Invite only pleasant seeds to come up and sit in the living room of your consciousness. Never invite a guest who brings you sorrow and affliction. And tell your friends, "If you love me, please water the wholesome seeds in me every day." One wonderful seed is mindfulness. Mindfulness is the Buddha in us. Use every opportunity to touch that seed and help it to manifest on the upper level of your consciousness.

The fourth practice is to keep a wholesome seed as long as possible once it has manifested. If mindfulness is maintained for fifteen minutes, the seed of mindfulness will be strengthened, and the next time you need the energy of mindfulness, it will be easier to bring up. It is very important to help the seeds of mindfulness, forgiveness, and compassion to grow, and the way to do this is to help them be present in your mind consciousness as long as possible. This is called transformation at the base — *ashraya paravritti*. This is the true meaning of virya paramita, the perfection of diligence.

࿇

The fifth crossing-over is dhyana paramita, the perfection of meditation. Dhyana is pronounced *zen* in Japanese, *chan* in Chinese, *thien* in Vietnamese, and *son* in Korean. Dhyana, or meditation, consists of two aspects.[7] The first is stopping (shamatha). We run our whole life chasing after one idea of happiness or another. Stopping is to stop our running, our forgetfulness, our being caught in the past or the future. We

---

[7] See chap. 6.

come home to the present moment, where life is available. The present moment contains every moment. Here we can touch our ancestors, our children, and their children, even if they have not been born yet. Shamatha is the practice of calming our body and emotions through the practice of mindful breathing, mindful walking, and mindful sitting. Shamatha is also the practice of concentrating, so we can live deeply each moment of our life and touch the deepest level of our being.

The second aspect of meditation is looking deeply (vipashyana) to see the true nature of things. You look into the person you love and find out what kinds of suffering or difficulty she has within herself and what aspirations she holds. Understanding is a great gift, but your daily life conducted in mindfulness is also a great gift. Doing everything mindfully is the practice of meditation, as mindfulness always nourishes concentration and understanding.

༄

The sixth petal of the flower is prajña paramita, the perfection of understanding. This is the highest kind of understanding, free from all knowledge, concepts, ideas, and views. Prajña is the substance of Buddhahood in us. It is the kind of understanding that has the power to carry us to the other shore of freedom, emancipation, and peace. In Mahayana Buddhism, prajña paramita is described as the Mother of All Buddhas. Everything that is good, beautiful, and true is born from our mother, prajña paramita. She is in us; we only need to touch her to help her manifest herself. Right View is prajña paramita.

There is a large literature on prajña paramita, and the *Heart Sutra* is one of the shorter discourses in that collection. The *Diamond Sutra* and the *Ashtasahasrika Prajñaparamita (Discourse in 8,000 Verses)* are among the earliest discourses in that collection. Prajña paramita is the wisdom of nondiscrimination.

If you look deeply into the person you love, you'll be able to understand her suffering, her difficulties, and also her deepest aspirations. And out of that understanding, real love will be possible. When someone is able to understand us, we feel very happy. If we can offer understanding to someone, that is true love. The one who receives our understanding will bloom like a flower, and we will be rewarded at the same time. Understanding is the fruit of the practice. Looking deeply means to be there, to be mindful, to be concentrated. Looking deeply into any object, understanding will flower. The teaching of the Buddha is to help us understand reality deeply.

Let us look at a wave on the surface of the ocean. A wave is a wave. It has a beginning and an end. It might be high or low, more or less beautiful than other waves. But a wave is, at the same time, water. Water is the ground of being of the wave. It is important that a wave knows that she is water, and not just a wave. We, too, live our life as an individual. We believe that we have a beginning and an end, that we are separate from other living beings. That is why the Buddha advised us to look more deeply in order to touch the ground of our being, which is nirvana. Everything bears deeply the nature of nirvana. Everything has been "nirvanized." That is the teaching of the *Lotus Sutra*. We look deeply, and we touch the suchness of reality. Looking deeply into a pebble, flower, or our own joy, peace, sorrow, or fear, we touch the ultimate dimension of our being, and that dimension will reveal to us that the ground of our being has the nature of no-birth and no-death.

We don't have to *attain* nirvana, because we ourselves are always dwelling in nirvana. The wave does not have to look for water. It already is water. We are one with the ground of our being. Once the wave realizes that she is water, all her fear vanishes. Once we touch the ground of our being, once we touch God or nirvana, we also receive the gift of non-fear.

Non-fear is the basis of true happiness. The greatest gift we can offer others is our non-fear. Living deeply every moment of our life, touching the deepest level of our being, this is the practice of prajña paramita. Prajña paramita is crossing over by understanding, by insight.

Perfect understanding is present in all the other perfections. Perfect understanding is like a container. If the container is not baked well in the kiln, there will be cracks, and the liquid in it will flow out. Prajña paramita is the mother of all the paramitas, the Mother of All Buddhas. Prajña paramita is like the wings of the bird that can carry it anywhere. Without Right Understanding, none of the other paramitas can go very far.

⁂

These are the practices of the Six Paramitas offered by the Buddha. Each of the six contains the other five. Understanding is giving, meditation is giving, continued practice is giving, inclusiveness is giving, and mindfulness training is giving. If you practice giving deeply, you are also practicing understanding, meditation, and so on. In the same light, we see that giving is mindfulness training, understanding is mindfulness training, meditation is mindfulness training, continued practice is mindfulness training, and inclusiveness is mindfulness training. If you practice one paramita deeply, you practice all six. When there is understanding and insight, meditation will be true meditation, continued practice will be true continued practice, inclusiveness will be true inclusiveness, mindfulness training will be true mindfulness training, and giving will be true giving. Understanding increases the quality of the other five practices.

Look into your situation and see how rich you are inside. See that what you have in the present moment is a gift. Without waiting any longer, begin to practice right away. The moment you begin to practice, you'll feel happy right away. The

Dharma is not a matter of time. Come and see for yourself. The Dharma can transform your life.

When you are caught in your sorrow, your suffering, your depression, your anger, or your fear, don't stay on the shore of suffering. Step over to the shore of freedom, non-fear, and non-anger. Just practice mindful breathing, mindful walking, and deep looking, and you will step onto the shore of freedom and well-being. You don't have to practice five, ten, or twenty years to be able to cross over to the other shore. You can do it right now.

CHAPTER TWENTY-SIX

The Seven Factors of Awakening

The Seven Factors of Awakening *(sapta-bodhyanga)* are mind-fulness, investigation of phenomena, diligence, joy, ease, con-centration, and letting go. Bodhyanga is made up of two words: *bodhi* and *anga*. Bodhi ("awakening," "enlighten-ment") comes from the root *budh-*, which means "to wake up," to be aware of what is going on within and all around you. A Buddha is "One Who Is Awakened." *Anga* means limb. Sapta-bodhyanga can also be translated as the Seven Limbs, or Factors, of Enlightenment.

After sitting in meditation at the foot of a *ficus religiosa*, known by Buddhists as the bodhi tree, when the morning star arose, the Buddha realized enlightenment and said, "How amazing that all living beings have the basic nature of awakening, yet they don't know it. So they drift on the ocean of great suffering lifetime after lifetime." It means that the potentialities of the Seven Factors of Awakening are already in us, but we don't know it.

It is said that the Buddha was reluctant at first to share the insight he experienced under the bodhi tree. Only after con-tinuing his meditation did he realize that many beings would benefit if he offered concrete ways to help them wake up. The Seven Factors of Awakening offer a description of both the characteristics of awakening as well as a path to awaken-ing. Imagine a tree with seven large limbs, each representing one Factor of Awakening. Every year, each of these branches grows longer and sends out new shoots with new leaves. Enlightenment is growing all the time. It is not something that happens once and is then complete. It is reassuring that the Buddha regarded joy and ease among these seven elements.

The First and main Factor of Awakening — the first limb of the bodhi tree — is mindfulness (smriti). Smriti literally means "remembering," not forgetting where we are, what we are doing, and who we are with. Mindfulness always arises in the context of a relationship with ourselves, other people, or things. It is not something we keep in our pocket and take out when we need it. When we see a friend on the street and recognize her, we have not taken "recognition" out of our pocket. It arose in the context of the situation. Our breathing, walking, movements, feelings, and the phenomena around us are all parts of the "relationship" in which mindfulness arises. With training, every time we breathe in and out, mindfulness will be there, so that our breathing becomes a cause and condition for the arising of mindfulness.

You might think, "I am the cause for mindfulness being present." But if you look around, you will never find an "I." The telephone's ring, the clock's chime, your teacher, and your Sangha can be favorable causes for mindfulness being present. Imagine yourself doing walking meditation on a beach, when suddenly the thought arises, "Do I have enough money in the bank?" If you return your awareness to your feet making contact with the sand, that is enough to bring you back to the present moment. You can do this because you have practiced walking meditation before. But it is your feet and not "I" that remind you to be present.

In the *Discourse on the Four Establishments of Mindfulness,* the Buddha asks, "If you practice the Four Establishments of Mindfulness, how long will it take to become enlightened?" First he answers, "Seven years," but then he says, "It can be as short as half a month." It means that awakening is always available. It only needs favorable conditions. The sun is there, even when it is behind the clouds. The Buddha said,

"By practicing the Four Establishments of Mindfulness, you will realize the Seven Factors of Awakening."[1]

Investigation of phenomena (dharma-pravichaya) is the Second Factor of Awakening. We humans love to investigate things. Often we want the results of our investigations to fit a certain mold or prove a certain theory, but at times, we are open and allow things simply to reveal themselves. In the latter case, our knowledge and our boundaries expand. When we want to investigate the bud on the branch of the tree, we might ask, "Where have you come from? Where are you going? Are you really that small?" The bud might reply, "I will grow into a leaf — green in the summer, orange in the fall. Then I will fall to the earth, and in two years I'll become a part of the earth. I am really not small. I'm as large as the earth." With mindfulness, investigation takes us deeply into life and into reality.

The Third Factor of Awakening is virya, which means energy, effort, diligence, or perseverance. Energy comes from many sources. Sometimes just thinking about what we might gain in the future gives us energy. In Buddhism, the sources of our energy are mindfulness, investigation, and faith in the practice. When we look deeply, we see that life is a miracle beyond our comprehension. But for many young people today, life is meaningless. Many thousands of young people commit suicide every year. In some countries, more young people die from suicide than from traffic accidents. We need to help young people cultivate the life-energy that comes from experiencing the wonders of life. We need to help their lives have meaning.

Even if we are in pain, if we can see meaning in our life, we will have energy and joy. Energy is not the result of good health alone or the wish to achieve some goal — material or spiritual. It is a result of feeling some meaning to our life.

---

[1] *Satipatthana Sutta.* See Thich Nhat Hanh, *Transformation and Healing.*

Making an effort at the wrong time or place dissipates our energy. Sitting in meditation for lengthy periods before we have developed good concentration might cause us to dislike meditation, and even to stop sitting altogether. When Siddhartha practiced meditation under the bodhi tree, his concentration was already highly developed. When Kashyapa told Ananda that Ananda would not be invited to attend the first Council of the Buddha's disciples because he did not have a high enough degree of awakening, Ananda sat in meditation all night, and by dawn he realized "the fruit of arhatship."[2] When Ananda arrived at the council, Kashyapa and the others recognized that he had had a breakthrough. His shining presence was proof enough.

The Fourth Factor of Awakening is ease *(prashrabdhih)*. Diligence is always accompanied by ease. In the so-called Third World, one often feels more ease than in the "overdeveloped" countries of the First World. Here, everyone is under enormous pressure, and people need stress-reduction programs. Their stress comes from constant thinking and worrying and from their lifestyles. We have to learn ways to bring our energy from our head down to our abdomen. At least once every fifteen minutes, we need to practice letting go.

When we are sick, we stay in bed and do nothing. Often we don't even eat or drink. All of our energy is directed toward healing. We need to practice resting even when we are not sick. Sitting meditation, walking meditation, and mindful eating are good opportunities for resting. When you feel agitated, if you are able to go to a park or a garden, it is an opportunity for rest. If you walk slowly and remember to take it easy, if you are able to sit and do nothing from time to time, you can rest deeply and enter a state of true ease.

---

[2] "The fruit of arhatship": the transformation of all afflictions.

The Fifth Factor of Awakening is joy *(priti)*. Joy goes with happiness (sukha), but there are differences. When you are thirsty and a glass of water is being served to you, that is joy. When you are actually able to drink the water, that is happiness. It is possible to develop joy in your mind, even when your body is not well. This will, in turn, help your body. Joy comes from touching things that are refreshing and beautiful, within and outside of ourselves. Usually we touch only what's wrong. If we can expand our vision and also see what is right, this wider picture always brings joy.

The Sixth Factor of Awakening is concentration (samadhi). *Sam-* means together, *a-* is bringing to a certain place, and *-dhi* is the energy of the mind. We collect the energy of our mind and direct it toward an object. With concentration, our mind is one-pointed and still, and quite naturally it stays focused on one object. To have mindfulness, we need concentration. Once mindfulness is developed, concentration, in turn, becomes stronger.

Concentration is not wholesome in itself. A thief needs concentration to break into a house. The object of our concentration is what makes it beneficial or not. If you use meditative concentration to run away from reality, that is not beneficial. Even before the time of the Buddha, many meditators practiced concentration to remove themselves from the world. Practicing this kind of concentration, the Buddha was not able to liberate himself from suffering. So he learned to use his concentration to shine light upon his suffering, and he was able to go deeply into life and develop understanding, compassion, and liberation.

The Seventh Factor of Awakening is equanimity, or letting go (upeksha). Equanimity is an aspect of true love.[3] It is far from indifference. Practicing equanimity, we love everyone equally.

---

[3] See chap. 22 on the Four Immeasurable Minds.

In the *Kakacupama Sutta (Example of the Saw),* the Buddha says, "Even if robbers cut your limbs off with a saw, if anger arises in you, you are not a follower of my teachings. To be a disciple of the Buddha, your heart must bear no hatred, you must utter no unkind words, you must remain compassionate, with no hostility or ill-will."[4] As a young monk, I memorized these words and even put them to music. This teaching touches our most noble intention, but it is the opposite of our strong habit energies. To transform these habit energies and realize our noblest intention, the Buddha and the Venerable Shariputra taught us: (1) to practice equanimity in the face of harsh words; (2) to learn not to feel annoyance, bitterness, or dejection; and (3) not to feel elated when praised, because we know that any praise is not for us as an individual, but for many beings, including our parents, teachers, friends, and all forms of life.

In the *Greater Discourse on the Example of the Elephant's Footprint,*[5] Shariputra shows the way to meditate on the Four Great Elements in order to practice equanimity. When we meditate on the elements of earth, water, fire, and air inside and outside our bodies, we see that we and they are the same. When we transcend our idea of a separate self, our love will contain equanimity, knowing that we and others are truly the same.

These Seven Factors are limbs of the same tree. If mindfulness is developed and maintained, the investigation of phenomena will meet with success. Joy and ease are wonderful feelings nourished by diligence. Concentration gives rise to understanding. When understanding is there, we go beyond comparing, discriminating, and reacting, and realize letting go. Those who arrive at letting go have the bud of a half-smile, which proves compassion as well as understanding.

---

[4] *Majjhima Nikaya* 21.

[5] *Majjhima Nikaya* 28.

The Seven Factors of Awakening, if practiced diligently, lead to true understanding and emancipation. The Buddha said that the Four Immeasurable Minds of love practiced with the Seven Factors of Awakening bring Complete, Perfect Enlightenment. The Seven Factors of Awakening are, therefore, the practice of love.

CHAPTER TWENTY-SEVEN

The Twelve Links of
Interdependent Co-Arising

The Twelve Links of Interdependent Co-Arising (*pratitya samutpada*, literally "in dependence, things rise up") is a deep and wonderful teaching, the foundation of all of Buddhist study and practice. Pratitya samutpada is sometimes called the teaching of cause and effect, but that can be misleading, because we usually think of cause and effect as separate entities, with cause always preceding effect, and one cause leading to one effect. According to the teaching of Interdependent Co-Arising, cause and effect co-arise *(samutpada)* and everything is a result of multiple causes and conditions. The egg is in the chicken, and the chicken is in the egg. Chicken and egg arise in mutual dependence. Neither is independent. Interdependent Co-Arising goes beyond our concepts of space and time. "The one contains the all."

The Chinese character for cause 因 has the character "great" inside of a rectangle. Cause is great, yet, at the same time, limited. The Buddha expressed Interdependent Co-Arising very simply: "This is, because that is. This is not, because that is not. This comes to be, because that comes to be. This ceases to be, because that ceases to be." These sentences occur hundreds of times in the discourses of both the Northern and Southern transmissions. They are the Buddhist genesis. I would like to add this sentence: "This is like this, because that is like that."

In the sutras, this image is given: "Three cut reeds can stand only by leaning on one another. If you take one away,

221

the other two will fall." For a table to exist, we need wood, a carpenter, time, skillfulness, and many other causes. And each of these causes needs other causes to be. The wood needs the forest, the sunshine, the rain, and so on. The carpenter needs his parents, breakfast, fresh air, and so on. And each of those things, in turn, has to be brought about by other conditions. If we continue to look in this way, we'll see that nothing has been left out. Everything in the cosmos has come together to bring us this table. Looking deeply at the sunshine, the leaves of the tree, and the clouds, we can see the table. The one can be seen in the all, and the all can be seen in the one. One cause is never enough to bring about an effect. A cause must, at the same time, be an effect, and every effect must also be the cause of something else. Cause and effect inter-are. The idea of a first or only cause, something that does not itself need a cause, cannot be applied.

After the Buddha passed away, many schools of Buddhism began to describe Interdependent Co-Arising more analytically. In the *Visuddhimagga (Path of Purification)* of the Theravada School, Buddhaghosa listed twenty-four kinds of "conditions" (Pali: *paccaya*), "the necessary and sufficient conditions for something to arise": (1) root-cause, (2) object, (3) predominance, (4) priority, (5) continuity, (6) co-nascence, (7) mutuality, (8) support, (9) decisive support, (10) pre-nascence, (11) post-nascence (a cause can be born after the effect), (12) repetition, (13) karma, (14) karma-result, (15) nutriment, (16) faculty, (17) dhyana, (18) path, (19) association, (20) dissociation, (21) presence, (22) absence, (23) disappearance, and (24) non-disappearance.

In the Sarvastivada School, four kinds of conditions *(pratyaya)* and six kinds of causes were taught, and this later became part of the teachings of the Vijñanavada School of Buddhist psychology. According to this analysis, all four kinds of conditions must be present for every thing that exists.

The first of the four kinds of conditions is the "cause condition," "seed condition," or "root condition" *(hetu-pratyaya)*, just as the seed is the cause condition of the flower. There are said to be six kinds of "cause conditions":

(1) Motivating or creative force *(karana-hetu)*. Each conditioned dharma is the "general cause" for all things except itself. It is a copresent cause, offering no obstacles, because no dharma constitutes an obstacle to the arising of dharmas prone to arising. This condition has the function of empowering and not restricting.

(2) Concurrent condition *(sahabhu-hetu)*. Sometimes two root conditions need to be present at the same time. If we draw a line "AB," A and B both have to be there. The same is true of lamp and lamplight. All pairs of opposites are like that; one cannot be present without the other. Above and below come into existence at the same time, as do the ideas "being" and "nonbeing." These coexistent dharmas mutually condition one another.

(3) Seed condition of the same kind *(sabhaga-hetu)*. Similars cause similars. Rice produces rice. Wholesome causes bring about wholesome effects. Faith and joy, for example, make a stable practice possible. And unwholesome causes bring about unwholesome effects.

(4) Associated condition *(samprayukta-hetu)*. A wholesome and an unwholesome seed support each other in giving rise to something. This is called "association" or "correspondence," and it applies only to mental events. Someone gives money to his church because he feels guilty about the wrong livelihood that has allowed him to make the money. The seed of guilt due to wrong livelihood is unwholesome. Giving is wholesome. The result is that the elders of the church tell him that they want him to transform his livelihood more than they want his money. This will hurt his pride, but can lead to much happiness in the future and can help alleviate his guilt.

THE HEART OF THE BUDDHA'S TEACHING

(5) Universal condition *(sarvatraga-hetu)*. The cause is present everywhere, in every part of our body as well as throughout the universe. The Six Elements of earth, water, fire, air, space, and consciousness are examples of universal conditions.

(6) Ripening condition *(vipaka-hetu)*. In our store consciousness, not everything ripens at the same time. When we bring home bananas, some ripen before the others. When we hear a Dharma talk, some of the seeds sown ripen right away, while others might take many years. A seed of one kind can also transform and ripen into something different. At first, an orange is a blossom, then it is something green and sour, and later it ripens into a sweet fruit. A seed of love can ripen as a seed of anger. When we begin our sitting meditation, we may feel confined and agitated. After a while, our meditation may ripen into something quite relaxing and enjoyable.

The second kind of condition, according to the Sarvastivadins, is called "condition for development" *(adhipati-pratyaya)*. This can help certain seeds develop or can obstruct their development. Everyone has a seed of faith, or confidence, for example. If you have friends who water this seed in you, it will grow strong. But if you meet only favorable conditions, you will not realize how precious this seed is. Obstacles along the path can help our determination and compassion grow. Obstacles teach us about our strengths and weaknesses, so that we can know ourselves better and see in which direction we truly wish to go. One could say that the Buddha's practice of austerity was unfavorable to the development of his path, but if he had not undertaken those practices and failed in them, he would not have learned and later taught the Middle Way. When your intention is strong, unfavorable conditions will not dishearten you. In difficult moments, you will stick to your friends, fortify your convictions, and not give up.

The third kind of condition is the "condition of continuity" *(samanantara-pratyaya)*. For something to exist there needs to be a continuous succession, moment after moment. For our practice to develop we need to practice every day — walking meditation, listening to Dharma teachings, practicing mindfulness of the four foundations in all our activities, staying with the same Sangha, and practicing the same teachings. If we put a frog on a plate, it will jump right off. If you do not practice steadily, you'll be like a frog on a plate. But when you decide to stay in one place until your practice fully develops, we can say that you have reached the state of "froglessness" and have begun to practice "continuity."

The fourth kind of condition is "object as condition" *(alambana-pratyaya)*. If there is no object, there cannot be a subject. For us to have confidence, there has to be an object of our confidence. When we feel despair, we feel despair about something — our idea of the future, our idea of happiness, or our idea of life. When we are angry, we have to be angry at someone or something. According to the Buddha, all phenomena are objects of mind. When we perceive the image or sign of any phenomenon, we know that the object of our perception resides within our own consciousness.

~

Can we live in a way that helps us see the causes that are present in the effects and the effects that are present in the causes? When we see this way, we begin to have insight into Interdependent Co-Arising, and this is Right View. In early Buddhism, we speak of Interdependent Co-Arising. In later Buddhism, we use the words interbeing and interpenetration. The terminology is different, but the meaning is the same.

After hearing the Buddha teach about Interdependent Co-Arising, Ananda said, "Venerable Lord, the teaching of Interdependent Co-Arising appears to be deep and subtle, but I find it quite simple." The Buddha replied, "Do not say that, Ananda. The teaching of Interdependent Co-Arising is indeed deep and subtle. Anyone who is able to see the nature of Interdependent Co-Arising is able to see the Buddha."[1] Once you can see into the nature of Interdependent Co-Arising, you will be guided by your insight and you will not lose your practice.

The teaching of impermanence is implicit in the teaching of Interdependent Co-Arising. How could we live if we were not nourished by multiple causes and conditions? The conditions that make it possible for us to exist and to change come from what is not us. When we understand impermanence and nonself, we understand Interdependent Co-Arising.

In this gatha, Nagarjuna links Interdependent Co-Arising with emptiness:

> *All phenomena that arise interdependently,*
> *I say that they are empty.*
> *Words come to an end, because their message is false.*
> *Words come to an end, because there is a Middle Way.*[2]

All teachings of Buddhism are based on Interdependent Co-Arising. If a teaching is not in accord with Interdependent Co-Arising, it is not a teaching of the Buddha. When you have grasped Interdependent Co-Arising, you bring that insight to shine on the three baskets *(tripitaka)* of the teachings.[3] Interdependent Co-Arising allows you to see the Buddha, and the Two Truths[4] allow you to hear the Buddha. When you are able to see and hear the Buddha, you will not lose your way as you traverse the ocean of his teachings.

The Buddha said that there are twelve links *(nidanas)* in

---

[1] *Mahanidana Sutta, Digha Nikaya* 15.

[2] *Mahaprajñaparamita Shastra.*

[3] The three baskets are Sutras (teachings of the Buddha), Vinaya (rules of conduct), and Abhidharma (systematized presentations of the teachings).

[4] See chap. 17.

the "chain" of Interdependent Co-Arising.[5] The first is ignorance (avidya). *Vidya* means seeing, understanding, or light.
Avidya means the lack of light, the lack of understanding, or
blindness. Although ignorance is usually listed as the first
link, it does not mean that ignorance is a first cause. It is also
possible to begin the list with old age and death.

The second link is volitional action (samskara), also translated as formations, impulses, motivating energy, karma formations, or the will to cling to being. When we have a lack of
understanding, anger, irritation, or hatred can arise.

The third link is consciousness (vijñana). Consciousness
here means the whole of consciousness — individual and collective, mind consciousness and store consciousness, subject
and object. And consciousness here is filled with unwholesome and erroneous tendencies connected with ignorance
that are of the nature to bring about suffering.

The fourth link is mind/body, or name and form (nama
rupa). "Name" (nama) means the mental element and
"form" (rupa) means the physical element of our being.
Both mind and body are objects of our consciousness. When
we look at our hand, it is an object of our consciousness.
When we touch our anger, sadness, or happiness, these are
also objects of our consciousness.

The fifth link is the six *ayatanas,* which are the six sense
organs (eyes, ears, nose, tongue, body, and mind) accompanied by their objects (forms, sounds, smells, tastes, tactile objects, and objects of mind). These six ayatanas do not exist
separately from mind/body (the fourth link), but are listed
separately to help us see them more clearly. When a sense
organ comes into contact (the sixth link) with a sense object,
there has to be sense consciousness (which lies within the

---

[5] The earliest discourse in which the Buddha talked about a chain of
causes was the *Mahanidana Sutta, Digha Nikaya* 15, although in that discourse, only nine links are given. In later teachings, the list was expanded
to twelve.

The Wheel of Life

Figure Six

third link). We are beginning to see how the Twelve Links inter-are, how each link contains all the other links.

The sixth link is the contact (sparsha) between sense organ, sense object, and sense consciousness. When eyes and form, ears and sound, nose and smell, tongue and taste, body and touch, and mind and object of mind come into contact, sense consciousness is born. Contact is a basis for feelings. It is a universal mental formation, present in every mental formation.

The seventh link is feelings (vedana), which can be pleasant, unpleasant, neutral, or mixed. When a feeling is pleasant, we may become attached (the ninth link).

The eighth link is craving *(trishna)*, or desire. Craving is followed by grasping.

The ninth link is grasping, or attachment *(upadana)*. It means we are caught in the thralls of the object.

The tenth link is "coming to be" *(bhava)*, being, or becoming. Because we desire something, it comes to be. We have to look deeply to know what we really want.

The eleventh link is birth *(jati)*.

The twelfth link is old age (or decay) and death *(jaramarana)*.

Ignorance conditions volitional actions. Volitional actions condition consciousness. Consciousness conditions mind/body. And so on. As soon as ignorance is present, all the other links — volitional actions, consciousness, mind/body, and so on — are *already* there. Each link contains all the other links. Because there is ignorance, there are volitional actions. Because there are volitional actions, there is consciousness. Because there is consciousness, there is mind/body. And so on.

In the Five Aggregates, there is nothing that we can call a self. Ignorance is the inability to see this truth. Consciousness, mind/body, the six senses and their objects, contact, and feeling are the effect of ignorance and volitional actions.

Because of craving, grasping, and coming to be, there will be birth and death, which means the continuation of this wheel, or chain, again and again.

When artists illustrate the Twelve Links of Interdependent Co-Arising, they often draw a blind woman to represent ignorance; a man gathering fruit in the jungle or a potter at work to illustrate volitional actions; a restless monkey grasping this and that for consciousness; a boat to represent mind/body; a house with many windows for the six senses and their objects; a man and a woman close to each other to represent contact; a man pierced by an arrow for feeling; a man drinking wine for craving or thirst; a man and a woman in sexual union or a man picking fruit from a tree to represent attachment or grasping; a pregnant woman for coming to be; a woman giving birth for birth; and an old woman leaning on a stick or a man carrying a corpse on his back or his shoulder for old age and death.

Another way that artists sometimes depict the Twelve Links is to draw an embryo in the womb for consciousness; the child just before birth for mind/body; the child from one to two years old, when his or her life is dominated by touching, for the six senses and their objects; the same child from three to five years old for contact; and an adult for desire or attachment.

There do not have to be exactly twelve links. In the *Abhidharma* texts[6] of the Sarvastivada School, it says that you

---

[6] There is a collection ("basket") of Buddhist teachings called *Abhidharma* ("super Dharma"). These are extended explanations of the teachings the Buddha gave. At first, in order to lend credence to their work, the authors of the *Abhidharma* tried to make these writings look like discourses of the Buddha. In the second stage, these writings were accepted as independent and given the name *Abhidharma*. During the third stage, as *Abhidharma* developed, it became more and more analytical. This fine and detailed analysis is often dry and difficult to understand. Sometimes it is analysis just for the sake of analysis, rather than guidance for the practice to help us transform our suffering. The fourth and final stage of *Abhidharma* was to shorten and simplify the long, detailed analyses so that they became easier to understand.

can teach one, two, three, four, or five, up to twelve links. The one link belongs to the unconditioned realm (asam-skrita). The two links are cause and effect. The three links are past, present, and future. The four links are ignorance, volitional actions, birth, and old age and death. The five links are craving, grasping, coming to be, birth, and old age and death. The six links are past cause, present cause, future cause, past result, present result, and future result. Because ignorance and volitional actions exist in consciousness, and the six ayatanas exist in name and form, in the *Mahanidana Sutta* the Buddha lists only nine links. At other times Buddha taught ten links, omitting ignorance and volitional actions.

Sometimes when the Buddha taught Interdependent Co-Arising, he began with old age and death and the suffering that accompanies them. In the sutras that do not include ignorance and volitional actions as links, the Buddha ends by saying that mind/body is conditioned by consciousness, and consciousness is conditioned by mind/body. The Buddha never wanted us to understand the Twelve Links in a linear way — that there is a line going from ignorance to old age and death or that there are exactly and only twelve links. Not only does ignorance give rise to volitional actions, but volitional actions also give rise to ignorance. Each link in the chain of Interdependent Co-Arising is both a cause and an effect of all the other links in the chain. The Twelve Links inter-are.

In the tendency to see the teachings of the Buddha as an explanation of how things are rather than as a support and guide to the practice, the Twelve Links have been misunderstood in many ways. One way has been to see them as a way to explain why there is birth and death. The Buddha usually began the Twelve Links with old age and death to help us get in touch with suffering and find its roots. This is closely linked to the teachings and practice of the Four Noble Truths. It was after the lifetime of the Buddha that teachers more often than not began with ignorance, to help prove why there is birth and death. Ignorance became a kind of first cause, even though the Buddha always taught that no first cause can be found. If ignorance exists, it is because there are causes that give rise to and deepen ignorance. The Buddha was not a philosopher trying to explain the universe. He was a spiritual guide who wanted to help us put an end to our suffering.

Two other theories based on the Twelve Links evolved after the lifetime of the Buddha. One was called the Three Times and the other the Two Levels of Cause and Effect. According to these theories, ignorance and volitional actions belong to the past; birth and old age and death belong to the future; and all the other links from consciousness to coming to be belong to the present. It is true that ignorance and volitional actions existed before we were born, but they also exist in the present. They are contained within all the other links, which include the so-called links of the present and future.

Regarding the Two Levels of Cause and Effect, at the first level, ignorance and volitional actions are said to be causes, and consciousness, mind/body, the six ayatanas, and contact are said to be effects. At the second level, feelings, craving, grasping, and coming to be in this life lead to birth and old age and death in a future life. Theories like these are not entirely inaccurate, but we have to be able to go beyond them. All commentaries and theories contain some misunderstanding, but we can still feel gratitude to these commentators and theorists for taking the teachings in a new direction to help people transform, while basically conforming to teachings of the Buddha.

When we hear from commentators that some links are causes (namely ignorance and volitional actions), and others are effects (namely birth and old age and death), we know

The Three Times and Two Levels of Cause and Effect

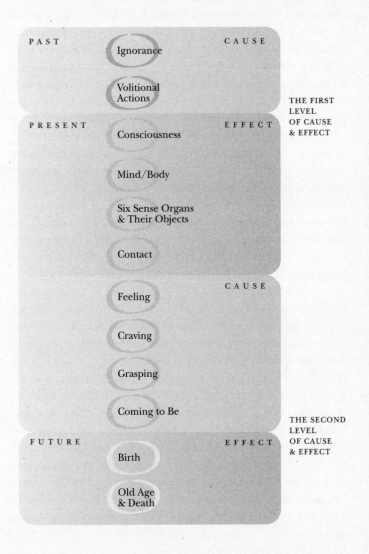

Figure Seven

233

that this is not consistent with the Buddha's teaching that everything is both a cause and an effect. To think that ignorance gives rise to volitional actions, which later give rise to consciousness, which then gives rise to mind/body would be a dangerous oversimplification. When the Buddha said, "Ignorance conditions volitional actions," he meant that there is a relationship of cause and effect between ignorance and volitional actions. Ignorance nourishes volitional actions, but volitional actions also nourish ignorance. Ignorance activates consciousness by producing feelings of discomfort, craving, boredom, intention, and aspiration, so these feelings are called volitional actions. Once these feelings are active in consciousness, they make ignorance stronger. The tree gives rise to and nourishes its leaves, but the leaves also nourish the tree. Leaves are not just the children of the tree. They are also the mother of the tree. Because of the leaves, the tree is able to grow. Every leaf is a factory synthesizing sunshine to nourish the tree.

The interbeing of leaf and tree is parallel to the interbeing of the Twelve Links of Interdependent Co-Arising. We say that ignorance conditions volitional actions, but ignorance also conditions consciousness, both through volitional actions and directly. Ignorance conditions mind/body as well. If there were no ignorance in mind/body, mind/body would be different. Our six organs and the six objects of these organs also contain ignorance. My perception of the flower is based on my eyes and on the form of the flower. As soon as my perception becomes caught in the sign "flower," ignorance is there. Therefore, ignorance is present in contact, and it is also present in feelings, craving, grasping, coming to be, birth, and old age and death. Ignorance is not just in the past. It is present now, in each of our cells and each of our mental formations. If there were no ignorance, we would not become attached to things. If there were no ignorance, we would not grasp the objects of our attachment. If there were

The Interbeing of the Twelve Links

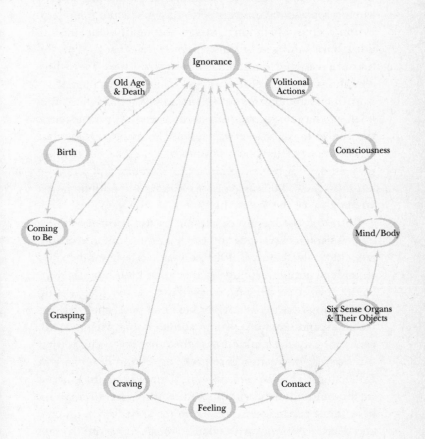

Ignorance conditions and is conditioned by the other eleven links.
This web would be too difficult to discern
if arrows were drawn from each link to all of the other links,
but those lines should be envisioned here.

Figure Eight

no ignorance, the suffering that is manifesting right now would not be there. Our practice is to identify ignorance when it is present. Grasping is in volitional actions, feelings, coming to be, birth, and old age and death. Our infatuations, our running away from this or toward that, and our intentions can be seen in all the other links. Every link conditions every other link and is conditioned by them.

With this understanding, we can abandon the idea of a sequential chain of causation and enter deeply the practice of the Twelve Links of Interdependent Co-Arising. Although it says in the sutra that consciousness brings about mind/body, that mind/body brings about the six ayatanas, and so on, we must understand this as a way of speaking and nothing more. We have to see the Twelve Links in a broad, open way.

Consider, for example, craving as the fruit of feeling. Sometimes a feeling does not lead to craving, but to aversion. Sometimes the feeling is not accompanied by ignorance, but by understanding, lucidity, or loving kindness, and the outcome will not be craving or aversion. To say that feeling brings about craving is not precise enough. Feeling with attachment and ignorance brings about craving. We must link each of the Twelve Links with all the other links. This is what the *Heart Sutra* means when it tells us, "No Interdependent Co-Arising." The Twelve Links are "empty," because each of them would not exist without all the others. Feeling cannot be without craving, grasping, coming to be, birth, old age and death, ignorance, volitional actions, and so on. In each of the Twelve Links, we see the presence of the other eleven. Feeling can lead to craving, non-craving, or equanimity.

Ignorance is avidya, the lack of light. Vidya is understanding or wisdom. The presence of light means the absence of darkness. The presence of day means the absence of night. The presence of ignorance means the absence of understanding. The Buddha said, "When ignorance comes to an end, understanding arises."[7] Ignorance leads to volitional actions, the will to live. When you are angry, you want to do something. But does understanding lead to the will to die? No, it leads to the will to live, also. In understanding there is loving kindness and compassion, and when you are compassionate, loving, and understanding, you want to do something to help alleviate the suffering. Anger, hatred, and ignorance are forms of energy. Understanding and compassion are also forms of energy.

On one side, there are actions for grasping things or satisfying our desires. On the other side is the volition to be present in order to help alleviate suffering. That is the intention of Buddhas, bodhisattvas, and all people of goodwill. They have love, understanding, and therefore the willingness to be present amidst the suffering in order to bring relief, comfort, and joy. The expression "volitional action," or "will to live" has to be understood in these two ways: (1) to live in order to experience pleasure for oneself alone or to oppress others, or (2) to be present in order to help. Social workers do not go into slum areas because they want power or riches. They go because they want to serve, to fulfill their need of loving. That is also a volitional action.

When the Buddha looks at a flower, he knows that the flower is his own consciousness. There is nothing wrong in having consciousness. It is only when we water unwholesome seeds — ignorance, hatred, jealousy, anxiety — that consciousness causes suffering to ourselves and others. Consciousness is the base for distinguishing, planning, helping, and doing good work. That kind of consciousness is present in the Buddha and the bodhisattvas. The Buddha said, "How lovely is the city of Vaishali." He said, "Ananda, don't you think that the rice fields are lovely? Shall we go into town and

---

[7] *Samyutta Nikaya* IV, 49 and 50.

share the Dharma?" These statements are based on lucid consciousness, consciousness full of understanding, care, and love.

We have to water the seeds of our own lucid consciousness. There is ignorance in us, but there is also wisdom. The seed of awakening is also present in each link. In compost there are flowers; and in flowers there is compost. If we know how to make compost, it will quickly become flowers. If we know how to look after flowers, they will last longer. Don't think there is only ignorance in the Twelve Links. There is also the seed of awakened wisdom. If you throw away the Twelve Links, you will not have the means to arrive at peace and joy. Don't throw away your ignorance, volitional actions, or consciousness. Transform them into understanding and other wonderful attributes.

As you can see, there is also a positive side to the Twelve Links, although Buddhist teachers since the time of the Buddha seem to have overlooked this. We need to find words to describe the Interdependent Co-Arising of positive states of mind and body, and not just of negative states. The Buddha taught that when ignorance ends, there is clear understanding. He didn't say that when ignorance ends, there is nothing. What does clear understanding condition? Clarity, the absence of ignorance, gives rise to the desire to act with love and compassion. This is called the Great Aspiration (mahapranidhana) or mind of awakening (bodhichitta) in Mahayana Buddhism. When you practice the Four Noble Truths, you see that you can liberate yourself and other beings, and you stop running away from and destroying yourself. The positive side of volitional actions is the motivating energy called the Great Aspiration that propels us toward the beautiful and the wholesome, rather than toward the hell realms.

Just as volitional actions condition consciousness, the Great Aspiration conditions wisdom. When our ignorance has been transformed, what we have been calling conscious-ness becomes wisdom. Consciousness is described in the Vijñanavada schema in terms of eight consciousnesses, and these are transformed into Four Wisdoms. When the seeds of awakening, love, and compassion in our store consciousness have been developed and matured, our store consciousness (alayavijñana) is transformed and becomes the Great Mirror Wisdom that reflects the reality of the cosmos. All the seeds that can become the Great Mirror Wisdom are already present in our store consciousness. We only have to water them. Great Mirror Wisdom is the outcome of the vow to save beings as our volitional action.

When we invoke the name of Avalokiteshvara, this is the willingness and capacity of being there, listening, responding to suffering, and helping beings. When we invoke the name of Samantabhadra, that is the willingness and capacity of act-ing mindfully and joyfully to serve others. When we invoke the name of Manjushri, that is the willingness and capacity of looking deeply, understanding, and being the eyes of the world. With this kind of will, guided by clear understanding, our consciousness becomes an instrument of engagement in the world. The presence of a Buddha is an example of this kind of volitional action, an offering of consciousness of what is going on, the willingness to help, and knowing what to do and how to do it in order to alleviate the suffering in the world. That consciousness manifests in mind/body, just as it does for everyone else. But the quality of the Buddha's mind/body is different from ours, and we can see and feel that.

We have to learn the ways to use our consciousness as a tool of transformation. Our six sense organs — eyes, ears, nose, tongue, body, and mind — can contribute toward the arising of Great Mirror Wisdom. We see that the Buddha also has six senses that enter into contact with six sense objects, but he knows how to guard his senses so that more internal knots will not be tied. The Buddha uses his six senses skillfully and realizes wonderful things. The first five consciousnesses become the Wisdom of Wonderful Realization. We can use these five consciousnesses to serve others. Mind consciousness, upon emancipation, becomes the Wonderful Observation Wisdom, wisdom that can see things as they are.

When the six senses and their objects make contact, this contact gives rise to a pleasant, unpleasant, or neutral feeling. When a bodhisattva sees a child suffering, she knows how it feels to suffer, and she also has an unpleasant feeling. But because of that suffering, concern and compassion arise in her and she is determined to act. Bodhisattvas suffer like the rest of us, but in a bodhisattva, feelings do not give rise to craving or aversion. They give rise to concern, the desire and the willingness to stay in the midst of suffering and confusion, and to act.

When a bodhisattva sees a beautiful flower, she recognizes that the flower is beautiful. But she also sees the nature of impermanence in the flower. That is why there is no attachment. She has a pleasant feeling, but it does not create an internal formation. Emancipation does not mean that she suppresses all feelings. When she comes into contact with hot water, she knows it is hot. Feelings are normal. In fact, these feelings help her dwell in happiness, not the kind of happiness that is subject to sorrow and anxiety, but the kind of happiness that nourishes. When you practice breathing, smiling, being touched by the air and the water, that kind of happiness does not create suffering in you. It helps you be strong and sane, able to go further on your way toward realization. Buddhas, bodhisattvas, and many others have the capacity of enjoying a pleasant feeling, the kind of feeling that is healing and rejuvenating without becoming attached. The feeling that we have when we see people oppressed or starving can give rise in us to concern, compassion, and the willingness to act with equanimity, not with attachment.

The Wisdom of Equality comes from the seventh consciousness, manas. Manas is the number one discriminator. It says, "This is me. This is mine. This is not mine." That is manas's specialty. We have to keep this consciousness, so that it can become the Wisdom of Equality. Our consciousness has to be transformed and not thrown away. It is the same with the Five Aggregates. We don't say, "The Five Aggregates are suffering," and throw them away. If we do, there will be nothing left — no nirvana, no peace, and no joy. We need an intelligent policy for taking care of our garbage.

Wonderful Observation Wisdom transforms manas into the Wisdom of Equality. We are one. We are equal. I may think that you are my enemy, but while touching the ultimate dimension, I see that you and I are one. Sometimes we only need to touch the Earth once, and the Wisdom of Equality appears right in the heart of our manas consciousness. Wonderful Observation Wisdom takes the place of the sixth consciousness, mind consciousness. Before the disappearance of ignorance, the sixth consciousness gives rise to many wrong perceptions, like seeing a rope as a snake, and a lot of suffering. Thanks to "transformation at the base" — the store-consciousness becoming Great Mirror Wisdom — the sixth consciousness can be transformed into Wonderful Observation Wisdom.

The fourth wisdom, Great Mirror Wisdom, brings about miracles. In the past, our eye consciousness made us infatuated or put us in the dark. Now, with our eyes open, we can see the Dharmakaya, the teaching body of the Buddha. When our mind is clear like a calm river, the sixth consciousness is Wonderful Observation Wisdom and our store consciousness is Great Mirror Wisdom.

Clear understanding conditions the Great Aspiration and wisdom. If consciousness conditions mind/body, what does wisdom condition? We have body and mind, bodhisattvas have body and mind, and the Buddha has a body and a mind. We should not throw away our body and mind in order to experience liberation. We use the term Nirmanakaya (transformation body) to describe the bright side of mind/ body. In this body and mind, there is no longer ignorance, volitional actions, or wrong consciousness. The function of this body and mind is to awaken and liberate living beings. Love and compassion can manifest in hundreds of thousands of different forms. Avalokiteshvara can appear as a child, a politician, or as a beautiful woman with a voice as clear as the song of the *kalavinka* bird, the Indian cuckoo. A bodhisattva can be beautiful or ugly, poor or rich, healthy or sick. Any mind/body that has the function to bring about love, understanding, and happiness is the transformation body of the Buddha.

If mind/body conditions consciousness on one side and the six ayatanas on the other, and the transformation body conditions wisdom on one side, what does it condition on the other? We can say that it conditions the result body (Sambhogakaya), which is the fruit of deep practice that is said to be marked by thirty-two signs. Every body is a collection of the Five Aggregates and has mental and physiological components (name and form). In the case of the Sambhogakaya, the physiology and the psychology contain clarity, bodhichitta, and the Four Wisdoms as means for teaching the path, and do not contain ignorance.

Even within a Buddha's mind/body, there is contact. The Buddha drinks water and wears warm clothes. If he is not protected from the cold, he will become ill. When the six sense organs of the Buddha are in contact with the six sense objects, the Buddha has feeling, but that feeling does not lead to grasping and attachment. Contact in a Buddha (Sambhogakaya) is purified and mindful, and feelings are the same. The Sambhogakaya is wholly protected, because he practices guarding his six sense organs and their objects. We can also practice shining the light of mindfulness on the contacts that take place between our sense organs and sense objects. If we do not guard these contacts, even if we sit in a meditation hall for twelve hours a day, we are not practicing. When we walk, talk, eat, or whatever we do, if we guard our senses, the contacts that take place between our sense organs and sense objects will be clear and calm.

As far as the positive side of the Twelve Links is concerned, contact becomes mindfulness of contact, and feeling becomes mindfulness of feeling. Every contact of the senses and every feeling has clarity and calmness. When feelings and contact are protected, they lead not to craving but to love, compassion, joy, and equanimity — the Four Immeasurable Minds.[8] With mindfulness, we see feelings as painful, pleasant, or neutral. When we see people suffering or in pain or when we see them enjoying themselves in a foolish way, a feeling in us gives rise to the energy of loving kindness — the desire and the capacity to offer real joy, and this leads to the energy of compassion — the desire and the capacity to help living beings put an end to their suffering. This energy gives rise to joy in us, and we are able to share our joy with others. It also gives rise to equanimity — not taking sides or getting carried away by the images and sounds brought to us through contact and feelings. Equanimity does not mean indifference. We see the ones we love and the ones we hate equally, and try our best to make both of them happy. We accept the flowers and the garbage with neither attachment nor aversion. We treat both with respect. Equanimity means to let go, not to abandon. Abandoning causes suffering. When we are not attached, we are able to let go.

The Four Immeasurable Minds are the basis for freedom. When we are in touch with things by means of the mind of love, we do not run away or seek, and that is the basis of freedom. Aimlessness takes the place of grasping. When we have

---

[8] See chap. 22.

freedom, what seemed to be suffering becomes Wondrous Being. It can also be called the Kingdom of God or the Pure Land. Someone who is free has the ability to establish a Pure Land, a place where people do not need to run. Wondrous Being is beyond being and nonbeing. If a bodhisattva needs to manifest being, if he needs to be born in this world, he will be born in this world. There is still life, but he is not caught in ideas of being, nonbeing, birth, or death.

Wondrous Being is the equivalent to the "coming to be" of the conventional Twelve Links. Wondrous Being is the basis for being born without getting caught in wrong ideas about birth and death. The leaf has the appearance of being born and dying, but it is not caught in either. The leaf falls to the earth without any idea of dying, and is born again by decomposing at the foot of the tree and nourishing the tree. The cloud has the appearance of dying in becoming rain, but it feels no sorrow or pain. There are people who suffer when they see a leaf die. In the age of Romanticism, there were young people who picked up fallen flower petals, buried them, wept, and wrote epitaphs. When a leaf is born, we can sing Happy Continuation. When a leaf falls, we can sing Happy Continuation. When we have awakened understanding, birth is a continuation and death is a continuation, birth is an appearance and death is an appearance. People also appear to be born, grow old, and die.

We study the Twelve Links of Interdependent Co-Arising in order to diminish the element of ignorance in us and to increase the element of clarity. When our ignorance is diminished, craving, hatred, pride, doubt, and views are also diminished; and love compassion, joy, and equanimity are increased. This happens in all twelve nidanas. After clarity, there is bodhichitta, the Great Aspiration. The key is the guarding of the six senses and mindfulness of feelings and contact. This is the place we can enter into the cycle and begin to transform it.

In his first Dharma talk, the Buddha cautioned his disciples not to be attached to either bhava or abhava, being or nonbeing, because bhava and abhava are just constructs of the mind. Reality is somewhere in between. When we present the Twelve Links in the usual way, if we say there is no attachment, it means there will be no being, that we are aspiring to abhava. But this is exactly what the Buddha did not want. If you say that the purpose of the practice is to destroy being in order to arrive at nonbeing, this is entirely incorrect. With nonattachment, we see both being and nonbeing as creations of our mind, and we ride the wave of birth and death. We don't mind birth. We don't mind death. If we have to be born again to continue the work of helping, that is okay. We know that nothing is born and nothing can die. We have the wisdom of no-birth and no-death. We know that there is birth, old age, and death, but we also know that these are only waves on which bodhisattvas ride. Birth is okay and death is okay, if we know that they are only concepts in our mind. Reality transcends both birth and death.

In the eleventh century in Vietnam, a monk asked his meditation master, "Where is the place beyond birth and death?" The master replied, "In the midst of birth and death." If you abandon birth and death in order to find nirvana, you will not find nirvana. Nirvana is in birth and death. Nirvana is birth and death. It depends on how you look at it. From one point of view, it is birth and death. From another, it is nirvana.

Let us not present the teaching of the Buddha as an attempt to escape from life and go to nothingness or nonbeing. Bodhisattvas vow to come back again and again to serve, not because of craving but because of their concern and willingness to help. The practice of mindful living develops the same kind of wisdom, concern, and loving kindness in us, so we can serve. It is time for us to present the teaching of Interdependent Co-Arising in a way that is easy and ap-

Twelve Links: The Two Aspects of Interdependent Co-Arising

	WHEN CONDITIONED BY DELUDED MIND	WHEN CONDITIONED BY TRUE MIND
(1)	Ignorance *(avidya)*	Clear Understanding *(vidya)*
(2)	Volitional Actions *(samskara)*	Great Aspiration *(mahapranidhana)*
(3)	Consciousness *(vijñana)*: *First Five Consciousnesses* *Manovijñana* *Manas* *Alayavijñana*	Four Wisdoms: *Wisdom of Wonderful Realization* *Wonderful Observation Wisdom* *Wisdom of Equality* *Great Mirror Wisdom*
(4)	Mind/Body *(nama rupa)* *(Nirmanakaya)*	Transformation Body
(5)	Six Sense Organs & Their Objects *(ayatanas)*	Result Body *(Sambhogakaya)*
(6)	Contact *(sparsha)*	Mindfulness of Contact
(7)	Feeling *(vedana)*	Mindfulness of Feeling
(8)	Craving *(trishna)*	Four Immeasurable Minds *(Brahmaviharas)*
(9)	Grasping *(upadana)*	Freedom *(apranihita)*
(10)	Coming to Be *(bhava)*	Wondrous Being
(11)	Birth *(jati)*	Wisdom of No-Birth
(12)	Old Age and Death *(jaramarana)*	Wisdom of No-Death

Figure Nine

Twelve Links: The Two Aspects of Interdependent Co-Arising

WHEN CONDITIONED BY:

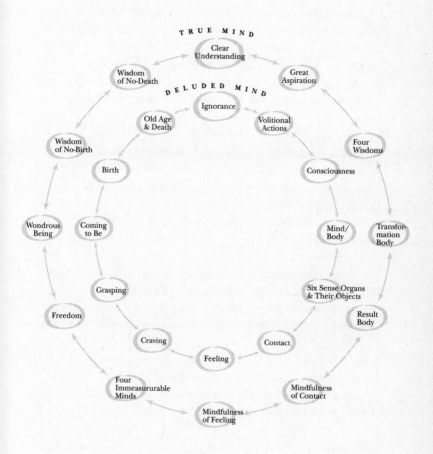

Figure Ten

THE HEART OF THE BUDDHA'S TEACHING

proachable for the people of our time. Those who teach the Twelve Links need to understand their positive side, also. When we are motivated by our mind of love, all Twelve Links become brighter.

There is co-arising conditioned by deluded mind and co-arising conditioned by true mind. The world, society, and the individual have been formed by a cycle of conditions based on deluded mind. Naturally, in a world based on deluded mind, there is suffering and affliction. But when conditions are based on true mind, they reflect the wondrous nature of reality. Everything depends on our mind. Imagine one thousand people whose minds are full of misperceptions, wrong views, envy, jealousy, and anger. If they come together, they will create a hell on Earth. The surroundings they live in, their daily lives, and their relationships will all be hellish. If two people full of misunderstanding live together, they create a hell realm for each other. How much greater the hell of one thousand people!

To make hell into paradise, we only need to change the mind on which it is based. To change the minds of one thousand people, it may be necessary to bring in some element from the outside, like a Dharma teacher or a group of people practicing the Dharma. Imagine one thousand people who do not have wrong perceptions, anger, or jealousy, but who have love, understanding, and happiness. If these people come together and form a community, it will be paradise. The mind of the people is the basis of paradise. With your deluded mind, you make hell for yourself. With your true mind, you make paradise. If two people come together with true mind, they make a small paradise for themselves. If a third person wants to join them, they should be careful. "Should we let him join us or not?" If their paradise is solid, they can allow him to join. With two true minds, there is hope that one deluded mind can be gradually transformed.

Later, there will be three true minds, and this small paradise will continue to grow.

Many volumes have been written about the Twelve Links of Interdependent Co-Arising based on deluded mind. We have to open a new door and teach the practice of the Twelve Links based on true mind in order to bring about a world of peace and joy.

CHAPTER TWENTY-EIGHT

Touching the Buddha Within

In 1968, I was in India with Samdech Maha Ghosananda, a leader of Cambodian Buddhism, and Sister Chân Không, my dear student, friend, and colleague. For several days we sat together on Vulture Peak until sunset, and I realized that in former times the Buddha had looked at the same setting sun with the same eyes. Afterwards, we walked down the mountain slowly and mindfully, not saying a word, and since that day, I have continued to walk in the same way.

Vulture Peak is beautiful, and Europe, Asia, Africa, Australia, North and South America are also beautiful. When there is mist on the mountains, it is beautiful, and when there is no mist, it is also beautiful. All four seasons are beautiful. You are beautiful, and your friends are beautiful. There is nothing to stop you from being in touch with life in the present moment. The question is, Do you have eyes that can see the sunset, feet that can touch the earth? If the Buddha were to transmit his eyes to you, would you know how to use them? Don't think that happiness will be possible only when conditions around you become perfect. Happiness lies in your own heart. You only need to practice mindful breathing for a few seconds and you'll be happy right away. Confucius said, "What greater joy can there be than putting into practice what you have learned?"

Sometimes we feel as though we are drowning in the ocean of suffering, carrying the burden of all social injustice of all times. The Buddha said, "When a wise person suffers, she asks herself, 'What can I do to be free from this suffering? Who can help me? What have I done to free myself from this suffering?' But when a foolish person suffers, she asks herself, 'Who has wronged me? How can I show others that I am the victim of wrongdoing? How can I punish those who have caused my suffering?'" Why is it that others who have been exposed to the same conditions do not seem to suffer as much as we do? You might like to write down the first set of questions and read them every time you are caught in your suffering.

Of course, you have the right to suffer, but as a practitioner, you do not have the right not to practice. We all need to be understood and loved, but the practice is not merely to expect understanding and love. It is to practice understanding and love. Please don't complain when no one seems to love or understand you. Make the effort to understand and love them better. If someone has betrayed you, ask why. If you feel that the responsibility lies entirely with them, look more deeply. Perhaps you have watered the seed of betrayal in her. Perhaps you have lived in a way that has encouraged her to withdraw. We are all co-responsible, and if you hold onto the attitude of blame, the situation will only get worse. If you can learn how to water the seed of loyalty in her, that seed may flower again. Look deeply into the nature of your suffering so you will know what to do and what not to do to restore the relationship. Apply your mindfulness, concentration, and insight, and you will know what nourishes you and what nourishes her. Practice the First Noble Truth, identifying your suffering; the Second Noble Truth, seeing its sources; and the Third and Fourth Noble Truths, finding ways to transform your suffering and realize peace. The Four Noble Truths and the Noble Eightfold Path are not theories. They are ways of action.

We begin the practice by seeking meaning for our life. We know that we don't want to run after fame, money, or sensual pleasure, and so we learn the art of mindful living. In time, we develop some understanding and compassion, and we find that these are the energies we can use to alleviate our suffering and the suffering of others. This already gives some meaning to our life.

We continue the practice, looking deeply into the Five Aggregates that comprise the self,[1] and we touch the reality of no-birth and no-death that is in us and in everything. This touching brings us the greatest relief. It removes all of our fears, offers us true freedom, and gives real meaning to our life.

We need places where we can go to sit, breathe quietly, and look and listen deeply. When we have difficulties at home, we need a room like that where we can take refuge. We also need parks and other peaceful places where we can practice walking meditation alone and with others. Educators, architects, artists, legislators, businessmen — all of us have to come together to create spaces where we can practice peace, harmony, joy, and deep looking.

There is so much violence in our schools. Parents, teachers, and students need to work together to transform the violence. Schools are not just places for transmitting technical know-how. They must also be places where children can learn to be happy, loving, and understanding, where teachers nourish their students with their own insights and happiness. We also need places in hospitals where family members, health care workers, patients, and others can sit, breathe, and calm themselves. We need City Halls where responsible people can look deeply into local problems. We need Congress to be a place where our real problems are truly addressed. If you are an educator, a parent, a teacher, an architect, a health care worker, a politician, or a writer, please

---

[1] See chap. 23.

help us create the kinds of institutions we need for our collective awakening.

Our legislators need to know how to calm themselves and communicate well. They need to know how to listen and look deeply and to use loving speech. If we elect unhappy people who don't have the capacity to make their own families happy, how can we expect them to make our city or our nation happy? Don't vote for someone just because he or she is handsome or has a lovely voice. We are entrusting the fate of our city, our nation, and our lives to such people. We have to act responsibly. We need to create communities of deep looking, deep sharing, and real harmony. We need to be able to make the best kinds of decisions together. We need peace, within and without.

The heart of the Buddha is in each of us. When we are mindful, the Buddha is there. I know a four-year-old boy who, whenever he is upset, stops what he is doing, breathes mindfully, and tells his mommy and daddy, "I am touching the Buddha within." We need to take care of the healthy seeds that are in us by watering them every day through the practice of mindful breathing, mindful walking, mindfully doing everything. We need to touch the Buddha within us. We need to enter our own heart, which means to enter the heart of the Buddha. To enter the heart of the Buddha means to be present for ourselves, our suffering, our joys, and for many others. To enter the heart of the Buddha means to touch the world of no-birth and no-death, the world where water and wave are one.

When we begin the practice, we bring our suffering and our habit energies with us, not just those of twenty or thirty years, but the habit energies of all our ancestors. Through the practice of mindful living, we learn new habits. Walking, we know that we are walking. Standing, we know that we are standing. Sitting, we know that we are sitting. Practicing this way, we slowly undo our old habits and develop the new habit of dwelling deeply and happily in the present moment. With mindfulness in us, we can smile a smile that proves our transformation.

The heart of the Buddha has been touched by our being wonderfully together. Please practice as an individual, a family, a city, a nation, and a worldwide community. Please take good care of the happiness of everyone around you. Enjoy your breathing, your smiling, your shining the light of mindfulness on each thing you do. Please practice transformation at the base through deep looking and deep touching. The teachings of the Buddha on transformation and healing are very deep. They are not theoretical. They can be practiced every day. Please practice them and realize them. I am confident that you can do it.

PART FOUR

Discourses

Discourse on
Turning the Wheel of the Dharma
Dhamma Cakka Pavattana Sutta

This is what I have heard. At one time the World-Honored One was staying near Varanasi at Isipatana in the Deer Park. At that time the World-Honored One addressed the group of five monks, saying, "Bhikkhus, there are two extremes that a monk should avoid. What are the two?

"The first is the devotion to sensual desire and the pleasure resulting from sensual desire. Such devotion is base, pedestrian, worldly, ignoble, and unbeneficial. The second is devotion to harsh austerity. Such devotion is painful, ignoble, and unbeneficial. By not following either of these extremes, the Tathagata has realized the Middle Way that gives rise to seeing and understanding. This seeing and understanding are at the bases of peace, knowledge, full awakening, and nirvana.

"What is the Middle Way, bhikkhus, that the Tathagata has realized that gives rise to seeing and understanding, when that seeing and understanding are at the bases of peace, knowledge, full awakening, and nirvana?

"It is the Noble Eightfold Path, consisting of Right View, Right Thinking, Right Speech, Right Action, Right Livelihood, Right Diligence, Right Mindfulness, and Right Concentration. This is the Middle Way, bhikkhus, that the Tathagata has realized that gives rise to seeing and understanding when that seeing and understanding are at the bases of peace, knowledge, full awakening, and nirvana.

"Here, bhikkhus, is the Noble Truth of suffering. Birth is

suffering. Old age is suffering. Sickness is suffering. Death is suffering. Sorrow, grief, mental anguish, and disturbance are suffering. To be with those you dislike is suffering. To be separated from those you love is suffering. Not having what you long for is suffering. In other words, to grasp the Five Aggregates as though they constitute a self is suffering.

"Here, bhikkhus, is the Noble Truth of the cause of suffering. It is the desire to be born again, delight in being born again, attached to the pleasures found in this and that. There is the craving for sense pleasures, for becoming, and for not becoming any more.

"Here, bhikkhus, is the Noble Truth of ending suffering. It is the fading away and ending of craving without any trace. It is giving up, letting go of, being free from, and doing away with craving.

"Here, bhikkhus, is the Noble Truth of the Path that leads to the end of suffering. It is the Noble Eightfold Path of Right View, Right Thinking, Right Speech, Right Action, Right Livelihood, Right Diligence, Right Mindfulness, and Right Concentration.

"Monks, when I realized the Noble Truth of suffering, seeing, understanding, insight, wisdom, and light arose in me with regard to things I had not heard before.

"When I realized that the Noble Truth of suffering needs to be understood, seeing, understanding, insight, wisdom, and light arose in me with regard to things I had not heard before.

"When I realized that the Noble Truth of suffering has been understood, seeing, understanding, insight, wisdom, and light arose in me with regard to things I had not heard before.

"When I realized the Noble Truth of the causes of suffering, seeing, understanding, insight, wisdom, and light arose in me with regard to things I had not heard before.

"When I realized that the causes of suffering need to be

given up, seeing, understanding, insight, wisdom, and light arose in me with regard to things I had not heard before.

"When I realized that the causes of suffering have been given up, seeing, understanding, insight, wisdom, and light arose in me with regard to things I had not heard before.

"When I realized the Noble Truth of ending suffering, seeing, understanding, insight, wisdom, and light arose in me with regard to things I had not heard before.

"When I realized that the ending of suffering needs to be experienced, seeing, understanding, insight, wisdom, and light arose in me with regard to things I had not heard before.

"When I realized that the ending of suffering has been experienced, seeing, understanding, insight, wisdom, and light arose in me with regard to things I had not heard before.

"When I realized the Noble Truth of the Path that leads to the end of suffering, seeing, understanding, insight, wisdom, and light arose in me with regard to things I had not heard before.

"When I realized that the Path that leads to the end of suffering needs to be practiced, seeing, understanding, insight, wisdom, and light arose in me with regard to things I had not heard before.

"When I realized that the Path that leads to the end of suffering has been practiced, seeing, understanding, insight, wisdom, and light arose in me with regard to things I had not heard before.

"As long as insight and understanding of the Four Noble Truths in their three stages and twelve aspects, just as they are, had not been realized, I could not say that in the world with its gods, maras, brahmas, recluses, brahmans, and humans, someone had realized the highest awakening.

"Monks, as soon as insight and understanding of the Four Noble Truths in their three stages and twelve aspects, just as they are, had been realized, I could say that in this world with its gods, maras, brahmas, recluses, brahmans, and humans, someone had realized the highest awakening, that understanding and seeing have arisen, that the liberation of my mind is unshakable, that this is my last birth, that there is no more becoming."

When the World-Honored One had spoken, the five monks rejoiced in their hearts. Upon hearing the Four Noble Truths, the pure eye that sees the meaning of the teachings without attachment arose in the monk Kondañña. He realized that everything that is of the nature to arise is of the nature to cease.

When the Dharma Wheel had thus been turned by the World-Honored One, the Earth gods proclaimed, "Near Varanasi at Isipatana in the Deer Park, the highest Wheel of the Dharma has been set in motion. It cannot be turned back by recluses, brahmans, gods, maras, brahmas, or anyone in any world."

When the four kings heard the Earth gods' proclamation, they proclaimed, "Near Varanasi at Isipatana in the Deer Park, the highest Wheel of the Dharma has been set in motion. It cannot be turned back by recluses, brahmans, gods, maras, brahmas, or anyone in any world."

When the gods of the Thirty-Third Heaven, the gods of the Realm of the Dead, the Tushita gods, the gods who rejoice in creation, the gods who have power through control of others, and the gods in the company of Brahma heard the four kings' proclamation, they proclaimed, "Near Varanasi at Isipatana in the Deer Park, the highest Wheel of the Dharma has been set in motion. It cannot be turned back by recluses, brahmans, gods, maras, brahmas, or anyone in any world."

At that hour, at that moment, in an instant of time, the proclamation reached the world of Brahma, and the Ten-Thousand World Systems shook and shook again. An immeasurable splendor was seen throughout the world, surpassing the splendor of all the gods.

Inspired, the World-Honored One spoke: "Indeed, Kondañña has understood. Indeed, Kondañña has understood." Thus, Kondañña received the name Kondañña Who Understands.

Samyutta Nikaya V, 420

Discourse on the Great Forty
Mahacattarisaka Sutta

This is what I have heard. At one time the Lord was staying near Savatthi in the Jeta Grove in Anathapindika's Park. At that time the World-Honored One addressed the bhikkhus, saying, "O bhikkhus."

"O Teacher," the bhikkhus respectfully replied.

The World-Honored One said, "Bhikkhus, I am going to teach you about the Noble Right Concentration, what are its causes and what are its accompanying factors. Please listen carefully and give all your attention as I speak."

"Yes, Lord," the bhikkhus respectfully replied.

The World-Honored One spoke, "What, bhikkhus, are the causes and accompanying factors that adorn Right Concentration? They are Right View, Right Thinking, Right Speech, Right Action, Right Livelihood, Right Diligence, and Right Mindfulness. When one-pointedness of mind is accompanied by these seven factors, it is called the Noble Right Concentration adorned with its causes and accompanying factors.

"In the following example, Right View comes first. Why does Right View come first? When there is wrong view and one knows it is wrong view, it is already Right View. When there is Right View and one knows it is Right View, that is also Right View. What is wrong view? It is the view that there is no point in giving alms, offering alms, or ceremonial offerings. That there is no ripening of the fruit of wholesome or un-wholesome actions. That this world does not exist and neither does the other world. That there is no birth from parents, and no beings are born spontaneously. That no monks or brahmans have perfected the Path, are going in the right direction, have experienced for themselves the special understandings, or are able to illuminate our understanding of this world or the other world.

"What, bhikkhus, is Right View? Bhikkhus, there are two kinds of Right View. There is Right View in which not all the leaks have been stopped. It gives rise to merit but still results in attachment. Then there is Right View that is noble in which the leaks have been stopped. It is supramundane and an element of the Path. What is Right View in which not all the leaks have been stopped? It is the view that there is a point in giving alms, offering alms, and ceremonial offerings. That there is ripening of the fruit of wholesome and unwholesome actions. That this world exists and so does the other world. That there is birth from parents, and there are beings who are born spontaneously. That monks and brahmans have perfected the Path, are going in the right direction, have experienced for themselves the special understandings, and are able to illuminate our understanding of this world or the other world.

"What is Right View in which the leaks have been stopped? It is understanding, understanding as one of the Five Faculties, understanding as one of the Five Powers, understanding as the enlightenment factor called investigation of phenomena in someone whose mind is noble, whose mind has no leaks, who has been provided with the Noble Path, and who is practicing the Noble Path. That, bhikkhus, is Right View that is noble, without leaks, supramundane, and a limb of the Path.

"He who makes an effort to give up wrong view and take upon himself Right View has Right Diligence. He who by means of mindfulness gives up wrong view and dwells taking

Right View upon himself has Right Mindfulness. These three phenomena revolve around Right View. They are Right View, Right Diligence, and Right Mindfulness.

"In the following example, Right View comes first. Why does Right View come first? When there is wrong thinking and one knows it is wrong thinking, it is already Right View. When there is Right Thinking and one knows it is Right Thinking, it is also Right View. What is wrong thinking? It is thinking that leads to desire, hatred, and harming.

"What is Right Thinking? Bhikkhus, there are two kinds of Right Thinking. There is Right Thinking in which not all the leaks have been stopped. It gives rise to merit but still results in attachment. Then there is Right Thinking that is noble in which the leaks have been stopped. It is supramundane and an element of the Path. What is Right Thinking in which not all the leaks have been stopped? It is the thinking that leads to giving up desire, hatred, and harming. That is Right Thinking in which not all the leaks have been stopped, that gives rise to merit but still results in attachment.

"What is Right Thinking that is noble, in which the leaks have been stopped, that is supramundane and an element of the Path? It is logical reasoning, initial reflection, thinking, application of mind, implanting in mind, and formation of speech in someone whose mind is noble, whose mind has no leaks, who has been provided with the Noble Path and is practicing the Noble Path. That, bhikkhus, is Right Thinking that is noble, without leaks, supramundane, and an element of the Path.

"He who makes an effort to give up wrong thinking and take upon himself Right Thinking has Right Diligence. He who by means of mindfulness gives up wrong thinking and dwells taking Right Thinking upon himself has Right Mindfulness. These three phenomena revolve around Right Thinking. They are Right View, Right Diligence, and Right Mindfulness.

"In the following example, Right View comes first. Why does Right View come first? When there is wrong speech and one knows it is wrong speech, it is already Right View. When there is Right Speech and one knows it is Right Speech, that is also Right View. What is wrong speech? It is lying, slandering, harsh words, and frivolous conversation.

"What is Right Speech? Bhikkhus, there are two kinds of Right Speech. There is Right Speech in which not all the leaks have been stopped. Then there is Right Speech that is noble in which the leaks have been stopped. What is Right Speech in which not all the leaks have been stopped? It is abstention from lying, slandering, harsh words, and frivolous conversation.

"What is Right Speech in which the leaks have been stopped? It is holding back from, desisting, resisting, and abstaining from the four kinds of wrong speech in someone whose mind is noble, whose mind has no leaks, who has been provided with the Noble Path, and who is practicing the Noble Path.

"In the following example, Right View comes first. Why does Right View come first? When there is wrong action and one knows it is wrong action, it is already Right View. When there is Right Action and one knows it is Right Action, it is also Right View. What is wrong action? It is the destruction of life, taking what is not given, and sexual misconduct.

"What is Right Action? Bhikkhus, there are two kinds of Right Action. There is Right Action in which not all the leaks have been stopped. Then there is Right Action that is noble in which the leaks have been stopped. What is Right Action in which not all the leaks have been stopped? It is abstention from destroying life, from taking what is not given, and from sexual misconduct.

"What is Right Action in which the leaks have been stopped? It is holding back from, desisting, resisting, and abstaining from the three wrong bodily actions in someone whose mind is noble, whose mind has no leaks, who has been provided with the Noble Path, and who is practicing the Noble Path.

"He who makes an effort to give up wrong action and take upon himself Right Action has Right Diligence. He who by means of mindfulness gives up wrong action and dwells taking Right Action upon himself has Right Mindfulness. These three phenomena revolve around Right Action. They are Right View, Right Diligence, and Right Mindfulness.

"In the following example, Right View comes first. Why does Right View come first? When there is wrong livelihood and one knows it is wrong livelihood, it is already Right View. When there is Right Livelihood and one knows it is Right Livelihood, that is also Right View. What is wrong livelihood? It is hypocritical and indistinct speaking, fortune telling, trickery and covetousness, and wanting to make profit out of profit.

"What is Right Livelihood? Bhikkhus, there are two kinds of Right Livelihood. There is Right Livelihood in which not all the leaks have been stopped. Then there is Right Livelihood that is noble in which the leaks have been stopped. What is the Right Livelihood in which not all the leaks have been stopped? It is when the noble disciple gives up wrong livelihood and makes his living by Right Livelihood.

"What is the Right Livelihood in which the leaks have been stopped? It is holding back from, desisting, resisting, and abstaining from wrong livelihood in someone whose mind is noble, whose mind has no leaks, who has been provided with the Noble Path, and who is practicing the Noble Path.

"He who makes an effort to give up wrong livelihood and take upon himself Right Livelihood has Right Diligence. He who by means of mindfulness gives up wrong livelihood and dwells taking Right Livelihood upon himself has Right Mindfulness. These three phenomena revolve around Right Livelihood. They are Right View, Right Diligence, and Right Mindfulness.

"In the following example, Right View comes first. Why does Right View come first? Right Thinking arises in someone who has Right View. Right Speech arises in someone who has Right Thinking. Right Action arises in someone who has Right Speech. Right Livelihood arises in someone who has Right Action. Right Diligence arises in someone who has Right Livelihood. Right Mindfulness arises in someone who has Right Diligence. Right Concentration arises in someone who has Right Mindfulness. Right Understanding arises in someone who has Right Concentration. And Right Liberation arises in someone who has Right Understanding. Therefore, bhikkhus, the Path of the practitioner in training has eight factors, and the Path of the practitioner who is an arhat has ten factors.

"In the following example, Right View comes first. Why does Right View come first? Wrong view is overcome in someone who has Right View. All the other unwholesome, wrong states that arise dependent upon wrong view are also overcome. All the other wholesome states that arise dependent upon Right View are practiced to fulfillment.

"Wrong thinking is overcome in someone who has Right Thinking, etc.

"Wrong speech is overcome in someone who has Right Speech, etc.

"Wrong action is overcome in someone who has Right Action, etc.

"Wrong livelihood is overcome in someone who has Right Livelihood, etc.

"Wrong diligence is overcome in someone who has Right Diligence, etc.

"Wrong mindfulness is overcome in someone who has Right Mindfulness, etc.

"Wrong concentration is overcome in someone who has Right Concentration, etc.

"Wrong understanding is overcome in someone who has Right Understanding, etc.

"Wrong liberation is overcome in someone who has Right Liberation, etc.

"Thus, bhikkhus, there are twenty factors supporting the wholesome and twenty factors supporting the unwholesome. This Dharma teaching on the Great Forty has been set in motion and cannot be turned back by any monk, brahman, god, Mara, Brahma, or anyone in the world."

Majjhima Nikaya 117

Discourse on Right View
Sammaditthi Sutta

This is what I have heard. At one time the Lord was staying near Savatthi in the Jeta Grove in Anathapindika's Park. At that time the Venerable Sariputta addressed the bhikkhus.

"Friend," the bhikkhus respectfully replied.

The Venerable Sariputta said, "How does a noble disciple practice Right View, a view that is upright? How does he or she obtain unshakable confidence in the Dharma? How can he or she arrive at the true Dharma?"

"Friend Sariputta, we have traveled a long way to be in your presence and we are happy to learn the meaning of these words. Please explain your statements, and after we have heard your teachings, we will bear them in mind."

"Please listen, friends, and give your full attention to what I say. Friends, when a noble disciple understands the unwholesome and the roots of the unwholesome as well as the wholesome and the roots of the wholesome, then that disciple has Right View, a view that is upright. He or she is endowed with unshakable confidence in the Dharma and has arrived at the true Dharma. Friends, destroying life, taking what is not given, and sexual misconduct are unwholesome. Lying, slandering, harsh words, and frivolous conversation are unwholesome. Covetousness, ill-will, and wrong views are unwholesome. The roots of the unwholesome are greed, hatred, and delusion.

"Abstaining from destroying life, from taking what is not given, and from sexual misconduct; abstaining from lying, slandering, harsh words, and frivolous conversation; not coveting, not harboring ill-will, and practicing Right View are wholesome. The roots of the wholesome are the absence of greed, hatred, and delusion.

"When a disciple understands the unwholesome and its roots and the wholesome and its roots, he or she entirely transforms the tendency to greed, removes the tendency toward hatred, and discontinues the tendency toward the 'I am' view. He or she transforms delusion, gives rise to understanding, and right now in this very life puts an end to suffering."

"Well said, friend," the delighted bhikkhus spoke, and asked, "Is there yet another teaching on how a disciple practices Right View?..."

"Friends, when a noble disciple understands nourishment, the making of nourishment, the cessation of nourishment, and the Path that leads to the cessation of nourishment, that disciple practices Right View. Friends, there are four kinds of nourishment that support beings who have already come to be and those who are seeking a new existence. They are edible food, coarse or fine; the food of sense impressions; the food of intention; and the food of consciousness. Nourishment originates where greed originates, and nourishment ceases when greed ceases. The Path that leads to the cessation of nourishment is the Noble Eightfold Path. When a disciple understands this, he or she entirely transforms these tendencies.

"Yet another teaching on Right View is that when the noble disciple understands suffering, the making of suffering, the cessation of suffering, and the Path leading to the cessation of suffering, he or she has Right View. Birth, old age, sickness, death, grief, lamentation, pain, discontent, and agitation are suffering. Not to have what you want is suffering. In short, grasping the five skandhas is suffering. The creation of suffering is the thirst to be born again, which is associated with a delight in and attachment to the various pleasures found here and there. It is the thirst for the desire realm, the realm of being, and the realm of nonbeing. The stopping of suffering is disappearance of desire, the ending of ideas, the giving up of, letting go of, liberation from, and refusal to dwell in the object of desire. The Path leading to the cessation of suffering is the Noble Eightfold Path.

"Another teaching on Right View is that when a noble disciple understands old age and death, the making of old age and death, the cessation of old age and death, and the Path leading to the cessation of old age and death, he or she has Right View. Old age is the decrepitude of being in the various worlds of living beings. It includes broken teeth, gray hair, wrinkled skin, the dwindling of the life force, and the weakening of the sense organs. Death is the passing away of living beings from the various worlds of living beings, their shifting to other existences, their decomposition, disappearance, and death, the completion of their time, the disunion of the skandhas, and the laying down of the body. Old age and death originate where birth originates. The cessation of birth is the cessation of old age and death. The Path leading to the cessation of old age and death is the Noble Eighfold Path.

"Another teaching on Right View is that when a noble disciple understands birth, the making of birth,... he or she has Right View. Birth is the arising of beings in the various worlds of beings, their appearance, rebirth, manifestation of the skandhas, and acquisition of sense organs and sense objects. Birth originates where becoming originates. The cessation of becoming is the cessation of birth. The Path leading to the cessation of birth is the Noble Eightfold Path.

"Another teaching on Right View is that when a noble disciple understands becoming,... he or she has Right View. There are three becomings: becoming in the world of desire, becoming in the world of fine matter, and becoming in the nonmaterial world. Becoming originates where grasping originates and ceases where grasping ceases...

"Another is that when a noble disciple understands grasping,... he or she has Right View. There are four kinds of grasping: the grasping of sensual desire, views, rules and rituals, and a belief in a separate self. Grasping originates where thirst originates. Grasping ceases where thirst ceases, and the Noble Eightfold Path...

"A further teaching on Right View is that when a noble disciple understands thirst,... he or she has Right View. There are six classes of thirst: thirst for forms, sounds, smells, tastes, touch, and objects of mind. Thirst originates where feelings originate and thirst ceases where feelings cease...

"A further teaching on Right View is that when a noble disciple understands feelings,... he or she has Right View. There are six classes of feelings: feelings that arise from eye contact, ear contact, nose contact, tongue contact, body contact, and mind contact. Feelings originate where contact originates and cease where contact ceases...

"A further teaching on Right View is that when a noble disciple understands contact,... he or she has Right View. There are six classes of contact: eye contact, ear contact,... Contact originates where the six sense organs and objects originate...

"A further teaching on Right View is that when a noble disciple understands the six sense doors,... he or she has Right View. The six sense doors are the eye door, ear door,... The six sense doors originate where the mind/body originates...

"A further teaching on Right View is that when a noble disciple understands the mind/body,... he or she has Right View. The mind element consists of feelings, perceptions, volitions, contact, and mental attention. The body element consists of the Four Great Elements and the form that results from the Four Great Elements. The mind/body originates where consciousness originates...

"A further teaching on Right View is that when a noble disciple understands consciousness,... he or she has Right View. There are six classes of consciousness: eye consciousness, ear consciousness,... Consciousness originates where the impulses originate...

"A further teaching on Right View is that when a noble disciple understands impulses,... he or she has Right View. There are three kinds of impulses: body impulses, speech impulses, and mind impulses. Impulses originate where ignorance originates...

"A further teaching on Right View is that when a noble disciple understands ignorance,... he or she has Right View. Ignorance is the failure to recognize suffering, the making of suffering, the cessation of suffering and the Path leading to the cessation of suffering. Ignorance originates where the leaks originate...

"A further teaching on Right View is that when a noble disciple understands the leaks,... he or she has Right View. There are three leaks: the leak of sensual desire, the leak of being, and the leak of ignorance. The three leaks originate where ignorance originates..."

Majjhima Nikaya 9

Index

Note: Page numbers in italics indicate figures. Page numbers followed by "n" indicate footnotes.

A

Abhidharma (Buddhist psychology), 230n; on attention, 64; on the links of Interdependent Co-Arising, 230–231; on mental formations, 71

acceptance: in calming, 26

action: as the measure of realization, 98; of non-action, 39–40, 122, 157–158, 191; from suffering, 85–86; understanding and, 82–83; volitional *(See* formations); *"What Am I Doing?"* practice, 61. *See also* Right Action

active concentration, 105–106

afflictions *(kleshas)*, 74; as causes of suffering, 22–23; seeds of, 206–207, *208;* as the source of perceptions, 53–54, 179

aggregates. *See* Five Aggregates

agitation, 74–75; stopping and calming, 24–26

aimlessness *(apranihita)*, 152–154

alayavijñana. See store consciousness

alcohol: not consuming, 96–97

Amida Buddha: contemplating, 76n

Ananda: and the Buddha, 49, 77,

Ananda *(continued)*
165, 190, 225–226; on phenomena, 77; realization of, 217

Anapanasati Sutta (Discourse on the Full Awareness of Breathing), 68

anatman. See nonself

anger *(vyapada)*, 78–79, 186; embracing, 25–26, 72–73, 195–196, 203–205

animitta. See signlessness

anitya. See impermanence

anxiety *(domanassa)*, 78, 154

appreciation. *See* reverence for life

apranihita (aimlessness), 152–154

arising (creating) (of suffering) *(samudaya)*, 9–11, *10;* cessation of *(See* cessation (of suffering)); looking deeply into, 37–38; as no arising, 122; realizing, 39–40; recognizing, 31–38; stopping, 38, 39

arising (of things). *See* Interdependent Co-Arising

arya ashtangika marga. See Noble Eightfold Path

ashrava (setbacks), 31, 74

attachment (grasping) *(upadana)*, 229

attention *(manaskara)*, 64; nourishing the object of, 65–66

Avalokiteshvara (Kwan Yin), 79n, 86–87, 88, 172, 242; invoking the name of, 239. *See also Heart Sutra*

Avatamsaka Sutra: on being ourselves, 152–153; on dharmas, 128

avidya. See ignorance

awakening. *See* liberation; mind of love/awakening

ayatanas. See sense organs and their objects

B

balani (Five Powers), 184–191

being. *See* coming to be

being ourselves, 152–153

beings: inanimate, 127, 152. *See also* human beings; living beings

beloved: paying attention to, 65–66

bhava. See coming to be

bijas. See seeds (of consciousness)

birth *(jati),* 229

birth and death: as continuation, 245; the place beyond, 245; reality of, 124, 126, 127, 137–139, 140, 151, 152, 245

bliss: body of, 158–159, 160, 242. *See also* joy *(mudita/priti)*

bodhichitta. See mind of love/awakening

Bodhidharma: and Emperor Wu, 61

bodhisattvas, 242; Buddha eye in the hands of, 82–83; feelings of, 240

bodhyanga. See Seven Factors of Awakening

body (form) *(rupa),* 176; calming, 25–26; looking deeply at, 177; mindfulness of, 68–71, 176–177, 219; *nama rupa* (mind/body), 36n, 227; resting, 26–27; transformation of, 110

body of bliss *(Sambhogakaya),* 158–159, 160, 242

body of the Dharma *(Dharmakaya),* 156–158, 160

body of transformation *(Nirmanakaya),* 159–160, 242

books: as food, 32–33, 96; writing, 91

bowing, 52

Brahmaviharas. *See* Four Immeasurable Minds

breath counting, 71

breathing. *See* mindful breathing

Buddha: and Ananda, 49, 77, 165, 190, 225–226; contact with sense objects, 242–243; as the Dharmakaya, 156–158, 160; enlightenment, 214; entering the Heart of, 3–5, 128, 250–254; humanity of, 3, 129–130; interbeing with Dharma and Sangha, 166; meaning of the word, 187, 214; native language, 16; as the Nirmanakaya, 159–160, 242; as not a philosopher, 232; practice and enlightenment, 6, 42; practicing mindfulness of, 76n; practicing with, 111–112; presence, 239; reciting the name of, 20, 76n; reluctance to teach, 200; as the Sambhogakaya, 158–159, 160, 242; and Shariputra, 198–202; and the sick monk, 165; smile, 173; and Subhadda, 49; suffering of, 205; taking refuge in, 161–164; as the Tathagata, 158n; teachings (*See* teachings of the Buddha); three bodies of, 156–160, 241–242; as true or false, 166; as in us, 162–163; as Vairochana, 158; and Vatsigotra, 17–18

Buddha nature *(Buddhata):* the seed of Buddhahood, 52, 56, 187–188, 238

Buddhaghosa: conditions of Interdependent Co-Arising, 222

Buddhism: as a practice, 56; schools, 13–17

Buddhist psychology. *See Abhidharma*

"Butterflies over the Golden Mustard Fields" (poem) (Nhat Hanh), 140–141

C

calming, 25–26, 66, 210; meditation practices, 76. *See also* stopping

capacity. *See* inclusiveness

cause and effect: vs. Interdependent Co-Arising, 221

causes: of Interdependent Co-Arising, 223–224; of mindfulness, 215; of suffering, 22–23, 31–38, 182

cessation (of ignorance), 109

cessation (of suffering) *(nirodha)*, *10,* 11; as no cessation, 122; realizing, 43; recognizing, 41–42; as well-being, 41, 45–46

changing the peg, 207–209

children: teaching and helping, 150–151, 216, 252

chitta. See mind

chitta samskara. See mental formations

collective practice, 34, 167, 181, 197, 248–249

coming to be (being/becoming) *(bhava)*, 229; and nonbeing, 245

compassion *(karuna)*, 169, 172–173; in listening, 86–89; in writing, 90–91

concentration *(samadhi)*, 105, 107, 186, 218; and insight, 186; kinds, 105–106; mindfulness and, 186, 187; practices, 107, 110–111, 146–155; *shamatha* as, 210; wrong, 218. *See also* meditation; Right Concentration

Concentration on Aimlessness/ Nonself, 111, 152–154

Concentration on Emptiness/ Nirvana, 111, 147–148

Concentration on Signlessness/ Impermanence, 110, 111, 148–150

concepts. *See* ideas

conditioned realm, 79–80

conditions of Interdependent Co-Arising, 222–225

Confucius: on his own maturation, 39; on joy in practice, 250; on silence, 92

conscious breathing. *See* mindful breathing

consciousness *(vijñana)*, 36, 180–181, 227, 237–238; aspects, 12n, 110, *208,* 227; as collective and individual, 75, 181; as discriminative wisdom, 145; as a nutriment, 36–37; as the object of concentration, 108; as a tool of transformation, 239–240; transforming, 181, 238–239, 241. *See also* mind; mind consciousness; store consciousness; thinking

consuming mindfully, 96–97, 197

contact (with sense objects) *(sparsha)*, 32–34, 96, 227; in a Buddha, 242–243

contemplations on interdependence, impermanence, and compassion, 80

continuity: and Interdependent Co-Arising, 224–225

craving *(kama/ trishna)*, 78–79, 229; as the cause of suffering, 22–23; freedom from, 78–79

creating of suffering. *See* arising (creating) (of suffering)

"Cuckoo Telephone" (poem) (Nhat Hanh), 12

D

dana. See giving

death: old age and death, 229. *See also* birth and death

deep ecology, 127

deep listening. *See* mindful listening

deep looking. *See* looking deeply

dependent origination. *See* Interdependent Co-Arising

Descartes, René: on existence, 59

desire. *See* craving

desire realm, 79

developing thought *(vichara)*, 60

development conditions: and Interdependent Co-Arising, 224

Dharma, 164; asking about, 49; body of (*See* Dharmakaya); interbeing with Buddha and Sangha, 166; as a raft, 136; taking refuge in, 156, 161–164; Three Dharma Seals, 21–22, 131–145; as true or false, 166; as in us, 163. *See also* sutras (discourses); teachings of the Buddha; turning the wheel of the Dharma; *and specific sutras*

Dharma Seals. *See* Three Dharma Seals

Dharma talks, 17; opening to, 12–13

Dharmakaya (Dharma body), 156–158, 160, 241

dharma-pravichaya (investigation of phenomena), 76, 216

dharmas. See phenomena

dhatus (Eighteen Elements), 76–77

dhyana. See meditation

Diamond Sutra, 126, 210; dialectics, 129; on human beings, 147; on perceptions, 179–180; on signs (images), 148, 149, 151

diligence (effort/energy) *(virya)*, 185, 192, 206–209, 216–217; sources, 100–103, 216–217; wrong, 99. *See also* Right Diligence

Discourse in 8,000 Verses, 210

Discourse on Knowing the Better Way to Live Alone, 68

Discourse on Right View: text, 271–275

Discourse on the Four Establishments of Mindfulness, 67–68, 215–216

Discourse on the Full Awareness of Breathing, 68

Discourse on the Great Forty: text, 263–269

Discourse on the Many Realms, 77

Discourse on Turning the Wheel of the Dharma, 7–8, 22, 28, 122, 245; text, 257–261

discriminative perception *(vikalpa)*, 134

discriminative wisdom *(vijñana)*, 145

Doan Van Kham: poem, 151

drinking mindfully, 96–97

drishta dharma sukha viharin, 23, 173–174

dukkha. See suffering

"dwelling happily in things as they are", 23, 173–174

dying: assisting others, 66, 68

E

ease *(prashrabdhih)*: practicing with, 101, 217

eating mindfully, 32, 96, 147

education (for children): reforming, 150–151, 252

effort. *See* diligence

Eight Concepts, 139

Eight No's of the Middle Way, 139

Eight Right Practices, 11, 49–118; interbeing of, 50, *57*, 58, 118; interbeing of the Five Mindfulness Trainings and, 97–98, 118. *See also* Noble Eightfold Path; *and individual right practices*

Eighteen Elements *(dhatus)*, 76–77

eightfold path: ignoble, *30*, 46. *See also* Noble Eightfold Path

elements: Eighteen Elements *(dhatus)*, 76–77; Four Great Elements, 77; recognizing in the body, 69–70, 219; Six Elements, 77–78

embracing: the body, 176, 177; in calming, 26, 72–73. *See also* inclusiveness

emotions. *See* feelings

emptiness *(shunyata)*, 135, 146–148; in Interdependent Co-Arising, 226. *See also* interbeing; nonself encouragement (of ourselves): in turning the wheel of the Dharma, 29–31, *30,* 38–39, 42, 43–44

engagement in the world, 8, 239

enlightenment. *See* liberation

equality: Wisdom of Equality, 110, 174–175, 241

equanimity *(upeksha),* 169, 174–175, 218–219, 243; as letting go, 35, 78

exploitation: preventing, 94–95, 197

extinction. *See* nirvana

F

faith *(shraddha),* 161–162, 165, 185

faiths: preserving our own, 169

fearlessness (non-fear): realizing, 152, 177, 178, 180, 211–212

feelings (emotions) *(vedana),* 71, 229; of bodhisattvas, 240; looking deeply into, 178; mindfulness of, 71–73, 177–178; stopping and calming, 24–26; suffering as a feeling, 141

Fifth Mindfulness Training, 96–97, 197

First Mindfulness Training, 94, 197

First Noble Truth, 9, 19–23; turning the wheel of, 29–31, *30,* 117. *See also* suffering

Five Aggregates *(skandhas),* 23n, 36n, 176–183; interbeing of, 181–182; looking deeply into, 182; the Twelve Links of Interdependent Co-Arising in, 229–230. *See also* body; consciousness; feelings; mental formations; perceptions

Five Faculties *(indriyani),* 184–185, 186

Five Mindfulness Trainings, 94–98, 118, 196–197; collective practice of, 34, 197; Fourth, 84, 87, 89, 197. *See also* Right Mindfulness

Five Powers *(balani),* 184–191

Five Remembrances, 123–124

flower watering, 206–209

food: as a nutriment, 31–32; other nutriments as, 31–38

forbearance: vs. inclusiveness, 198

forgetfulness: stopping, 24–25

form. *See* body

form realm, 79

formations (volitional actions) *(samskara),* 73, 126, 180, 227; positive vs. negative, 237, 238

formless concentration, 107–110

formless realm, 79, 107–110

Four Dhyanas, 106–107

Four Establishments of Mindfulness, 67–81, 215–216

Four Great Elements *(mahabhuta),* 77

Four Immeasurable Minds, 36, 169–175, 199n, 205, 243–244. *See also* compassion; equanimity; joy; love

Four Noble Truths, 3–46, 9–11, *10,* 45–46; interbeing of, 44–45, 128; turning the wheel of, 28–40, *30,* 41–44, 117–118, 128, 238; value, 8. *See also individual noble truths*

Four Reliances, 144–145

Four Standards of Truth, 143

Four Wisdoms, 110, 239

Fourfold Right Diligence, 100

Fourth Mindfulness Training, 84, 87, 89, 197

Fourth Noble Truth, 11, 43, 46, 127–128; turning the wheel of, *30,* 43–44. *See also* Noble Eightfold Path

freedom, 194–195; as aimlessness, 152–154; basis of, 243; from craving, 78–79; and happiness, 78; practicing, 195; realizing, 177, 178, 180. *See also* liberation

freshness: offering, 195

"The Fruit of Awareness Is Ripe" (poem) (Nhat Hanh), 4–5

G

Gavampati: on the Four Noble Truths, 44–45

giving (generosity) *(dana)*, 94–95, 193–196

grasping (attachment) *(upadana)*, 229

Great Aspiration *(mahapranidhana)*, 238, 244

Great Mirror Wisdom, 110, 239, 241

Greater Discourse on the Example of the Elephant's Footprint: on equanimity, 219

ground of being. *See* nirvana

Guishan, Master: on diligence, 102

H

habit energies *(vashana)*: "Hello, Habit Energy" practice, 61–62; recognizing, 25, 191; stopping, 24–25, 67

happiness *(sukha)*, 9, 78; of bodhisattvas, 240; capacity for, 188–191; "dwelling happily in things as they are", 23; freedom and, 78; ideas of, 54; vs. joy, 173–174, 218; letting go of obstacles to, 35, 78; moment of, 153–154; as not individual, 135; nutriments of, 31–38; practicing, 42–43, 189–191; realizing, 43, 191, 250; recognizing, 41–42; Right Concentration and, 106; and suffering, 3–4, 43, 78; transforming suffering into, 42–43; without setbacks, 31. *See also* joy

healing *(shamatha)*, 66, 217; preconditions, 24–27; teaching as, 143

hearing. *See* mindful listening

Heart Sutra, 210; teachings, 122, 124, 135, 137, 153, 183, 236

Holy Truths. *See* Four Noble Truths

human beings, 126, 129, 151–152; protecting, 94, 126–127, 147, 197. *See also* others; persons

Huong Hai, Master: poem on concentration, 105–106

I

ideas (concepts/notions): Eight Concepts, 139; as keys, 140; no idea, 55–56, 63; transcending, 129–130, 137, 139. *See also* signs (images) *(lakshana)*

ignoble eightfold path, *30*, 46

ignorance *(avidya)*, 78, 227; cessation of, 109; as a first cause, 232; and understanding, 236–237

ill-being. *See* suffering

illness. *See* sickness

images. *See* signs

impartiality. *See* Wisdom of Equality

impermanence *(anitya)*, 21, 131–133, 136, 139; Concentration on Impermanence, 110; in Interdependent Co-Arising, 226; and nirvana, 136; and nonself, 132; value of, 132–133

inclusiveness *(kshanti)*, 188–191, 193, 198–206; developing, 205

indriyani (Five Faculties), 184–185, 186

initial thought *(vitarka)*, 60

injustice: understanding, 203–205

insight. *See* understanding (insight/wisdom)

intention. *See* volition

interbeing: of Buddha, Dharma, and Sangha, 166; of cause and effect, 221–222; and cloning, 181–182; of the Eight Right Practices, 50, *57*, 58, 118; of the Five Aggregates, 181–182; of the Five Mindfulness Trainings and the Eight Right Practices, 97–98, 118; of the Four Immeasurable Minds, 175; of the Four Noble Truths, 44–45, 128; Interdependent Co-Arising as, 225; with others, 125–126, 135; realizing, 148; of the Six Paramitas, 202, 212; of subject and object, 53, 80;

interbeing *(continued)*
of the Twelve Links of Interdependent Co-Arising, 229, 231, 234–236, *235*

interdependence: contemplation on, 80

Interdependent Co-Arising *(pratitya samutpada)*, 221–249; vs. cause and effect, 221; conditioned aspects: true mind vs. deluded mind, *246, 247,* 248–249; conditions and causes, 222–225; emptiness in, 226; impermanence in, 226; as interbeing, 225; links (*See* Twelve Links of Interdependent Co-Arising); realizing, 148

interest: practicing with, 101

intoxicants: not consuming, 96–97

investigation of phenomena *(dharma-pravichaya)*, 76, 216

J

jaramarana (old age and death), 229

jati (birth), 229

joy *(mudita/priti)*, 78, 169, 173–174; vs. happiness, 173–174, 218; practicing with, 42–43, 100–103; 121–122, 189–191; as self-enjoyment, 159; and suffering, 19, 121–122; true joy, 43, 123, 127–128. *See also* body of bliss; happiness

K

Kakacupama Sutta: on equanimity, 219

kama. See craving

karma: of livelihood, 114–116. *See also* action

karuna. See compassion

Kashyapa: and Ananda, 217

Kayagatasati Sutta, 68

killing: in daily living, 94; in making a living, 115–116; in thinking or speech, 93

kleshas. See afflictions

knowledge. *See* understanding (insight/wisdom)

koan practice, 44

Kondañña, 7

kshanti. See inclusiveness

Kshitigarbha (bodhisattva), 188–189

kung-an practice, 44

Kwan Yin. *See* Avalokiteshvara

L

lakshana. See signs (images)

Lavoisier, Antoine: on birth and death, 138

legislators: electing, 252–253

letter writing: as Right Speech, 90–91

letting go, 35, 78; practicing, 78, 217, 219

liberation (awakening/enlightenment), 125; of the Buddha, 214; factors of, 76n, 101, 214–220; suffering as the means of, 3, 5, 38, 42, 45; Three Doors of Liberation, 145, 146–155; time required for, 215. *See also* freedom; realization

life: helping young people find meaning in, 150–151, 216, 252; nirvana as in this very life, 140; not wasting, 102–103; reverence for, 94, 132–133; seeking meaning for, 251–252

life span, 127, 152

listening. *See* mindful listening

livelihood: karma of, 114–116; wrong, 113–114, 117. *See also* Right Livelihood

living beings: Buddha nature of, 187; vs. inanimate beings, 127, 152; protecting, 94, 126–127, 147, 197. *See also* human beings

looking deeply *(vipashyana)*, 124, 205, 210, 211; into the arising (creating) of suffering, 37–38; into birth and death, 138; at the body, 177; in calming, 26;

looking deeply *(continued)*
into feelings, 178; into the Five
Aggregates, 182; at imperma-
nence/nonself, 132; into mental
formations, 180; miracle of
mindfulness of, 66; into
perceptions, 54–56, 179; at
phenomena, 81; stopping and,
24; into suffering, 29–31, 37–38,
45, 128–129, 250–252. See also
understanding (insight/wisdom)

Lotus Sutra: on Avalokiteshvara,
79n, 172; on Wondrous Sound,
90

love *(maitri),* 169, 170–172; mind
of, 62, 238, 243, 244; possessive,
175; practicing, 170–172, 220,
251; true love, 170, 174, 175; and
understanding, 66–67, 171, 211

loving speech, 84, 87, 89

M

mahabhuta (Four Great Elements),
77

mahapranidhana (Great Aspiration), 238, 244

Mahasanghika School, 13

Mahayana Buddhism, 13, 16–17,
210

Maitreya Buddha, 167, 172

maitri. See love

manas consciousness, 109–110, 241

manaskara. See attention

Manjushri: invoking the name of,
239

manovijñana. See mind consciousness

Many-Schools Buddhism, 13–17

Mara, 17n

marga. See Noble Eightfold Path

McNamara, Robert: Nhat Hanh
and, 204

media: impacts of, 32–34, 96

meditation (meditative concentration) *(dhyana),* 60, 209–210;
aspects, 24, 209–210; calming
practices, 76; collective practice,

meditation *(continued)*
167; Four Dhyanas, 106–107;
levels, 106–110; and mindfulness, 186; without practicing the
precepts, 82; sitting meditation,
56, 99–100, 191; telephone
gatha, 92; walking meditation,
91, 148; wrong diligence in, 99.
See also concentration; looking
deeply; stopping

mental formations *(chitta samskara),*
71, 73–75, 180; changing the
peg, 207–209; looking deeply
into, 75, 180; as seeds (*See* seeds
(of consciousness)); wholesome
and unwholesome, 73–74

mere recognition, 68–69, 74

Middle Way, 7–8; diligence in, 101

mind *(chitta):* calming, 25–26;
mental formations, 71, 73–75;
mindfulness of, 73–75; *nama
rupa* (mind/body), 36n, 227;
objects of (*See* phenomena);
resting, 26–27; suppressing, 14–
15. *See also* consciousness; Four
Immeasurable Minds; mind
consciousness

mind consciousness *(manovijñana),*
12n, 74–75, 110, 187, *208*

mind of love/awakening
(bodhichitta), 62, 238, 243, 244

mindful breathing, 70–71; and
anger, 72; discourse on, 68;
effects, 70, 72; and listening, 88–
89; and Right Thinking, 59–60;
verse, 70–71

mindful consuming, 96–97, 197

mindful listening, 12–13, 86–89,
92–93, 197

mindfulness *(smriti),* 64–65, 185,
187, 210, 215; of the body, 68–
71; in breathing (*See* mindful
breathing); of Buddha, 76n;
causes of, 215; collective practice
of, 34, 167, 181, 197, 248–249;
coming back to the present
moment, 64; and concentration,
186, 187; in consuming, 96–97,
197; discourse on, 67–68;

mindfulness *(continued)*
in drinking, 96–97; in eating, 32, 96, 147; effects, 81, 210, 243; establishments (objects) of, 67–81; as a factor of awakening, 215–216; of feelings, 71–73; as generosity, 94–95; identifying seeds of consciousness, 51–52; in listening, 12–13, 86–89, 197; making the other present, 65; meditation and, 185; of the mind, 73–75; nourishing the object of attention, 65; of phenomena, 76–81; practicing, 33, 34, 55, 67–84, 87–89, 94–98, 117, 118, 197; relieving others' suffering, 65–66; responsibility of persons practicing, 154–155, 251; as reverence for life, 94; and Right Thinking, 59–60; seeds of, *208,* 209; and sense impressions, 33, 34; Seven Miracles of Mindfulness, 65–67; in sexual behavior, 95–96; stopping and calming agitation, 24–26; stopping creating suffering, 38; trainings (*See* Five Mindfulness Trainings); transforming suffering, 67; using the help of others, 30, 38; and well-being, 41; in the workplace, 116–117. *See also* looking deeply; Right Mindfulness

Mindfulness Trainings. *See* Five Mindfulness Trainings

miracles: source of, 241

Mother of All Buddhas *(prajña paramita)*, 56, 210

mouth yoga, 70

movies: as food, 32–33, 96

mudita. See joy

N

Nagarjuna: on Interdependent Co-Arising, 226; on the Third Dharma Seal, 22

nama rupa (mind/body), 36n, 227

Never-Despising (bodhisattva), 188

Nguyen Du: on insight, 109

Nhat Dinh, Master: freedom of, 40

Nhat Hanh, Thich: and Nhât Tri, 202–204, 205; as a novice monk, 101; and the peace rally reporter, 55; poems, 4–5, 12, 70–71, 140–141; and Robert McNamara, 204; on Vulture Peak, 250; youth, 5, 184

Nhât Tri, Thich: Nhat Hanh and, 202–204, 205

Nirmanakaya (transformation body), 159–160, 242

nirodha. See cessation (of suffering)

nirvana, 21, 129, 136–140, 245; as aimlessness, 153; Concentration on Nirvana, 111; and suchness, 211; and suffering, 122; as in this very life, 140

no idea (non-thinking), 55–56, 63

Noble Eightfold Path, *10,* 11, 46, 49–118; as no path, 122; practicing, 43–44, 46, 117–118; realizing, 44; recognizing, 43. *See also* Eight Right Practices

non-action: action of, 39–40, 122, 157–158, 191; aimlessness, 152–154

nonattachment. *See* equanimity

nonconception, path of, 55–56

non-fear. *See* fearlessness

non-harming *(ahimsa),* 79; as not killing, 94

nonself *(anatman),* 21, 132, 133–136; Concentration on Nonself, 111; and impermanence, 132; and nirvana, 136; seeing, 149–150; self as, 126. *See also* emptiness; interbeing

non-thinking (no idea), 55–56, 63

nothing to do (aimlessness), 152–154

nothingness: as the object of concentration, 108. *See also* emptiness

nutriments of happiness/suffering, 31–39

O

object: subject and, 53, 80

object conditions: and Interdependent Co-Arising, 225

objects of mind. See phenomena

obscurations. See afflictions

obstacles to development, 224

offering. See giving

old age: as nice, 125

old age and death (jaramarana), 229

others: assisting in dying, 66, 68; interbeing with, 125–126; making the other present, 65; relieving suffering caused by, 195–196; relieving the suffering of, 65–66, 188; using the help of, 30, 38

oxherding pictures: last picture, 39

P

paradise: creating, 248–249

paramitas. See perfections

paths (marga): ignoble eightfold path, 30, 46; of nonconception, 55–56. See also Noble Eightfold Path

patience. See inclusiveness

peace: capacity for, 188–191; offering, 195; recognizing, 41–42

perceptions (samjña), 52–55, 76, 178–180; afflictions as the source of, 53–54, 179; "Am I Sure?" practice, 60–61, 179; discriminative perception, 134; as erroneous, 52–53; looking deeply into, 54–56, 179; objects of (See phenomena); recognizing, 108–109

perfections (paramitas), 192–213, 193; interbeing of, 202, 212. See also diligence (effort); giving (generosity); inclusiveness; meditation; precepts; understanding (insight/wisdom)

persons (individuals), 151–152; persons (continued). responsibility of mindfulness practitioners, 154–155, 251; teaching and helping young people, 150–151, 216, 252; teaching as relevant to, 142–143, 143. See also human beings; others

phenomena (dharmas), 76, 80, 128; investigation of, 76, 216; mindfulness of, 76–81; things as they are, 23, 44; as us (not separate), 53, 80–81, 133–136. See also signs (images)

Plum Village, 55, 68, 102, 207

powers: Five Powers, 184–191

practicing: with the Buddha, 111–112; calming body and mind, 25–26, 76; collectively, 34, 167, 181, 197, 248–249; concentration, 107, 110–111; continuity in, 224–225; creating spaces for, 252; with ease, 101, 217; factors of awakening in, 101; the Five Powers, 187; the Five Remembrances, 123–124; the Four Noble Truths, 28–40, 30, 41–44, 117–118, 128, 238; freedom, 195; happiness, 42–43, 189–191; the ignoble eightfold path, 46; without intelligence, 20; with joy, 42–43, 100–103, 121–122, 189–191; with kung-ans, 44; letting go, 78, 217, 219; love and understanding, 170–172, 220, 251; mindfulness (See mindfulness); the Noble Eightfold Path, 43–44, 46, 117–118; not proving anything, 23; the precepts, 82; for psychotherapists, 41, 87, 88; resting while, 26–27; Right Diligence, 100–104; right now, 213; Right Thinking, 60–62; setbacks in, 31, 74; the Six Paramitas, 192–213; suffering and, 43–44, 103, 128–129; the teachings of the Buddha, 141–142; on the telephone, 91–92, 116 *prajña. See* understanding (insight/wisdom)

prajña paramita, 56, 210

Prasenajit, King, 165

prashrabdhih. See ease

pratitya samutpada. See Interdependent Co-Arising

precepts *(shila):* practicing, 82, 196–197. *See also* Five Mindfulness Trainings

presence: of the Buddha, 239; offering, 194; practicing *(See* mindfulness)

present moment: coming back to, 64; dwelling in, 173–174; as the moment of happiness, 153–154

priti. See joy

psychotherapists: practices for, 41, 87, 88

Pure Land, 192, 244

Q

Quang Duc, Thich: self-immolation, 81, 191

R

Rahula (son of the Buddha): the Buddha's instruction to, 198

Ratnakuta Sutra: on the Five Aggregates, 182–183

reading: as consuming, 32–33, 96; mindful, 12–13

reality, 147; touching, 55, 127, 136, 140, 148–149. *See also* nirvana; truth

realization: action as the measure of, 98; of Ananda, 217; in turning the wheel of the Dharma, *30*, 31, 39–40, 43, 44. *See also* liberation; understanding

realizing: arising (creating) (of suffering), 39–40; cessation (of suffering), 43; freedom, 177, 178, 180; interbeing, 148; Interdependent Co-Arising, 148; the Noble Eightfold Path, 44; suffering, 31; well-being, 41–46, 127

realms, 78–80; formless, 79, 107–110. *See also* elements

reciting the name of the Buddha, 20, 76n

recognition: in calming, 26; mere recognition, 68–69, 74; in turning the wheel of the Dharma, 29, *30*, 31–38, 41–42, 43

recognizing: arising (creating) (of suffering), 31–38; the body, 68–69; cessation (of suffering), 41–42; the elements of the body, 69–70, 219; feelings, 71–72; habit energies, 25, 191; mental formations, 74; the Noble Eightfold Path, 43; perceptions, 108–109; suffering, 29, 37

refuge. *See* taking refuge

Relevance to the Circumstance, 142–143

Relevance to the Essence, 142–143

reliance: Four Reliances, 144–145; on ourselves, 162–163

Remembrances, Five, 123–124

responsibility: as co-responsibility, 150, 251; of persons practicing mindfulness, 154–155; sexual, 95–96, 197

resting, 26–27, 66, 217

reverence for life, 94; impermanence and, 132–133

right *(samyak/samma):* vs. wrong, 11n

Right Action *(samyak karmanta),* 94–98; Right Concentration and, 106; and Right Livelihood, 98; Right Mindfulness and, 94, 97–98; Right Thinking and, 62

Right Concentration *(samyak samadhi),* 105–112, 117, 118; and Right Action, 106

Right Diligence (Effort) *(samyak pradhana),* 99–104, 118; gatha, 102; practices associated with, 100; Right Thinking and, 62

Right Livelihood *(samyag ajiva),*

Right Livelihood (continued)
113–118; Right Action and, 98;
as Right Mindfulness, 116–117

Right Mindfulness (samyak smriti),
56, 64–83, 117, 118; effects, 64,
79, 86; as a mother, 72; and
Right Action, 94, 97–98; Right
Livelihood as, 116–117

Right Speech (samyag vac), 84–93;
as loving, 84, 87, 89; mindful
listening and, 86–89; Right
Thinking and, 85; silence and,
92; telling the truth, 84–85, 89

Right Thinking (samyak samkalpa),
59–63, 117; conscious breathing
and, 59–60; practices related to,
60–62; and Right Diligence, 62;
and Right Speech/Action, 85;
and Right View, 59, 63

Right View (samyag drishti), 51–58,
103, 117, 210; discourse on: text,
271–275; as insight, 54, 117–118;
and Right Thinking, 59, 63; as
unexplainable, 54

rupa. See body

S

Saddharma Pundarika Sutra. See
Lotus Sutra

samadhi. See concentration

Samantabhadra: invoking the name
of, 239

Sambhogakaya (body of bliss),
158–159, 160, 242

Samiddhi Sutra: on practicing
happiness, 191

samjña. See perceptions

samskara. See formations

samudaya. See arising (creating) (of
suffering)

samyak (right): vs. wrong, 11n. See
also individual Right Practices

Sangha, 164–165; interbeing with
Buddha and Dharma, 166;
taking refuge in, 161–164, 164–
165; as true or false, 166; as in
us, 163

sapta-bodhyanga. See Seven Factors
of Awakening

Sarvastivada School, 13, 15–16;
conditions of Interdependent
Co-Arising, 222–225. See also
Abhidharma

Satipatthana Sutta (Discourse on the
Four Establishments of Mindfulness), 67–68, 215–216

saving the world, 83, 126–127, 154–
155, 239–249

scanning the body, 69, 176

School of Youth for Social Service
(Vietnam), 202

schools: of Buddhism, 13–17;
transforming, 150–151, 252

Second Mindfulness Training, 94–
95, 197

Second Noble Truth, 9–11, 46;
turning the wheel of, 30, 31–40,
117. See also arising (creating)
(of suffering)

seeds (of consciousness) (bijas),
12n, 36, 51–52, 74–75, 181, 186–
187; of alcoholism, 97; of
Buddhahood, 52, 56, 187–188,
238; cause conditions, 223–224;
conditions for arising, 222–225;
identifying, 51–52; of Right View,
54, 56; watering, 51–52, 55, 100,
181, 186–187, 190, 206–209, 238;
wholesome/unwholesome, 51–
52, 74–75, 100, 186–187, 206–
209, 208

selective concentration, 106

selective touching, 52

self, 126, 151. See also nonself

self-enjoyment, 159

sense impressions: as a nutriment,
32–34, 96

sense organs, 23; transformative
function, 239–240

sense organs and their objects
(ayatanas), 227; contact between,
32–34, 96, 229, 242–243

setbacks (in practice) (ashrava), 31,
74

Seven Factors of Awakening
(*sapta-bodhyanga*), 76n, 101, 214–220

Seven Miracles of Mindfulness, 65–67

sexual responsibility, 95–96, 197

Shakyamuni. *See* Buddha

shamatha (stopping-calming-resting-healing), 24–27, 209–210; as concentrating, 210; miracles of mindfulness of, 66

Shariputra: Lion's Roar, 198–202; on Right View, 51; on seeing the causes of suffering, 38

shraddha (faith), 161–162, 165, 185

shunyata. See emptiness

sickness (illness): of our age, 78, 154; healing, 217; living in peace with, 205

signlessness *(animitta)*, 108–109, 148–152

signs (images) *(lakshana)*, 76, 148; breaking through, 108–109, 148–151; types, 151–152

silence: complete silencing, 123; and Right Speech, 92

sitting meditation, 56, 99–100; just sitting, 191

Six Elements, 77–78

Six Paramitas. *See* perfections

Six Realms, 78–79

six sense organs. *See* sense organs

skandhas. See Five Aggregates

smiling, 70, 102; the Buddha's smile, 173

smoking: stopping, 67

smriti. See mindfulness

social justice, 94–95; including injustice, 203–205

sounds: listening to, 92–93, 166

Source Buddhism, 13, 16–17

space: creating for practice, 252; as the object of concentration, 108; offering, 195

sparsha. See contact

speech: killing in, 93; from suffering, 85–86. *See also* Right Speech

stability: offering, 194

Sthaviravada School, 13

stopping *(shamatha)*, 24–25, 66, 209–210; using mindfulness, 38. *See also* calming

store consciousness *(alayavijñana)*, 12n, 36n, 74–75, 109, 180–181, 186, *208;* as the source of perceptions, 53–54; transformation of, 239. *See also* seeds (of consciousness)

student-teacher relationship, 144

Subhadda: the Buddha and, 49

subject: and object, 53, 80

suchness, 55–56, 149; and nirvana, 211

suffering *(dukkha)*, 9, *10*, 38, 78, 141; arising of (*See* arising (creating) (of suffering)); of the Buddha, 205; causes (roots), 22–23, 31–38, 182; cessation of (*See* cessation (of suffering)); everything as, 19–23; and happiness, 3–4, 43, 78; impermanence and, 132–133; and joy, 19, 121–122; living in peace with, 205; looking deeply into, 29–31, 37–38, 45, 128–129, 250–252; as the means of liberation, 3, 5, 38, 42, 45; and nirvana, 122; as no suffering, 122; as not a mark of all things, 21–22, 141; nutriments of, 31–38; and practicing, 43–44, 103, 128–129; realizing, 31; recognizing, 29, 37; as relative, 123; relieving others, 65–66, 86–89, 188; relieving suffering caused by others, 195–196; speech/action from, 85–86; Three Kinds of Suffering theory, 19–22; touching, 28–40; transforming, 42–43, 43–44, 67, 81–83, 103, 121–122, 160, 239–249; as Wondrous Being, 243–244

Sukhavati Sutra: on sounds, 92

suppressing ourselves, 14–15, 103, 202

Sutra of Forty-Two Chapters, 141

sutras (discourses), 17; opening to, 12–13. *See also* teachings of the Buddha; *and specific sutras*

T

Tai Xu, Master: on touching reality, 55

taking refuge, 156, 161–165, 166; verses, 161, 163, 167–168

Tamrashatiya School, 13, 15–16

Tang Hôi, Master, 36n

Tathagata, 158n

Tathagatagarbha, 158

teacher-student relationship, 144

teaching: authenticity of, 131, 141, 142–143, 166, 226; children, 150–151, 216, 252; image teaching vs. substance teaching, 55; relevance of, 142–143, 143; standards of truth, 143

teachings of the Buddha: deathbed gatha, 123; distortions of, 13–14; on the Four Immeasurable Minds, 169, 170; guides to, 142–145; on ignorance and understanding, 236–237; on inclusiveness, 198; on Interdependent Co-Arising, 221, 225–226, 231–232; on perceptions, 52–53; on phenomena, 77–80; practicing, 141–142; renewing, 17; repairing, 18; on suppressing the mind, 14; on taking refuge, 156, 163; on his own teachings, 3; three baskets, 226n; transmission streams, 13–17; on turning the wheel of the Dharma, 7–8, 22, 28, 122, 245, 257–261; understanding, 12–18, 142–145, 226. *See also* sutras (discourses); *and specific sutras*

telephone practice, 91–92, 116

television programs: as food, 32–33, 96

telling the truth, 84–85, 89

Theravada School, 16; conditions of Interdependent Co-Arising, 222

Thiên Hôi, Master: on the place of no-birth and no-death, 140, 245

things: inanimate, 127, 152; marks of all things (*See* Three Dharma Seals); as they are, 23, 44

thinking, 59; aspects (parts), 60; non-thinking, 63; stopping, 24–25; suppressing, 14–15; transforming, 62–63. *See also* Right Thinking

Third Mindfulness Training, 95–96, 197

Third Noble Truth, 11, 45–46, 127; turning the wheel of, *30,* 41–43. *See also* cessation (of suffering)

three baskets *(tripitaka),* 226n

three bodies of the Buddha, 156–160, 241–242

Three Concentrations. *See* Three Doors of Liberation

Three Dharma Seals, 21–22, 131–145; destroying as concepts, 139. *See also* impermanence; nirvana; nonself

Three Doors of Liberation, 145, 146–155. *See also* aimlessness; emptiness; signlessness

Three Jewels, 161–168

Three Kinds of Suffering theory, 19–22

Three Times theory, 232, *233*

Threefold Training, 82

Tolstoy, Leo: two enemies story, 134

touching: the Buddha within, 3–5, 128, 250–254; impermanence, 133; reality, 55, 127, 136, 140, 148–149; selective touching, 52; suffering, 28–40; what brings peace and joy, 42

Tran Thai Tong: on mindful steps, 39

transformation: body of, 159–160, 242; miracle of mindfulness of, 67 transforming: consciousness, 181, 238–239, 241; the cycle of the Twelve Links of Interdependent Co-Arising, 244, 245–248; suffering, 42–43, 43–44, 67, 81–83, 103, 121–122, 160, 239–249; thinking, 62–63

trishna. See craving

truth: Four Standards of Truth, 143; relative vs. absolute, 121–130, 143, 144–145; telling the truth, 84–85, 89. *See also* Four Noble Truths

Tue Trung, Master: on the Eight Concepts, 139

turning the wheel of the Dharma, 28–40, *30,* 41–44; the Buddha on, 7–8, 22, 28, 122, 245; discourse on: text, 257–261

Turning the Wheel Sutra: on the Five Aggregates, 182

Twelve Links of Interdependent Co-Arising, 221–249, 226–229; as empty, 236; illustrations of, *228,* 230; interbeing of, 229, 231, 234–236, *235;* misunderstandings of, 231–234; positive side, 236–244; studying, 244; teaching, 245–248; theories based on, 232–234, *233;* transforming the cycle, 244, 245–248; variations on, 230–231

Two Levels of Cause and Effect theory, 232–234, *233*

Two Realms, 79–80

Two Relevances, 142–143, 145

Two Truths, 121–130, 145

U

unconditioned realm, 79–80

understanding: injustice, 203–205; the teachings of the Buddha, 12–18, 142–145, 226; things as they are, 44

understanding (insight/wisdom) *(prajña),* 179–180, 186; and action, 82–83; and anger,

understanding *(continued)* 203–205; in calming, 26; concentration and, 186; Dharma talks and sutras as presentations of, 17; discriminative wisdom vs., 145; Four Wisdoms, 110, 239; ignorance and, 236–237; and love, 66–67, 171, 211; miracle of mindfulness of, 66–67; offering, 196; *prajña paramita,* 56, 210; Right View as, 54, 117–118; source of, 109, 118. *See also* realization; Right View

upadana (grasping/attachment), 229

V

Vairochana, 158

vashana (habit energies): stopping, 24–25

Vatsigotra: the Buddha and, 17–18

Vibhajyavada School, 13

vichara (developing thought), 60

Vietnam War, 5, 202–205

views: all as wrong, 56. *See also* Right View

vijñana. See consciousness; discriminative wisdom

Vijñanavada School: conditions of Interdependent Co-Arising, 222–225; on mental formations, 74

vikalpa (discriminative perception), 134

Vimalakirti: on sickness and suffering, 3

violence: transforming, 150–151, 252

vipashyana. See looking deeply

virya. See diligence

vitarka (initial thought), 60

Vô Ngôn Thông: on silence, 92

volition: as a nutriment, 34–36. *See also* encouragement

volitional actions. *See* formations

Vulture Peak: Nhat Hanh on, 250

W

walking meditation, 91, 148

wave-water metaphor, 124–125, 127, 136, 140, 211

well-being: cessation of suffering as, 41, 45–46; realizing, 41–46, 127

Wheel of Life: links of Interdependent Co-Arising, *228,* 230

will. *See* volition

wisdom: discriminative vs. nondiscriminative, 145; Four Wisdoms, 110, 239. *See also* understanding (insight/wisdom)

Wisdom of Equality, 110, 174–175, 241

Wisdom of the Great Mirror, 110, 239, 241

Wisdom of Wonderful Observation, 110, 240, 241

Wisdom of Wonderful Realization, 110, 240

Wondrous Being, 244

Wondrous Sound (bodhisattva), 90

workaholism, 61–62

world: engagement in, 8, 239; saving, 83, 126–127, 154–155, 239–249

writing: as Right Speech, 90–91

Y

young people: teaching and helping, 150–151, 216, 252

Plum Village is a retreat community in southwestern France where monks, nuns, laymen, and laywomen practice the art of mindful living. Visitors are invited to join the practice for at least one week. For information, please write to:

Plum Village
13 Martineau
33580 Dieulivol
France